Leadership Team Coaching in Practice

Leadership Team Coaching in Practice

Case studies on developing high-performing teams

Edited by
Peter Hawkins

KoganPage

First published in Great Britain and the United States in 2014 by Kogan Page Limited
Second edition 2018

2nd Floor, 45 Gee Street	c/o Martin P Hill Consulting	4737/23 Ansari Road
London	122 W 27th St, 10th Floor	Daryaganj
EC1V 3RS	New York, NY 10001	New Delhi 110002
United Kingdom	USA	India

www.koganpage.com

© Peter Hawkins and the individual contributors 2014, 2018

The right of Peter Hawkins and the individual contributors to be identified as the authors of this work has been asserted by them in accordance with the Copyright, Designs and Patents Act 1988.

ISBN   978 0 7494 8238 1
E-ISBN   978 0 7494 8239 8

British Library Cataloguing-in-Publication Data

A CIP record for this book is available from the British Library.

Library of Congress Cataloging-in-Publication Data

Names: Hawkins, Peter, 1950- author.
Title: Leadership team coaching in practice : case studies on developing high-performing teams / Peter Hawkins.
Description: Second Edition. | New York : Kogan Page Ltd, [2018] | Revised edition of the author's Leadership team coaching in practice, [2014]
Identifiers: LCCN 2018015737 (print) | LCCN 2018018844 (ebook) | ISBN 9780749482398 (ebook) | ISBN 9780749482381 (pbk.)
Subjects: LCSH: Teams in the workplace–Management. | Leadership. | Employees–Coaching of. | Executive coaching.
Classification: LCC HD66 (ebook) | LCC HD66 .H38553 2018 (print) | DDC 658.4/022–dc23

Typeset by Integra Software Services, Pondicherry
Print production managed by Jellyfish
Printed and bound by CPI Group (UK) Ltd, Croydon, CR0 4YY

Nemo solus satus sapit.
(TITUS MACCIUS PLAUTUS, 254–184 BC)

No individual person can be wise enough on their own.
(QUOTED BY THE CADBURY REPORT
ON BOARD GOVERNANCE, 1992)

CONTENTS

11   Developing an effective 'team of teams' approach in Comair   169

Barbara Walsh, Danny Tuckwood (Metaco), Erik Venter (CEO), Geraldine Welby-Cooke (Head of Od), Tracey Mccreadie (Manager of Service Delivery, Ops) and Justin Dell (Manager of Ground Ops) (all in Comair), Peter Hawkins (Metaco, Supervisor)

12   Empowering the next generation of team leaders in fast-moving startups   188

Shannon Arvizu

13   Evaluation and assessment of teams and team coaching   207

Peter Hawkins

14 Coaching the board: How coaching boards is different from coaching executive teams, with case examples from the private, public and voluntary sectors   234

Peter Hawkins and Alison Hogan

15 Embodied approaches to team coaching   253

Peter Hawkins and David Presswell

16 Developing the personal core capacities for systemic team coaching   270

Peter Hawkins

17 Training systemic team coaches 286

Peter Hawkins and John Leary-Joyce

18 Systemic team coaching – where next? 300

Peter Hawkins and Krister Lowe

FOREWORD

An organization isn't a machine; it's a living organism. Since the industrial revolution, it's been customary to think about the production of goods and services as though they all still emerged from factories. Business (or management) schools grew out of engineering schools, inheriting their mechanistic model and language. But what Peter Hawkins and his associates demonstrate is that this mental construct, if it ever were true, no longer is. Companies don't have ideas, only people do – and it is the interactions between and among people from which innovation, insight and value emerge. Leadership is about creating the conditions in which those are most likely to proliferate.

This book in itself ably demonstrates its own proposition. The output of a team of exceptionally gifted and experienced practitioners, their case studies combine to produce a highly coherent, practical and holistic approach to leadership team coaching. It grows from the shared experience of exceptional collaborators, proving – if proof were needed – that teams aren't about dumbing down but braining up. Most CEOs today recognize that they cannot achieve change alone, that they depend critically on the contributions of executives who understand how to get the best from each other. But recognition is the easy part: how to achieve such high-order collaboration is the hardest part of leadership. As companies emerge from the tight executional focus required to weather the economic crisis, leaders now confront the harder problem, which is the transformation of heroic soloists into fully functional and sustainable teams.

This takes time. Many leaders expect – or hope – that the smooth interaction of capable people will develop naturally. That almost never happens. Few executives, harried by key performance indicators, targets and share price, have the time or the skills to develop the social capital on which an organization's resilience, productivity and creativity depend. The single greatest motivator at work may be our connectedness to each other – but this is easily stunted or eroded by the day-to-day demands of work. That's where leadership team coaching comes in: helping already outstanding individuals to grow beyond their expertise by investing the time and attention required for true social capital to compound.

In his research at MIT into collective intelligence, Thomas Malone found that what makes groups particularly adept at problem solving is a high level of social sensitivity (groups that are well attuned to one another), equal levels of contribution (people are neither dominant nor passive) and having more women. Those are, in essence, the building blocks of great teams. The mortar, however, is more subtle: it is time spent together, expertly facilitated, that turns conflict into thinking and unfettered exploration into a shared sense of mission. Like so much in our working lives, we know when we've found it but when it's lacking, we aren't sure where to look.

Hawkins and his collaborators are expert guides. Reading these case studies, you can feel in their interventions and observations the decades of experience that they bring to their understanding of individuals and groups. You recognize at once that theirs is not abstract or academic inquiry but one driven by firsthand understanding of the urgency of execution. Both practical and wise, these coaches make the often bewildering and frustrating aspects of coaching leadership teams structured, disciplined and human.

In all organizations, whether commercial or not, I have always sensed a deep ambivalence around the very concept of team. Living in an age that so easily venerates heroic soloists, many wonder whether or not collaboration dilutes individuality, produces a lower common denominator and somehow diminishes those who contribute generously to the whole. Hawkins' illustrations should eliminate such anxieties once and for all. There is no doubt, reading these examples, that a great team both captures and expands the capacity and ability of every individual that contributes to it and that it is in working with and for each other that we find and grow the best of ourselves.

Margaret Heffernan

ACKNOWLEDGEMENTS

This book would not have been written without the many readers who responded so positively to the first, second and third editions of *Leadership Team Coaching*, particularly the many executives and team leaders who used the models and approaches and have been generous enough to share their experience.

The book is a practical follow-up showing how systemic and leadership team coaching works in practice with case studies from different countries and business sectors. It is very much a product of a team, and although it is my name on the cover I would like to thank all the other members of the team who have made it possible, by writing up the stories of their work and reflecting on what has worked and what they have learnt.

As well as those who have contributed chapters there have also been important inputs from all those who have taught on, or been students on, the seven diploma programmes in systemic team coaching as well as numerous master classes and shorter workshops that I, and my colleagues, have taught in many parts of the world. I would particularly like to thank John Leary-Joyce, Hilary Lines and Marion Gillie who have been great co-trainers and creative co-developers.

All the writers in this book would also like to salute and acknowledge all the teams and organizations that have been committed and courageous enough to open themselves and their work in team coaching in pursuit of discovering how to become a more effective team and make more of a difference not only to their organization but also their stakeholder world. A particular thank you goes to the CEOs and senior leaders who have gone further and been willing to write about their own experience in this process.

In preparing the text we have had enormous support from Fiona Benton and Julie Jeffery of Renewal Associates who have regularly turned mess and confusion into order and readability and ensured that references were hunted down and corrected. A big thank you to both of you for your flexibility and support.

Finally I would once more like to thank my wife and partner Judy Ryde for her love, patience, colleagueship, support and her many important contributions to the writing of this book and for accepting that our holiday suitcases are always full of half-written manuscripts.

Peter Hawkins
Professor of Leadership, Henley Business School
Emeritus Chairman, Bath Consultancy Group
Chairman, Renewal Associates
Honorary President of the Academy of Executive Coaching
Chairman of Metaco South Africa

INTRODUCTION TO THE SECOND EDITION

It is four years since I decided that, to accompany the second edition of *Leadership Team Coaching*, it would be helpful to have a book of example applications of systemic team coaching in a variety of countries, across different sectors and in organizations facing diverse challenges. I was keen to have the perspectives, not just of the team coach, but also from the CEO or team leader who was partnering the team coach in developing their team.

Much has happened in those four years. The interest in, and need for, systemic team coaching has grown exponentially, as more and more companies realize the need to move from individualistic heroic leaders to more collective leadership within the team, and greater collaboration and engagement beyond the team. Both our own training in systemic team coaching (see Chapter 17) and other parallel trainings (see Chapter 18), has increased in number and spread to most parts of the world, from China to South America, Scandinavia to South Africa, and Australia to California. The research on coaching trends shows that team coaching is predicted to be the fastest growing form of coaching in the next three years (Ridler Report, 2016; see Chapter 18) and increasingly we are seeing the development of eco-systemic team coaching (Hawkins, 2017) where team coaching becomes part not just of an organization-wide development and transformation process, but a development of the wider eco-system, with coaching of networks and partnerships.

The new literature that has emerged in the last four years also reflects this. The book *Teams of Teams* by General McChrystal and colleagues (2015), describing the radical culture change in the allied forces in post-war Iraq, dominated by regular and wide-spread violence, became a New York Times bestseller. The approach they adopted has been applied to many business organizations and described in both McChrystal's book and that of his colleague and sometime aide-de-camp, Chris Fussell (2017).

Although coming from a very different sector and culture, my own approach has developed along similar lines. In the first edition of this book, I included a joint case study with a CEO showing 'inter-team coaching' in a UK District Hospital (see Chapter 10). Since then, in the third edition of *Leadership Team Coaching* (Hawkins, 2017), I have developed approaches for expanding systemic team coaching into organization-wide transformation, and developed eco-systemic team coaching that coaches inter-organization relationships, partnerships and networks.

Increasingly there is a need to combine team coaching with organizational development, HR processes, leadership development and to find ways of coaching whole businesses. Large companies are increasingly employing fewer people and all the growth in employment is coming from business start-ups, small growth companies as well as the not-for-profit (or better termed 'for-benefit') sector. Yet we know that over half of all business start-ups fail within their first two years. This means that the need for coaching intact teams in large companies will plateau and even decrease in the next ten years, but the urgent need to coach business start-ups and growth companies will continue to grow sharply. So, in this new edition I have invited two new case studies, one from a young millennial team coach in California, describing the flexibility a team coach needs to ride the rollercoaster of coaching a young, fast-growing and changing business (Chapter 12) and the other from my colleagues at Metaco in South Africa, where they and I have been using a 'team of teams' approach to help a well-established regional airline business go through a period of rapid transformation (Chapter 11). This latter chapter is not only about a 'team of teams' but also written by a 'team of teams', with four authors from across the company and three external systemic team coaches all writing together! All the original case study authors have contributed their reflections four years down the line since they did the work, including what new learning this has led onto for them in their work as team coaches, team coach supervisors and business and team leaders.

This new edition also includes a major update in Chapter 3 detailing new case studies that have been published elsewhere and also a new Chapter 18, written jointly with Krister Lowe from the USA. This final chapter also includes a short case study of training partners in a global professional services firm (Deloitte) to become team coaches of their own teams – and shows the links between systemic team coaching, leadership development and organizational transformation.

Since the first edition we have also had new literature: from Christine Thornton bringing out a second edition (2016), Jennifer Britton in Canada bringing out a new book (Britton, 2013) and Anna Rod and Marita Fridjon bringing out a book based on their ORSC approach (Rod and Fridjon, 2016), and John Leary-Joyce and Hilary-Lines, both contributors to this book (see Chapters 4 and 17), writing *Systemic Team Coaching* (Leary-Joyce and Lines, 2017) adding their perspectives on this approach and the training necessary. Krister Lowe (see Chapter 18) has done a great job interviewing both authors, researchers and practitioners on his podcast (www.teamcoachingzone.com) and providing signposts to the best tools, evaluation instruments and books in the field. In 2018 Krister Lowe and a team of other editors are publishing *The Team Coaching Handbook* which will also integrate the best thinking and practice from around the world.

There has also been a growing literature on the need to develop a more systemic approach to all types of coaching (Einzig, 2017; Lawrence and Moore, 2018; Turner and Hawkins, 2017, 2018; Hawkins, 2014c, 2011b; Goldsmith, 2018). These authors argue that for too long leadership coaching has been 'expensive personal development for the already highly-privileged' (Hawkins, 2014c) and that coaching needs to deliver not just for the coachee but their wider stakeholder eco-system.

In addition, his period has brought new research on the future of leadership and leadership development (see Hawkins, 2017b). This new edition has drawn on much of this research and in the new Chapter 18 we show how systemic team coaching can play a key role in leadership development. This new section also includes a new short case study on systemic team coaching in developing senior partners in Deloitte, one of the world's 'big four' professional services firms.

The next five years will see even faster change than we have witnessed in the last five years. The demand for team coaching, transforming organizations, supporting business start-ups and growth companies and developing partnerships, networks and business eco-systems will all grow exponentially. Systemic team coaching will also need to undertake its own transformation and incorporate its own digitalization to streamline its offering, create better continuous evaluation and increase its reach and impact (see new Chapter 18 and Hawkins, 2017: Chapter 9). My hope is that this new updated and expanded second edition will assist team coaches globally in this important challenge.

Introduction 01

Highly effective teams – the latest research and development

Companies know that they derive greater creativity and innovation from teamwork – but what, they wonder, makes a great team?

(MARGARET HEFFERNAN, 2013: 228)

We must never forget that teams are living systems, not manufactured products that can be built to prescribed proportions, built to order, functionally correct. We need not a mechanistic science of teams but an ecology that can constantly enrich and renew our craft of team building and team coaching and a poiesis that can inspire our work and remind us that the mystery of whatever emerges in each team we encounter is always greater than what we think we know.

I have been in and around teams all my life, that is if we can see the family as a team, for it too must pull together to survive and to thrive. The family receives a commission from its wider tribe of grandparents, aunts, uncles, ancestors, from those who have gone before. From these expectations, the couple have to clarify their intentions, both privately together and publicly at their wedding or through Facebook or other means. They co-create first together and then awaken to the realization that the relationship has a life of its own, becoming a third voice in their being together. Then the children become part of the co-creation, each one changing the shape, the rhythm and the flow of the family living. The family is never an island; even the Swiss Family Robinson had to coexist alongside the other creatures that shared their castaway terrain. The family has to connect, with neighbours, relatives, friends, both ones they share and those of individual family members, with schools and work, tradesmen and visitors. Some families learn, develop and change with each play and challenge that life presents for them to participate in. Other families get stuck holding on to the familiarity of one particular time and way of being. In some, the individuals learn separately and go their own ways.

At age 50, life presented me with a whole new opening and perspective on understanding systems and the nature of teams. For in that year my wife and I came to live on the borders of Bath in the countryside, to restore an old Victorian walled garden and look after some fields and woodland copses. Our home sat high on the hill, overlooking a deep valley bordered by woods. At age 55 I worked with local schools, communities and the Woodland Trust to plant a new woodland on our side of the valley and I daily watch it grow and change from my desk in the upstairs study. There is an old saying describing the common human predicament of 'not being able to see the wood for the trees'. I think my wife and I were drawn to this location so we could daily see both the wood and the trees, and watch how the wood changes. For a wood is much greater than a collection of individual trees. Counting and labelling each tree in the wood tells you very little. To really understand the wood, you need to know its geology, the soil which feeds its roots, its topology, how it is nestled within the landscape and protected from some winds and open to others, the time the sun first alights upon its branches and when it leaves them, the streams that feed it, the animals, insects and birds that have come to inhabit it and how they fashion their occupation of different woodland locations and how they interplay, live and die, dependent on each other. Also how each species, including humans, have used the wood for their shelter and home building, foraging for food and, in the case of humans, firewood. You need to watch it through each of its seasons and in all weathers: the skeletal forms of the trees in winter, the crisp silence when it is full of snow, the spring awakening and the glory of the late April carpet of bluebells, celandine, ramsons or wild garlic flowers and delicate wood anemones, the dappled light of the full summer sun, the mushrooms and berries and multi-coloured dancing, falling leaves of late autumn. Watching carefully to see whether the ash or the oak is the last to come into leaf, to see when the first swallows arrive and listen to catch the call of the cuckoo as it passes through. There are rare moments too, like the time I watched two hares standing on their hind legs in pugilistic combat or when, at dusk, an owl swerved at speed in downward flight to catch a pipistrelle bat.

Woodlanders, those who live and work in the woods, know the woods from living in their interstices. Their knowledge is embodied and diurnal as they breathe differently each day in syncopation with the woods. As visitors we can never know the wood fully, but we can open all our senses and let it teach us how it lives. Woodlanders learn from their environment that everything resides in relationship with everything else, and that every organism is gifting itself to the great whole. That Death is an integral part of life, for as Andreas Weber writes (2017), it is the dying of organisms that feed the next cycle of living. He writes beautifully and poetically of watching a wood in winter, and how the dead trees were providing shelter and nourishment for woodpeckers, and other birds and insects, continuing in death to be part of 'the circle of giving' and the food chain, because modern man had not yet come along to remove them as 'dead waste' (Weber, 2017: 197). Roger Deakin (2007) tells us how woodlanders can tell a tree by the noise it makes in the wind, and can identify fungi by their smell. Most of us in so-called 'developed economies' have lost our connections with earth and the Earth that supports us. Woodlands are a diminishing resource. Every minute 41 hectares of trees are felled, the equivalent of 50 football fields (Fiaramonti, 2017: 2). In our human-centric ways of thinking we can easily forget that it is not large companies, banks and governments that produce the true wealth in the world, but the natural eco-systems that freely gift us warmth, light, air, and food. We have become indigenous orphans (Hawkins, 2017c) and still have much to learn from more indigenous people who live closer to the earth, such as Native Americans. Luther Standing Bear, Chief of the Oglala in Lakota, said in 1905:

> The old Lakota was wise. He knew that a man's heart away from Nature becomes hard; he knew that lack of respect for growing living things soon lead to a lack of respect for humans too.... The old people came literally to love the soil and they sat or reclined on the ground with a feeling of being close to a mothering power.

As 'teamlanders', those who live and work in teams, we too need to open our senses to listen, watch and experience the team through our bodies, be sensitive to how it changes, how it resides in its wider landscapes and watch the changing weather blowing through its branches. We need an ecology of teams and an ecological ethic of team working. This ethic is one that embraces stewardship and humility; sees interconnection and how every team is a system nested within other systems; is respectful of the past and alive to the moment of the present and also 'leans into the emergent future' (Scharmer and Kaufer, 2013), sensing what the world of tomorrow needs us to learn and do today. It is a practice, not of problems and solutions, but of constant challenges and co-created approaches and experiments – co-created by collective groups and between them and their wider systems.

Whether we lead teams, are team members, coach or study teams, we need an ethic of collaboration. The American and north European 20th-century zeitgeist that has come to dominate much of the thinking of dominant global corporations has been built on competition. President Roosevelt argued as long ago as 1912 that: 'competition was useful up to a certain point and no further'. But we have forgotten the limits to competition, along with the limits to growth. In 2013 the Salz report into Barclays Bank wrote: 'Winning at all costs comes at a price; collateral issues of rivalry, arrogance, selfishness and a lack of humility and generosity.'

Royal Bank of Scotland was even more caught in the grip of competition, where under Sir Fred Goodwin the purpose of the bank was to be the largest bank in the world! The cult of the heroic leader that dominated much business and leadership writing in the late 20th century was dangerously mixed with the leader's over-weaning ambition and the competition for greater status than one's peers. Heffernan (2013: 105) quotes one senior executive saying how: 'The desire for bigger and bigger profits was driven entirely by senior executives' desire for personal prestige and social status.'

Outscoring your peers, in salary, recognition, awards and so on, is a schismogenetic spiral (Bateson, 1972), where the accelerations in the rewards for one CEO drive acceleration in the demands of the others. We have seen an ever-accelerating gap between the earnings of senior executives and board directors and that of their employees, and this has continued unabated since the world economic crisis of 2008–09.

Team development can also get caught into this spiral, such as in the drive to become a high-performing team, where high performance is a destination, not a living process, and is measured by doing better than the teams around you. Team coaches, inspired by what was achieved with sports teams, became focused on helping teams run harder, win the race and outperform their colleagues. Team performance has too often been measured by the inputs (does the team have the right quality team players, the right structures and processes, the requisite meetings and so on) or outputs ('hitting its targets'!).

Instead we need to understand that a team's performance can only be truly understood through its capacity to co-create value with and for all its stakeholders. I address this issue more fully in Chapter 13 on the evaluation and assessment of teams where I argue that:

> A team's performance can best be understood through its ongoing ability
> to facilitate the creation of added value for the organization it is part of,
> the organization's investors, the team's internal and external customers and
> suppliers, its team members, the communities the team operates within and the
> more than human world in which we reside.

This is echoed in Chapter 14 on boards, where we quote Van den Berghe and Levrau (2013: 156, 179) on what makes an effective board: 'a board is effective if it facilitates the creation of value added for the company, its management, its shareholders and all its relevant stakeholders'.

This is part of the ethic of moving from the focus on creating 'shareholder value' to 'shared value' (Porter and Kramer, 2011). Shareholder value has dominated organizational attention for most of the last hundred years, reinforced by the writings of economist Milton Friedman who argued that the only social responsibility of a company was to increase the returns to its shareholders. Increasingly, both business leaders and academics are recognizing a broader imperative, that of creating 'shared value' (Porter and Kramer, 2011), and that a sustainable business needs to create short-term and long-term value for all its key stakeholders. Even Jack Welch, one of the iconic heroic leaders famed for turning around the fortunes of General Electric, has converted to this new paradigm, declaring that: 'strictly speaking, shareholder value is one of the dumbest ideas in the world' (quoted in Erdal, 2011).

As 'teamlanders' we can flourish only if we have a systemic perspective, an attitude of careful responsiveness and an ethic of collaboration. Heffernan (2013: 373) summarizes this beautifully:

> Innovative institutions and organizations thrive not because they pick and breed superstars but because they cherish, nurture and support the vast range of talents, personalities and skills that true creativity requires. Collaboration is a habit of mind, solidified by routine and predicated on openness, generosity, rigour and patience. It requires precise and fearless communication, without status, awe or intimidation. It's hard because it allows no passengers.

The woodland too is a team that allows no passengers; all species and eco-inhabitants have to play their part and contribute to the overall ecology. The woodland never stands still. Its living ecology is always learning and evolving in dynamic relationship to the systems in which it abides. Fungi turn old waste into new nutrients and mycelium transfers nutrients from one part of the wood to another. The woodland flourishes through every part responding to every other part, through every member attuning to the greater whole and participating in the constantly emerging future.

This book is a guidebook for 'teamlanders', that is, all of us who spend so much of our working life living in teams, dependent on teams to get our work done, connecting with and through other teams, developing and evolving the teams we lead and coach. It addresses important questions such as:

- How to create teams that function at more than the sum of their parts?

- How do we enable teams to learn and evolve?

- How can each team member be enabled by the team to achieve much more than they could by just working in parallel with others?

- How can we develop team meetings that we look forward to, are a joy to attend and leave us more focused, energized and connected than before we turned up?
- How do teams generate new thinking together, rather than just exchange the thoughts that the team members already know?
- How do teams align, so that the team members can connect with the team's stakeholders in a way that represents the whole team?

Much has been written about the study of, and research on, high-performing teams, and I have summarized much of this in my previous books (Hawkins, 2011, 2014, 2017). Less has been written about the craft of coaching and developing those teams, either as the team leader or as a specialist team coach, although this field is now beginning to grow rapidly. Much of this writing, including my own books, focuses on the models and techniques of coaching and developing teams. There is even less on case studies of how team leaders and team coaches have set about this process, what took place, what difference it made and what the team leaders and team coaches learnt in the process. This book sets out to address that imbalance.

The core of this book is a series of case studies of systemic team coaching from different countries (Australia, Finland, Canada, USA, South Africa, continental Europe and the UK, and shorter accounts from many others); different sectors (professional services, pharmaceutical, health service, airlines, building development, finance, local government); and focusing on different team challenges and contexts. A number of these case studies are written jointly by the CEO or team leader and an external team coach, emphasizing that this partnership is at the heart of effective team coaching.

Before we start the team case studies there are two chapters to help you approach and get the most value from reading the case studies. Chapter 2 describes the foundations of leadership team coaching and systemic team coaching, including defining these terms and presenting the five disciplines model of teams and team coaching which is referred to by many of the writers throughout the book. Chapter 3 gives guidance on how to read and engage with case studies and reviews all the limited number of major case studies that are already published.

Chapters 4 to 7 offer four very different case studies, but all find very different ways of utilizing Hawkins' five disciplines model of team coaching (Hawkins, 2011, 2014, 2017). The first (Chapter 4), by Hilary Lines and a team leader who has chosen to remain anonymous, focuses on the disciplines of *commissioning* and *clarifying* in a new leadership team in a professional services organization. Then in Chapter 5, two Canadian team coaches,

Catherine Carr and Jacqueline Peters, share how they coached two very different teams (one in local government and one in finance) to work more effectively in *co-creating* their collective work. In Chapter 6, Angela McNab, a new CEO in a UK National Health Service hospital, and Jacqui Scholes-Rhodes, her coach, show how they worked together to connect the hospital senior team with the wider leadership from across the hospital. Finally, in Chapter 7, Sue Coyne and Judith Nicol describe their joint coaching of a building development company, focusing on maximizing the *core learning* of the team.

Chapters 8 to 12 provide case studies of team coaching in very different contexts. David Jarrett describes coaching the Finnair leadership team in the context of the company needing to undertake a major organizational transformation and restructuring. Padraig O'Sullivan and Carole Field show the coaching of a pharmaceutical leadership team in Australia that is focused on the need to drive greater innovation. Chapter 10 is written jointly by Gavin Boyle (a hospital CEO) and me, with a focus on inter-team coaching involving a hospital executive team, the hospital board and the three new clinical directorate teams. Chapter 11 describes the 'Team of Teams' coaching in an African airline and Chapter 13 the coaching of an American high-tech growth company.

The book then turns to consider specific aspects of team coaching. Chapter 13 looks at ways of evaluating team development and team coaching, with new material about assessing team maturity and how this can inform the type of team coaching intervention that is needed. Chapter 14 looks at the critical area of board evaluation and coaching boards on their development, for although an increasing number of company and government organizations' boards are carrying out board evaluations, hardly any are following through and getting help to address the development issues that arise from the evaluation. From the growing volume of research it is clear that the majority of boards are failing the organizations that they should be stewarding as well as the wider system of the company's stakeholders (Kakabadse and Kakabadse, 2009; Kakabadse and Van den Berghe, 2013).

Chapter 15 looks at the use of embodied techniques in team coaching, recognizing that for teams to develop they need to move beyond the exchange of what they already know and access the deeper levels of '*the unthought known*', what they sense but currently do not have a language to think about or express. Our bodies know far more than our left brain neo-cortex rational minds and we need to use these other forms of knowing in being aware '*teamlanders*'.

Chapter 16 explores the key ways of looking, listening, thinking and being necessary for '*systemic team coaching*' and shows how we need a fundamentally different attitude of being to work systemically with the team as a whole in creating greater value in relation to its wider stakeholder eco-system.

Chapter 17 discusses the challenges of training effective systemic team coaches using the format of a letter to someone who is considering doing a team coaching training and a letter to the same person several years later who is now thinking of setting up a team coaching training themselves. This chapter is written by me, with John Leary-Joyce, based on our joint experience of training systemic team coaches in and from over 30 different countries.

The final chapter brings the book together, taking stock of the current state of team coaching, its place in the wider panoply of leadership and organizational development approaches and the evolution of human consciousness, and looks at the challenges ahead.

There are many routes through this book, depending on your interests and needs, but whichever order you read it in, I suggest that you read it dialogically, that is, as if you are in conversation with the various authors, exploring with them the challenges that their and your team face, and how they and you can go about addressing these and in the process growing the capacity and collective maturity of the team.

The need for leadership and systemic team coaching is enormous. Coaching teams is a new and young craft, although its roots go back through the whole of human history. There are no easy answers or foolproof methods. We are all in this together and need to collaborate and learn together, always in service of the wider eco-system.

I hope you enjoy your journey through the book.

What are leadership team coaching and systemic team coaching?

02

PETER HAWKINS

Introduction

It is now eight years since I wrote the first edition of *Leadership Team Coaching* and four years since I wrote the first edition of this book and much has happened since that time. The theories, models and methods have been further tested, experimented with and developed, not only in my own work, but also in the work of my many colleagues, supervisees and by the students on the many systemic team coaching programmes we have been teaching, both in the UK and internationally. I have also supervised many different team coaches and had the privilege of working with a number of students doing research and dissertations in the area of team coaching who have further developed the thinking – most notably the excellent doctoral work of Catherine Carr and Jacqueline Peters in Canada. This book is therefore a culmination of many discussions, supervisions and dialogues, and, reflecting this wider involvement, I am pleased that a number of students, supervisees, colleagues and trainees have written chapters for this book.

While my first book's models, theories and methods have helped refine the theoretical foundations and practical teaching of team coaching, it has proved much harder for trainees to shift their thinking and move their practice from team coaching to systemic team coaching. Increasingly

I have realized that this requires a *metanoia*, a fundamental shift in perspective and thinking, as well as shift in one's own being. It has become clear to me that to fully understand the 'systemic' in systemic team coaching requires personal change at several levels, each level deeper and more fundamental than the ones above it. The four levels, I have realized, are similar to, and build upon, the four levels of engagement that Nick Smith and I developed in our work on individual transformational coaching (Hawkins and Smith, 2014, 2018), where we described the levels as: data/definition; behaviours; emotional ground; and underlying assumptions, beliefs and motivations:

1 Data/definition: it is important to understand conceptually the differences between team coaching, leadership team coaching and systemic team coaching.

2 Behaviours: then to develop the different ways of attending, looking and hearing that are required to perceive systemically.

3 Emotional ground: the systemic team coach then has to develop how to be and engage systemically.

4 Assumptions, beliefs and motivations: while carrying out the learning and development in all of the first three levels, one needs to confront, confound and unlearn many assumptions and core beliefs that are so much part of our ways of seeing, thinking and language, particularly in Western cultures.

In 2015, I wrote an article for *Coaching at Work* called 'Cracking the Shell' showing the seven coaching assumptions we have to unlearn in order to work systemically (Hawkins, 2015) and much of the development to be a systemic team coach involves unlearning our previous assumptions and beliefs. When working with colleagues teaching a diploma course on systemic team coaching we were worried about feedback from the students. One large subgroup loved the teachings of the models and theory, but found the experiential work, which involved them reflecting on themselves, 'confusing' and 'a waste of time'. Another large subgroup hated 'being taught' and wanted to discover things for themselves and have more personal development. 'How do we meet both sets of needs?' asked one of my colleagues. 'The real challenge is that both groups need both forms of learning, probably especially the one they find difficult.' Responded another colleague: 'How do we make the importance of both types of learning clear to the students and also how they connect?' This is also my challenge in writing this chapter. I believe it is important to communicate clearly the differences between systemic team coaching and other forms of team facilitation and team coaching with a degree of academic rigour. I also firmly believe that 'the map is not the territory' and that learning to become a team coach cannot happen just by learning the theory, models and approaches. So in this chapter I will outline the definitions of systemic and leadership team coaching and in Chapter 16 I will address the deeper personal and spiritual development necessary to be an effective systemic team coach.

I will first set out the five disciplines model that is core to systemic and leadership team coaching and used directly or indirectly in all the case studies, and then explore the conceptual differences between team coaching, leadership team coaching and systemic team coaching and eco-systemic team coaching.

The five disciplines of effective teams and the five approaches to coaching them

The five disciplines model of effective teams was developed over many years of working with teams, to help teams recognize the need both (a) to focus on the task and the process and (b) to focus internally within the team and externally on their commissioners and all their key stakeholders. At the centre of the resulting five disciplines is the discipline of *Core Learning*, the team's capacity both to 'helicopter up' and see the wider systemic picture that connects all four of the other disciplines and to constantly learn and develop ever-increasing levels of both functioning and performance (see Figure 2.1). This model has been used to help many leadership teams in many different countries and many different sectors. It has been used in large global companies, professional services organizations, government departments and not-for-profit organizations, both small and local and large and international. It has been applied to company boards, executive leadership teams and divisional teams, as well as project and account teams. Across all these settings we have found many teams that were strong in one or even two of the disciplines, but were unaware of, or were undeveloped in, the other disciplines. So far, out of hundreds of teams we have never found a team that excelled in all five disciplines.

We have also discovered that the model strongly assists teams in being more aware of their own 'team profile' and areas they need to develop more. It also provides a framework for team coaches to think about where they can add the most value and the different team coaching approaches needed for each of the five disciplines.

Figure 2.1   The five disciplines of high-performing teamso

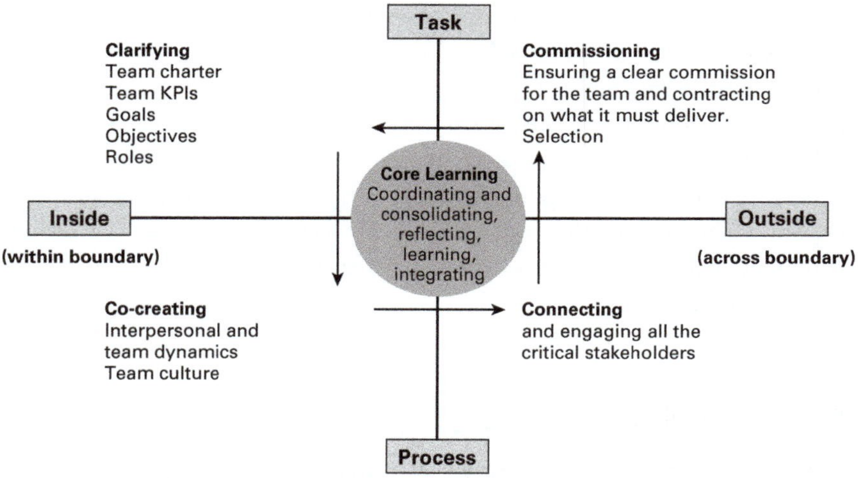

1 Commissioning: WHY we are a team

For a team to be successful it needs a clear commission from those who bring it into being. This includes a clear purpose and defined success criteria by which the performance of the team will be assessed. Once there is a clear commission, the role of the board (in the case of a leadership team, or more senior management in the case of other teams) is to appoint the right team leader whom they believe can deliver this mission. The team leader then has to select the right team members, who will have the right chemistry and diversity to work well together so the team will perform at more than the sum of their parts. Jim Collins (2001) describes this process as 'getting the right people on the bus', and in Hawkins (2017) there is a whole chapter (11) on selecting the right team players.

Richard Hackman (1990) emphasizes that the commission needs to include the support that the commissioners will give to the team. He argues that a good commission should include:

- targets;
- resources – eg people, financial, administrative, technical, accommodation;
- information;
- education – learning and development;

- regular, timely and appropriate feedback;
- technical and process assistance.

The team's commission is necessarily constantly changing. The team's commission does not just come from those above them in the organizational hierarchy, but also from the team's many stakeholders – its customers, suppliers, other parts of the organization, as well as the wider communities and natural environment of which it is a part.

2 Clarifying: WHAT we need to focus on as a team

Having ascertained its commission from outside itself and assembled the team, one of the first tasks for the new team is to jointly clarify its collective endeavour. The collective endeavour is a challenge the whole team find compelling and which they realize they can only achieve by working together. The team also needs to develop its own mission and team charter. The process of creating this mission together leads to higher levels of ownership and clarity for the whole team. This mission includes the team's:

- purpose;
- strategic narrative, goals and objectives;
- core values;
- vision for success;
- protocols and agreed ways of working;
- roles and expectations;
- team key performance objectives and indicators.

The team needs to ensure there is alignment between the team's mission and that of the wider organization as well as with the values and motivations of the individual team members.

The work of Richard Barrett (2006, 2010) shows that improving the alignment of individual, team and organizational values will greatly enhance team engagement and improve team performance.

3 Co-creating: HOW we work together as a team

Having a compelling collective endeavour, clear purpose, strategy, process and vision that everyone has signed up to is one thing; living it is a completely different challenge. If the mission is not going to stay just as a well-constructed group of words, but have a beneficial influence on performance, the team needs to constantly attend to how they creatively and generatively work together. This involves the team appreciatively noticing when they are functioning well, that is, at more than the sum of their parts, and also noticing and interrupting their own negative patterns, self-limiting beliefs and assumptions. A high-performing team also needs effective processes and agreed behaviours, both for their formal meetings and for engagement outside of meetings. This includes growing its collective capacity to handle conflict and contention in service of the greater system.

4 Connecting: WHO we need to engage with as a team to be create value

Being well commissioned, clear about what you are doing and co-creative in how you work together is necessary but not sufficient. The team only makes a difference and creates value through how they collectively and individually connect and engage with all their critical stakeholders. *Critical stakeholders* can be defined as both those individuals and groupings who are essential for the team to achieve its mission and those whom the team is in service of – both those from whom it receives value and those for whom it needs to create added value. It is through how the team engages in new ways to transform stakeholder relationships that they drive improvement in their own and the organization's performance.

Building on the research of Ancona and Caldwell (1992), Hawkins (2017: 50–51) identified three main strategies that teams use in connecting to their wider system:

a *Ambassadorial* – communicating about what the team is doing and raising its profile and reputation.

b *Scouting and Inquiry* – discovering what is happening and changing in and for customers, competitors, partners, investors, regulators, the wider environment and how these will create opportunities and threats for the team.

c *Partnering* – developing and managing partnerships with other teams inside the organization and beyond that can deliver greater value to the team's stakeholders than the team can do by themselves.

A high-performing team will have an effective and constantly updated stakeholder map, with role clarity on who has lead responsibility for each critical stakeholder. This relationship owner needs to ensure that all three processes are being handled well on behalf of the whole team.

Quality of stakeholder engagement is at the heart of team performance: 'research shows… it is not the amount of external communication that a team engages in which predicts successful team performance. Rather it is the type of external communication' (West, 1996: 110).

5 Core learning: HOW we continually learn to be more future-fit as a team

If a team only focuses on the first four disciplines they become better and better at playing today's game, but fail to develop the new and increased capacities to be future-fit for tomorrow's very different game. This fifth discipline sits in the middle and above the other four, and is the place where the team stands back, reflecting on their own performance and multiple processes and consolidating their learning ready for the next cycles of engagement. This discipline is also concerned with supporting and developing the learning and performance of every team member. Collective team learning and all the individual team members' learning goes hand-in-hand and all high-performing teams have a high commitment to both processes.

West (1996: 66–80) argues that successful teams attend to both team member well-being and long-term team viability by ensuring (a) social support between the team members, (b) team conflict resolution, (c) support for team members' learning and development and (d) a positive team climate. A key part of *core learning* is the team collectively attending to maintaining and developing these core elements.

How to evaluate the performance of each of the five disciplines

Since writing the second edition of *Leadership Team Coaching* (Hawkins, 2014), I have been asked, by both client teams and training programmes, 'how can we test or measure progress in each of the five disciplines?' This became a very useful springboard for further exploration, which led to developing the following measures, which can be used by team coaches or by teams to evaluate and monitor their own progress. These measures are designed to facilitate exploration and further development, not the scoring of achievements, ticking off accomplishments or self-blame. These review questions build on the questions in the high-performing team questionnaire but offer a different perspective. They are included here as they can be used as a way of reviewing the different case studies. Further and more detailed explorations of evaluating and assessing team performance and progress can be found in Chapter 13, including a questionnaire based on these questions:

1 Commissioning

   1.1 Has the team created an agreed upon and inclusive list of all their commissioners (all those who have a right to require something from the team)?

   1.2 Have they included their past and future commissioners – such as founders, future customers, possible potential buyers of the company?

   1.3 Does the team have a clear sense of what each commissioner needs from them to succeed and how they could inadvertently fail this commissioner?

2 Clarifying

   2.1 Has the team generatively co-created a mission, including purpose, strategy, core values and vision that is better than the team leader or any team member could have created by themselves?

   2.2 Has the team envisioned future emerging challenges?

   2.3 Have they stepped into the shoes and experience of each of their key stakeholders and clarified what their wider eco-system needs from them?

   2.4 Have they clarified their own aspirations?

   2.5 Have they field-tested their emerging clarity through dialogue with their commissioners, with their stakeholders and with those they lead?

   2.6 Have they tried to live their aspirations and behaviours in their own meetings and in their engagements with staff and stakeholders and refined them in the light of these trials?

   2.7 Have they developed two or three Team Key Performance Indicators that they are collectively accountable for?

3 Co-creating

   3.1 Is there shared ownership of the collective endeavour, team objectives and goals, and shared leadership? (See Hawkins, 2017: chapter 12.)

   3.2 Do all the team members hold each other mutually accountable for individual and team agreements?

3.3   Does the team generate new thinking together that is better than the individual thinking brought into the meetings?

3.4   How often do team members intervene in a way that enables improvements in the process and functioning of the team, by for example: interrupting old stuck patterns; raising awareness of what is happening live in the room; reframing problems or challenges; mediating conflict; enabling new connections; and so on?

4 Connecting

4.1   Does the team have a clear, shared and inclusive list of all their key stakeholders?

4.2   Have they clarified who will take the lead responsibility for each stakeholder connection on behalf of the team?

4.3   Do all the stakeholders feel engaged with the team and is the team kept well informed and well communicated with?

4.4   Do all the stakeholders feel able to influence what the team does and how it engages?

5 Core learning

5.1   Can each team member say what they have learnt and/or the capabilities and capacities they have developed in the past year, which they would not have learnt or developed without their involvement with the team?

5.2   Can the team identify what they have learnt together and the capacities they have collectively developed in the past year?

5.3   Does the team have a plan for how they will enable the learning and development of each team member?

5.4   Does the team have a plan for how they will enable the learning and development of the team as a whole?

Coaching the five disciplines

From the above questions it will be clear that the team coach needs to focus on very different questions in each of the five disciplines. These are summarized in Figure 2.2.

In Hawkins (2017: 100–22) I show the different coaching approaches needed in each discipline and later in the same book (pp 308–18) provide a range of tools and methods that can be used for each discipline.

Figure 2.2   The five disciplines model of team coaching: key questions

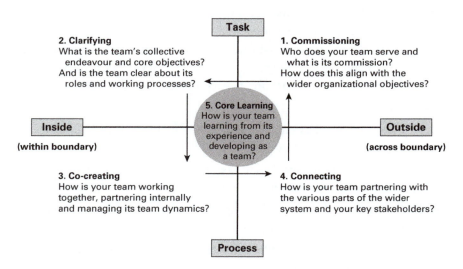

Defining systemic and leadership team coaching

In Hawkins (2017: 77) I defined *systemic team coaching* as:

> a process by which a team coach works with a whole team, both when they are together and when they are apart, in order to help them improve both their collective performance and how they work together, and also how they develop their collective leadership to more effectively engage with all their key stakeholder groups to jointly transform the wider business.

This definition and explanation showed how systemic team coaching builds on but is different from *leadership team coaching*, which I defined as 'team coaching for any team, not just the most senior, where the focus is on how the team collectively gives leadership to those who report to them and also how the team influences their key stakeholder groups' (Hawkins, 2017: 78).

I would now suggest that all effective leadership team coaching needs to be systemic to be successful (see Chapters 16 and 17).

The definition also shows how systemic team coaching is different from *performance team coaching*, which was the dominant approach to team coaching before I developed systemic team coaching: 'direct interaction with a team intended to help members make coordinated and task appropriate use of their collective resources in accomplishing the team's work' (Hackman and Wageman, 2005: 269); 'Helping the team improve performance, and the processes by which performance is achieved, through reflection and dialogue' (Clutterbuck, 2007: 77).

Systemic team coaching not only sees the team as a system, but as always existing within a larger system, most usually the organization, and in service of the organization's eco-system of stakeholders. Systemic team coaching therefore involves attending not only to the relationships within the team, but also to the relationships between the team (carried out on the team's behalf by any of the team members) and the team's stakeholders, which might include staff, customers, suppliers and partner organizations, investors, regulators, communities in which the organization operates, the more-than-human natural environment, professional or trade associations and others.

Since then I have developed the definition of systemic team coaching further in the light of the many teachings and discussions mentioned above. I also recognized that we can define it from a number of different perspectives:

By looking at the process: a process by which a team coach works with a whole team over an extended period of time both when the team is together and when it is apart.

By considering the intention or goal of the work: in order to help them improve both their collective performance and how they work together, and also how they develop their collective leadership to more effectively engage with all their key stakeholder groups to jointly transform the wider business and eco-system.

By looking at what the systemic team coach does: the systemic team coach contracts with the whole team and its key stakeholders, then co-inquires and co-discovers how the team is currently functioning internally and externally and how the team and its eco-system need the team to develop, then coaches the team to find these new ways of responding and engaging to create the needed difference.

By looking at how the systemic team coach needs to be, in order to successfully carry out the process and achieve the intention: the systemic team coach brings to the work a relational and systemic perspective, where they relate to the team, not as a client or subject of their coaching, but as a partner whom they stand alongside, both leaning into the future, sensing the needs emerging in their wider eco-system and experimenting with new ways of responding.

If we explore each of the phrases of this definition we can see more fully a number of separate elements:

- *With a whole team*: team coaching is different from coaching a series of team members or coaching the team leader on how they lead the team.

- *Both when the team is together and when it is apart*: some teams believe and act as if they are only a team when they are together, but the team functions between meetings, when its members are carrying out activities on behalf of the team. I sometimes use the analogy that the team meeting is like a football team practising on the training ground; the match is when the team members are out representing the team back in their own parts of the business.

- *In order to help the team improve both their collective performance and how they work together*: as Clutterbuck (2007), Hackman and Wageman (2005) and Hawkins and Smith (2006, 2013) all point out, team coaching is there not only to help create process improvement but also to impact on the collective performance of the team.

- *Develop their collective leadership*: often I will work with senior executives who have a mindset that they are only a member of the top team when they are attending the top-team meeting. High-performing leadership teams use their time together as a team to develop their collective capacity to spend the rest of the week leading all aspects of the business in a congruent and joined-up way which provides operational integration and transformational change aligned to the vision, mission, strategy and core values of the organization.

- *To more effectively engage with all their key stakeholder groups*: collective leadership is not just about running and transforming the business internally, but also about how the leadership team engages the various stakeholders in a congruent, aligned and transformational way. These stakeholders include customers, suppliers, partner organizations, employees, investors, regulators, boards, the communities in which the organization operates and the ecological environment that enables everything within it.

- *To jointly transform the wider business and eco-system*: the team needs to take responsibility beyond their locus of control for how they will deploy their influence to develop the wider business and larger eco-system in which they operate. This is partly carried out by focusing on how they will enable the leadership of others (staff, customers, suppliers, investors, and so on).

- *The systemic team coach contracts with the whole team and its key stakeholders*: for the work to be systemic the coach needs to contract not just with the team leader or even all the team members but also include contracting with some representatives of the wider system.

- *Co-inquires and co-discovers how the team is currently functioning internally and externally*: the work begins by a co-inquiry and co-discovery process between the systemic team coach and all the team members into the current reality.

- *How the team and its eco-system need the team to develop*: and also into the team's aspirations and the future needs of the wider system.

- *Then coaches the team to find this new way of responding and engaging to create the needed difference*: then comes the work of exploring, experimenting and rehearsing new ways of relating and responding to the emerging needs.

- *The systemic team coach relates to the team, not as a client or subject of their coaching, but as a partner whom they stand alongside*: systemic team coaching is not done to the team by the systemic team coach, but by the coach and the whole team working in partnership, both facing what is currently happening and what is required by the team and their eco-system.

- *Then co-inquires and co-discovers how the team is currently functioning internally and externally and how the team and its eco-system need the team to develop*: systemic team coaching always views the team in dynamic relationship with its eco-system; we can only discover the necessary development for the team by also looking at the needs of the team's eco-system as represented by all the stakeholders, as well as the team's aspirations and the relational space between the team and its eco-system.

- *Coaches the team to find these new ways of responding and engaging to create the needed difference*: the systemic team coach adds value through enabling the team to find new ways of perceiving, engaging and responding to their context, addressing their blind spots (Scharmer, 2013) and wilful blindness (Heffernan, 2011).

- *The systemic team coach brings to the work a relational and systemic perspective*: this is explored fully in Chapters 16 and 17.

In the third edition of *Leadership Team Coaching* I also went further to suggest that the world increasingly needs a further development of Systemic Team Coaching, which I termed eco-systemic team coaching. **Eco-Systemic Team Coaching** sees the team as co-evolving in dynamic relationship with its ever-changing eco-system of interconnected teams, with which it co-creates shared value. Eco-systemic coaching focuses on the interplay between the team and other connected teams (inter-team coaching). Its strategic dialogue involves its wider stakeholders ('coaching strategizing processes'), developing a team-based culture within an organization and across a network of enterprises ('coaching networks') or partnerships that bring people and organizations together in pursuit of a common goal ('coaching partnerships') (Hawkins, 2017). This new second edition has included two new case studies to reflect this development (Chapters 11 and 12).

Conclusion

For some, this model and these definitions may seem complex and dense, but for others their learning style will want to have defined the territory and mapped it out before they feel ready to go and explore the different team territories. Hopefully this chapter has also provided a rich frame and perspective through which the case studies can be viewed, and you might wish to return to it after you have read the cases, to see how they further inform and develop the theory, or contradict and reform it for you. I invite you to engage in your own dialogue between theory and practice in service of finding your own approach and meaning making.

Learning from case studies and an overview of published case studies

03

PETER HAWKINS, CATHERINE CARR
AND JACQUELINE PETERS

Introduction

One of the best ways to learn about leadership team coaching is to read case studies describing the work done by other team coaches and team leaders. However, it is important not just to absorb and copy what others have done, as every team has its own unique context, conditions and challenges. We provide guidance on ways of reading case studies dialogically; that is, reading as if you are in a generative conversation with the author. This means responding to what is written both appreciatively and critically, as well as reflecting on both their work and your own to maximize the learning you can glean from each case.

To date there has been a severe shortage of detailed case studies on all levels of team coaching, showing how the relationship between the team and the team coach has:

- developed over time;
- developed both the internal and external workings of the team;
- increased the effectiveness of the team to respond creatively and give leadership within their organization and their wider eco-system.

So in this introductory chapter we include an overview of some of the cases and case-based research that has been published elsewhere.

We have included a range of case studies drawn from different sectors and from different countries to provide a wide range of experiences the reader can draw upon. We have also tried to include case studies in which teams are addressing different challenges presented by the teams in question and in consequence focusing on different aspects of the five disciplines model of high performing teams.

The focus of the coach

Another perspective that you can apply to the case studies is to reflect on the work of the team coach and the nature of their engagement with the team and the wider system, and how this changes as the work develops overtime.

To help you with this process, Peter Hawkins has provided a framework in Table 3.1 that distinguishes between the different levels of team coaching. Please note this is not implying that the transformational levels of coaching are better or more important than those above them, only that they have a wider range of engagement and are more inclusive. Which level is required will depend on the context of the work, the challenges facing the team and the level at which the team and team coach are ready to engage.

Learning from interacting with the case studies

To get maximum value from these case studies we would encourage you as the reader to read these case studies dialogically; that is as if you are in a generative conversation with the authors. Whether you are a team coach, team leader or team member, we would invite you, as you are reading the chapter, to reflect on the following questions (perhaps writing your answers down either as you go along or when you have finished the chapter):

1 What did the team coach and team do that you could learn from?

2 What methods and tools did they use that you might find useful in your work?

3 What do you glean from the chapter about their way of being and engaging with the team that you could learn from?

Table 3.1 The level of team coaching and the team coaching disciplines

Level of team coaching	Focus	Goal or endeavour	Role of coach	Team coaching disciplines
Team facilitation	Team process	Better internal engagement	Enabling the team to do its work better	3
Team performance coaching	Team performance Task and process	Increased team performance	To help the team achieve its goals	2 & 3 (possibly 5)
Leadership team coaching	How the team gives leadership to its wider system	More effective shared leadership	To enable the team to lead more collectively and more effectively	2 & 3 and the internal aspects of 4
Systemic team coaching	Task, process and leadership in relation to the wider eco-system	The team better able to lead and co-create with its wider stakeholder eco-system	To help the team to engage and co-create more effectively with all its stakeholders	1, 2, 3, 4 & 5
Transformational systemic team coaching	The future emerging needs of the wider eco-system and how the team can respond	A team able to constantly transform in dynamic relationship with its eco-system	To enable the team to recognize and respond to the emerging needs and challenges of the wider eco-system in new transformative ways	1, 2, 3, 4 & 5

4　What did the team coach, team leader, or whole team fail to do that with the wisdom of hindsight you would have liked to have done in their place?

5　Which of the five disciplines did they attend to?

6　What might they have done to attend more fully to specific disciplines?

7　How did they engage with the wider system and bring a focus on the wider system into the coaching engagement?

8　If you had one piece of advice to the author(s) what would it be?

9　How does that advice to the authors also apply to you and your work?

10　If you were the team leader or team coach how would you go about developing the team further?

You might also like to apply the five discipline models and the evaluative measures mentioned in Chapter 2 to the work of the team in the case study, which might provide other indications of both what this work did achieve and what further progress you would encourage if you were leading or coaching this team.

In Chapter 13 we provide other approaches to evaluating team coaching including how to assess team maturity, which you might also find a useful lens through which to look at these cases.

New case studies since 2012

Since the publication of the first edition of this book, several authors have included a variety of short case descriptions in their books, including the first edition of this book (Hawkins, 2014b), Jennifer Britton (2013) in her book *From One to Many*, and Christine Thornton (2016) in the second edition of her book, *Group and Team Coaching*. Many case descriptions continue to include few or incomplete details on the actual methodology undertaken or the objective measures used to assess results, if indeed measures were embedded into the team coaching program. Case study research tends to cite outcomes that are primarily improvements in what are often termed mediators, including: 'learning, decision making, information sharing, communication, improved positive regard for each other and [increases in] individual contributions' (Peters and Carr, 2013). As in our 2012 review, few studies used objective assessment measures and where they did, we have noted that.

In order to support team coaches to learn how to both plan fulsome team coaching interventions and what to measure, we have selected case descriptions

Table 3.2 Comparison of team coaching case studies

Researcher/ practitioner (Date)	Subjects	Detailed approach/ intervention components	Primary team coaching approach*	Individual team member coaching	Team coaching outcomes according to participants
Mulec and Roth (2005)	Two global product development management teams in the pharmaceutical industry (Global)	Eight months of project team coaching included: Interviewing individual team members, action learning (attending team meetings and observing and coaching within that space), team leader coaching before team meetings, and concluding interviews with members about their learning	Leadership team coaching	Yes	• Change capacity • *Communication* • Creativity/innovation • Decision making • *Information sharing* • *Learning* • Meeting efficiency
C	Top management team of 9 members (Denmark)	One-year team coaching project included: 360 degree feedback, six individual sessions over a year, team coaching every two months (workshops and regular team meeting participation), team facilitation and extra individual coaching as needed	Leadership team coaching	Yes	• Cooperation • *Dialogue/communication* • Team *learning*

(Continued)

Table 3.2 (Continued)

Researcher/ practitioner (Date)	Subjects	Detailed approach/ intervention components	Primary team coaching approach*	Individual team member coaching	Team coaching outcomes according to participants
Blattner and Bacigalupo (2007)	Management team (US)	Team coaching project included: Team member interviews, Emotional Intelligence assessment and group profiling, two 12-hour offsite retreats scheduled three months apart	Leadership team coaching with some systemic focus	Yes	• *Communication* • Cooperation/ collaboration • *Decision making* • Focused dialogue • Positive team climate • Productivity • *Trust*
Anderson, Anderson and Mayo (2008)	Senior leadership team of ten members (US)	21-month engagement using a Leadership Insight Model included: Team leader coaching, interviews, team feedback session, coaching skills workshops, interactive consulting experiences, team member coaching, in the moment team coaching and interviews for evaluation	Transformational team coaching	Yes	Evaluation showed increases in: • Coaching others • Collaboration • *Communication* • Cross matrix initiatives • *Decision making* • Employee engagement scores • Engagement • Feedback • Individual *learning* • Meeting effectiveness • Team effectiveness (leadership team and leader's own team)

Authors	Setting	Intervention	Leadership focus	Outcomes
Kegan and Lahey (2009)	Senior marketing team in a Pharmaceutical company (US)	Six-month team coaching project included: Individual assessment, one-to-one coaching, team coaching sessions (one 2-day and two 1-day sessions), peer feedback, post-coaching survey and debrief session, and follow-up interviews three months later.	Team coaching	Yes	*Communication* • Individual *learning* • Team innovation • Peer feedback and coaching • Team building (dynamics) • *Trust*
Haug (2011)	Cross-functional management team of five (Germany)	Six-month project included: 20 observed meetings plus interviews and questionnaires, one-to-one coaching, email feedback on team meetings, and coach reflections	Team coaching	Yes	• Accelerated team development • Individual growth and development through one-to-one coaching • Planning • Problem solving • Productivity
Woodhead (2011)	Multi-disciplinary leadership team of three (UK)	Six-month project included: Six sessions for 2.5 hours per session, meeting once monthly, and final interviews	Leadership team coaching	Yes	• Clarity of shared goals • *Communication* • *Decision making* • Improved relationships • *Information sharing* • *Positive regard for each other* • Psychological safety • Team commitment

NOTE The italicized outcomes refer to those perceived most frequently by practitioners.

that included enough detail to fully assess either the team coaching approach and/or outcomes achieved. As a result, three of the case studies in Hawkins' book were highlighted in our review of the case studies since the 2014 edition, along with the four case descriptions discussed in Britton's book, and two additional studies by Gilchrest and Barnes (2013) and Cole (2017), which were published on the internet and were robust enough to include.

Hawkins and Boyle: executive, board and inter-team coaching creates a lever for systemic change

The Hawkins and Boyle (2014) case study described a systemic intervention with Yeovil Hospital Foundation Trust in the UK. This eighteen-month, multi-pronged approach focused on team coaching for the executive team with individual coaching for the CEO, inter-team coaching and contracting for three clinical divisional teams and a one-day board development workshop. The desired outcome the CEO wanted from the intervention was to restructure the organization from ten divisions into three. He also wanted to create a 'flagship model' for rural hospitals that could achieve greater quality of service while also increasing services and reducing costs – a tall order for any organization.

All the teams in the intervention completed a High Performing Team Questionnaire and *Descriptor Analysis* that probed five disciplines of high performance teams: Clarifying, Commissioning, Co-Creating, Connecting, and Core Learning (Hawkins, 2017). The assessment included doing a stakeholder analysis to determine what success looked like from multiple stakeholders' perspectives.

The new structure was launched in a one-day workshop with the three new clinical division teams, the executive team and the central functions team. The five teams all created their own mission and protocols for working within their team and with their stakeholders. They also discussed how they would help each other.

A full day board development event followed this session, where the board discussed the themes from the pre-session interviews and the *High Performing Board Questionnaire* (Hawkins, 2014). They identified ways to work with the executive team more effectively and move from a mindset of avoiding failure to a mindset of success. They also recognized that to achieve their challenging financial goals, they needed to focus more externally so the board decided to create new partnerships with other health organizations in their community.

The next several months focused on individual coaching for the CEO and team meetings with the executive.

At the end of the intervention, the board and executive team rated themselves and others rated the teams higher on the High Performing Team Questionnaire than they did nine months previously. The results from the three clinical divisional teams in the intervention were less clear and varied in their level of perceived improvement. Overall, all participants expressed satisfaction with the intervention.

We categorized this as a systemic team coaching approach because of the numerous stakeholder groups involved in the intervention, and the focus on using a restructuring of the organization to fuel organizational and systemic change, including stakeholders and partner organizations outside of the organization.

Jarrett: comprehensive team and leadership development programme supports cultural change to meet industry demands

The Finnair case study described a team coaching and cultural change project that was launched to achieve financial and business objectives, as described by David Jarrett (2014) and delivered by Bath Consultancy Group. They worked over a period of two years with the 10-member executive team and 120-member leadership group at Finnair. The airline industry was changing rapidly and the focus of the intervention was to support the organization to build a culture that was responsive to the strategic changes being made to the services, pricing and cost management structure.

The team coaching and leadership development intervention included initial interviews, assessment, 360° feedback for the executive team, a two-day leadership development event to identify the leadership behaviours required for the future, periodic team coaching sessions over two years and development for the next tier of leaders. The Finnair HR team supported the leadership and culture change by creating 'performance measurement, succession and talent processes, reward mechanisms and mentoring' approaches, which embedded the leadership behaviours required.

The most objective and compelling business outcome at the end of the two-year transformation and team coaching project was a correlated profit of about €14 million for the company, compared to a net loss of about €80 million on average for the four years prior to the team project. Other outcomes described were improved team dynamics, processes, team learning and team engagement.

We listed this as a systemic team coaching approach because the intervention included many teams in the organizational system. Also, there was a focus on tasks, processes, internal and external stakeholders and the organization and health system as a whole.

O'Sullivan and Field: linking team coaching to measures that matter

The pharmaceutical company example in the Hawkins (2014) book was written by Padraig O'Sullivan and Carole Field. They outlined a combined leadership and team development program delivered over approximately two years to the Australian subsidiary of a multi-national pharmaceutical company. The intervention began with a 5C assessment and one-to-one coaching for the Managing Director and expanded to the leadership team members individually and as a team. The team coaching consisted of individual coaching, a team launch, quarterly meetings and onboarding of new leaders and promoted peer coaching and shared leadership. At the organizational level, high potential leaders participated in a 'Rising Star' programme, which served as a model for talent and succession management for the Australian subdivision and for other affiliate offices across the company's Asian offices.

Business outcomes cited from the team coaching and leadership development program were 1) being recognized as one of the top 30 most innovative companies in Australia in 2012 by *Business Review Weekly* (BRW), and 2) being listed as one of the top 50 organizations to work in Australia by Great Places to Work, an international consulting group. In addition, employee engagement scores for the subsidiary were an average of 10 points higher than their benchmark organizations.

Anecdotal outcomes cited by the coaches and participants included improvements in the team's functioning and a new business strategy that garnered support from all team members.

We listed this as a systemic team coaching approach because the coaching focus moved from individual coaching to a leadership team focus and then to a systemic focus on how to create greater innovation within the organization. The work also sparked new talent management processes that expanded beyond Australia to the Asian operations of the company.

Miller: start with the individual coaching request and build to the team and organization levels

Miller's 2013 case study also showed how team coaching can start with one team or team leader and build to the entire organization. This extensive team coaching programme began with the intent to support a newly promoted senior leader with a challenged service team. Miller carried out a team offsite followed by six team coaching meetings. This was followed by individual coaching for the promoted leader and leadership team coaching for his team. The engagement ended with three offsites for the entire organization. The Team Diagnostic Assessment (TDI) was used to assess the effectiveness of the service team from team members' perspectives and showed a 30 per cent gain.

This case study is an example of leadership team coaching because the coaching engagement began with one challenged team but then expanded to the whole leadership team and included some organizational work to promote alignment, engagement and commitment.

Peters: consider coach training for leaders to build leadership capacity and to build a coaching culture

Peters (2013) built a team coaching programme for an oil and gas company, which included assessments, interviews, a team launch, team charter work, and ongoing team coaching. This case study highlighted the need to continue to support leadership teams in the pivotal transition from being coached to coaching themselves and other teams. In hindsight, Peters recommended adding in coach training with the executive team and senior team leaders to support their efforts at coaching their own teams. Outcomes included increased team effectiveness scores from an average of 6.0 to 7.5 and a significant increase in financial results over the 18 months of executive team coaching.

Peters' case study is also an example of systemic team coaching. She worked with the executive team and included a focus on how they were working together, their individual and team performance and their capacity to coach their teams. The coaching was expanded to include all six organizations' teams, however engagement and coaching sessions waned due to a serious economic downturn – a real challenge that all teams and coaches may face in their work together.

Public Service Agency: set consequential and challenging goals at the individual and organizational level

Finally, Britton's book showcased a government human resources agency who carried out a team coaching assignment to increase team effectiveness and, in particular, shared leadership and cross-functional collaboration. The coaches conducted initial team member interviews, followed by a single full team day and subsequent team leader coaching. This particular team coaching assignment focused on exploring individual behavioural styles, interests and talents. Amongst the positive outcomes, the team coaching increased the ability for junior staff to move into leadership roles.

We see this case study as an example of leadership team coaching in that the coaching focused on increasing shared leadership among the team members.

Sandahl: measure, measure and measure again

Phil Sandahl (2014) coached a health team and utilized a series of measures, highlighting how measurement can be effectively used. He met monthly with the health team over the course of a year for team coaching sessions.

Several measures were tracked, including the Team Diagnostic (TDI) assessment, which showed an increase of 30 per cent for productivity and 31 per cent for positivity. The team's patient satisfaction scores increased by 12 per cent and moved from the 18th percentile across the country to the 86th percentile. Each team took on one more patient per day. A return on investment analysis was done to demonstrate the financial savings and illustrated how patient satisfaction could increase revenue and avoid lawsuits.

Sandahl's case study is an example of performance team coaching because he worked with one team to increase their team performance.

Cole: bringing people together is half the work

In addition to practitioner case studies published in books and journals, several coaches and organizations provide case descriptions as part of their marketing materials. Some of these descriptions are more fulsome than others.

One such study was done by Cole (2017). He was brought in to repair senior leadership relationships between a CEO's two business divisions of a multinational conglomerate that had been separated out during an organizational restructuring. The groups were described as 'warring'. Cole did a two-day team coaching offsite (using the Society of Organizational Learning's (SoL) systemic coaching model, solution-focused and appreciative inquiry methods). They reportedly achieved 75 per cent of their team coaching connection and collaboration goals within the first six months. At the six-month follow-up, they committed to completing the final 25 per cent.

This case study is an example of leadership team coaching because Cole focused within a conglomerate to build internal cohesion, trust and collaboration.

Gilchrest and Barnes: keep flying the current plane but start building a new one

Coaches and organizations who focus on team coaching have increasingly published case descriptions as part of their marketing materials. Many are short descriptions without substantiating detail, however Gilchrest and Barnes (2013) outlined a detailed systemic team coaching case study conducted with the executive team at Rocela, a UK-based technology company. The company needed to make the shift from 'business as usual' to 'working on the business' in order to create a new business model and improve their ability to work together.

Company executives agreed to participate in five team coaching meetings over a year. The coaches used Hawkins' (2011) 5C model as the basis to address the future state needs of the company. After a year, coaches and participants stated that the team had a better team dynamic, higher quality thinking and decision making, and a new business strategy that garnered support from all team members.

We categorized this Gilchrest and Barnes study as a systemic team coaching initiative because the coaching focused on adapting to external facing needs of the company including creating a new business model to stay competitive.

Discussion

In the first edition of this book, we reviewed team coaching case studies up until 2012 and this time we have added case studies published between 2012 and 2017. The first set of studies documented a team coaching process and reported outcomes from the perspective of the team members. Later studies also include some outcomes based on perceptions of others external to the team such as client feedback (Sandahl, 2014), company feedback from the CEO or finance department (Jarrett, 2014; Cole, 2017), informal investor feedback (Peters, 2014) or external recognition such as awards (O'Sullivan and Field, 2014).

Table 3.3 Comparison of team coaching case studies since 2012

Researcher/ practitioner (Date)	Subjects	Detailed approach/ Intervention components	Primary team coaching approach*	Individual team member coaching	Team coaching outcomes according to participants
Miller in Britton (2013)	Senior Leader of financial institution, a service team, leadership team and country team (Canada)	Three-year programme included: • One-and-a-half day team offsite and six team coaching meetings • Staff feedback interviews and six individual leader coaching sessions • Five half-day leadership team offsites • Three offsites for the entire country team	Performance team coaching	Yes Team and team leader coaching	• Communication/ dialogue • Engagement • Financial results • Improved team effectiveness scores on Stellar Team Diagnostic from Team Coaching • Trust
Peters in Britton (2013)	Oil and Gas team (Canada)	18-month initiative: • Team interviews and a team debrief session • Two-day team offsite • Two-hour quarterly team meetings • One or two two-day team sessions per year	Transformation leadership team coaching	No	• Increased feedback and recognition • Adaptability • Communication • Completed team action plans • Goal alignment • Problem solving • Team effectiveness as measured on the team effectiveness Assessment (Peters, unpublished)

Public Service Agency, BC government in Britton (2013)	13-member team in government led by a Director (Canada)	Eight-month initiative included: • Team coaching orientation • Interviews with team members and stakeholder and a team debrief of results • One-day team launch session • Six team leader sessions • Follow-up team session	Leadership team coaching	Yes Team and team leader coaching	• Communication • New process for creating cross-functional projects
Sandahl in Britton (2013)	Direct Service Health Care Team (US)	13-month programme for direct patient care team included: • Monthly coaching sessions • Pre- and post-programme measures of Team Diagnostic assessment and the Press Ganey Patient Satisfaction survey	Performance team Coaching	No	• Financial results • Patient load • Positivity • Press Ganey Patient Satisfaction Score • Productivity • Team effectiveness as measured on the Team Diagnostic from Team Coaching International
Gilchrest and Barnes (2014)	Executive team at Rocelo, a technology company (UK)	One-year team coaching program based on Hawkins' (2014) 5C model included: • Assessment via team member interviews and observations of team meetings • Five team coaching meetings • Stakeholder feedback	Systemic team coaching	No	• New business strategy and structure • Decision making and higher quality thinking • Team dynamics

(Continued)

Table 3.3 (Continued)

Researcher/ practitioner (Date)	Subjects	Detailed approach/ Intervention components	Primary team coaching approach*	Individual team member coaching	Team coaching outcomes according to participants
Hawkins and Boyle in Hawkins (2014)	Yeovil Hospital Foundation Trust executive team, board and 3 clinical divisional teams (UK)	One-year programme included: • Team leader coaching • Team coaching • Board development	Systemic team coaching	Yes Team and team leader coaching	Team learning and development as measured on a High Performing Team Questionnaire (Hawkins, 2017)
Jarrett in Hawkins (2014)	Finnair: 10 executive team members and 120 leadership team members (Finland)	Two-year programme including: • Two-day multiple team workshops • Learning group follow-ups • 360° feedback questionnaires • Individual coaching • Leadership development including a 120-person Leader Summit	Systemic team coaching	Yes Team and team member coaching	• Delegation • Financial profit • Loyalty • Resilience • Shared leadership and responsibility • Trust

O'Sullivan and Field in Hawkins (2014)	Pharmaceutical subsidiary (Australia)	Leadership development over six years included: Individual coaching Team coaching 360° feedback	Systemic team coaching	Yes Team and team member coaching	• Employee engagement survey • Engagement • External awards (Top 30 Innovative workplace and Top 50 best places to work) • Innovative thinking
Cole (2017)	Senior leadership team of CEO and 9 direct reports in a business within a multinational conglomerate (Asia)	Two-day team coaching offsite (using solution-focused and appreciative inquiry methods) and six-month follow-up	Leadership team coaching	No	• Collaboration • Financial results • Progress tracking • Team connection • Structured meetings

In 2012, only one study (Anderson *et al*, 2008) reported an objective business result that was connected to the team coaching; this was an increase in the employee engagement results for the participating leadership team's division. By 2017, there were more team effectiveness questionnaires used and the results of these surveys often revealed that the teams subjectively assessed their teams as being more effective. In addition, Sandahl (2014) used a patient satisfaction assessment and O'Sullivan and Field (2014) used an employee engagement survey. Some studies recorded financial results (Jarrett, 2014; Peters, 2013; Sandahl, 2014) although these were sometimes noted as positive gains from the coaching and were at best correlated rather than causal results.

In both sets of case study reviews, practitioners noted many perceived benefits of the team coaching. The outcomes described most often are italicized in Table 3.2 and include: learning, decision making, information sharing, communication, trust, regard for each other, and individual contributions. In Table 3.3, the 2012 to 2017 case studies list similar outcomes and document increases in various team effectiveness scores as measured on formal and/or informal team effectiveness assessments (Hawkins and Boyle, 2013; Miller, 2013; Peters, 2013; Sandahl, 2013). Also noted in the outcomes of the latter studies were improvements in business strategies and cross-functional processes (Public Service Agency, 2013; Jarrett, 2014).

There are a variety of relationship-based outcomes listed in the team coaching case study literature (eg, positivity, trust, loyalty) and it is possible that the practitioners used approaches and had goals for the coaching that facilitated those kinds of outcomes. Further, case study researchers rely upon qualitative interviews, observations and feedback sessions, hence the kind of data they collect is often subjective and reflective in nature, often along the lines of relationship observations and outcomes. This aligns with Hackman's (1983) observation that team members may notice the quality of their relationship processes more readily than the impact of team structures, thus influencing what participants discuss as key coaching outcomes. At the same time, it is also possible that case study research may illustrate the genuine value and effect that team coaching can have on the quality of a team's relationships.

We can learn a lot from the case studies about what actual activities and processes are provided in a team coaching intervention. A common intervention element in many of the case studies was individual coaching of the team leader and team members. This observation contrasts with formative team coaching models (Clutterbuck, 2007; Hackman and Wageman, 2005; Hawkins, 2011; Kozlowski, Gully, Salas and Cannon-Bowers, 1996;

Wageman, Nunes, Burruss and Hackman, 2008), which all place less emphasis on individual coaching for all or most of the team members, except for
Clutterbuck's model (2007). Wageman *et al* (2008) and Hawkins (2011,
2017) do recommend that it may be beneficial to coach the leader as part of
the team coaching intervention, especially to support the development of the
team leader's team coaching skills.

Additionally, most of the coaching engagements detailed at least one or
more full-day events with their teams near the beginning of the team coaching process. These studies described team design activities that align with
the kinds of team launch actions alluded to by Hackman (2011), which
include defining the team's purpose, team member roles and responsibilities,
and working agreements. As Hackman (2011) and Wageman (2001) have
pointed out, there is great value in taking the time to focus on team design
because it has a great impact on team effectiveness.

When any of the case study teams were not at the beginning of the team
development cycle, it appeared that the team coach treated the beginning
of the coaching process as a new beginning, or mid-point review for the
team. The coach supported creating and/or renewing the foundational team
design elements such as purpose, goals, roles, working agreements, and so
on. This is a process linked to Hawkins' Discipline 2, 'Clarifying', and when
used in the mid-life of a team it is termed 'Re-clarifying'. This event-focused
launch or re-launch of the team creates the momentum for a team to refresh
and reset. This approach aligns with the idea that coaching interventions
are best matched for the times when the coaching can make the most difference: the beginning, middle or end of a team's work (Carr and Peters, 2012;
Gersick, 1988; Wageman, Fisher and Hackman, 2009).

Coaching engagements varied from one or two-day events and short
follow-up sessions (Cole, 2017) to six-year engagements (O'Sullivan and
Field, 2014) involving team coaching and other organizational development
initiatives.

Hawkins, as detailed in this book, has greatly advanced the field of
case study research by publishing many of the more robust case studies.
Practitioners who have trained in Hawkins' Systemic Team Coaching also
seem to be starting to publish their cases on the internet (eg, Gilchrest
and Barnes, 2014), which has helped to create some standardization in
approaches. Others such as Britton (2013) have contributed to the literature
by detailing studies with business measures, detailed agendas and the use of
team effectiveness assessments.

In 2017, the third edition of *Leadership Team Coaching* (Hawkins, 2017)
added a new focus on eco-systemic team coaching, with greater emphasis on

'team of team coaching', coaching networks, partnerships and whole start-up businesses. Included in that book are two case studies of eco-systemic team coaching: one of Saracens Rugby club and how they connect their sports team coaching with the coaching in both their business and their social change foundation; and Enspiral, a New Zealand-based network of small businesses and freelance workers. Eco-systemic team coaching creates a deeper marriage between team coaching and whole system and organizational development. Further case studies of this approach can be found in books by McChrystal (2015) and Fussell (2017), which apply a 'team of teams' approach to the Allied Forces in post-war Iraq, as well as applying what they collectively learnt from these experiences to a range of business organizations.

Future directions

As we review the case studies overall, it is worth pointing out three related studies in the coaching literature. Blackman, Moscardo and Gray's (2016) systematic review of business coaching noted 'While anecdotal accounts of positive personal experiences of coaching abound, the long-term credibility of coaching must rely on evidence-based studies with robust research, including quasi-experimental and experimental designs based on both cross-sectional and longitudinal designs' (p 476). This underscores the point that case study writers would be wise to do follow-up evaluations with their teams using qualitative and quantitative assessments and gather external stakeholder feedback more frequently to assess outcomes and substantiate team coaching participants' self-reported results.

The second and third studies to take note of were done by Lawrence and Whyte (2017) and Pliopas, Kerr and Sosinski (2014). These researchers highlight differences and similarities in the actual structure of coaching interventions. In addition to Hawkin's 5 Cs model, these studies provide coaches with the beginnings of a practice roadmap for team coaching: assessment, a one- to two-day team launch/workshop, individual coaching of the leader and/or other team members, training team members on coaching, ongoing team coaching sessions, and final sessions to review learning and plan next steps. Whether one coaching element is more useful than another, or whether coaching from an internal or external coach generates greater outcomes, are questions that remain for future research.

Overall, the call to action for team coaching research and practitioners remains: Going forward, the more objective business measures we can offer, the more compelling evidence we will have for leaders to pursue and commit to team coaching in business and work settings. Team building can be great fun, but team coaching demands more evidence of results – let's keep progressing the field.

Conclusion

This chapter has provided a series of synopses of team coaching case studies in the literature from before 2012 and from 2012 until 2017. These studies were drawn from a variety of countries; a wide range of types of organizations, including manufacturing, pharmaceutical, public health service; and different types of teams, including executive teams, regional sales teams and cross-functional teams. It has also described some methods for maximizing your learning from reading the case studies of team coaching carried out by others, including:

- how to reflect on what form of team coaching is being carried out using the Hawkins (2017) continuum of team coaching approaches;
- how to evaluate each of the case studies through the five lenses of the Hawkins (2017) five disciplines model;
- how to reflect on the relationship between the coach and the team being coached and how this developed over time; and
- how to reflect on how you might have handled the challenges and needs of the team differently if you were (a) the team leader and (b) the team coach.

Our hope is that you will be able to use these approaches when reading the case studies in the following nine chapters as well as the case vignettes in Chapters 14 and 15.

Coaching the commissioning and clarifying

04

A case study of a professional services leadership team

WRITTEN COLLABORATIVELY BY HILARY LINES AND RICHARD, THE TEAM LEADER

Enabling a new leadership team to move from formation to high performance is always challenging. But building a team to lead a newly created axis within a matrix organization, which runs against the grain of historical sources of power, influence and allegiance, is far tougher.

(LINES AND SCHOLES-RHODES, 2013: 177)

We wrote the above words in *Touchpoint Leadership* when we first described the work of the leadership team to be addressed in this case study. At that time, Hilary had been working as a co-inquirer and coach with the team for six months, and the case study focused on the application of the principles of *Touchpoint Leadership* to the work of the team. In this chapter we look back at the first 14 months of the development of the team and the role of team coaching in that process, drawing on the learning from the team and some of its stakeholders; and we map out the potential shape of the team coaching journey for the rest of the two-year programme.

Context for the work

A constant challenge for those businesses whose mission is to provide services aimed at transforming the performance of client organizations is to ensure that they organize their human talent both to best serve specific client and sector needs, and also to enable the development of a depth and breadth of expertise that is competitive and applicable to multiple business types. These interrelated goals of attending to client needs and building deep but versatile capability require active and highly tuned leadership to ensure that the two axes are held in creative rather than destructive tension (Trompenaars and Nijhoff Asser, 2010). Whichever axis the leadership decides will be uppermost in the matrix creates its own challenges that need to be managed (Lines and Scholes-Rhodes, 2013: 142–45).

In the organization that this team were part of, all consulting services staff were originally organized into sector-facing groups, as the primary 'home' of performance and career development, while virtually belonging to one of a number of practice communities, focused on capability. The business had come to realize that this structure was creating an impediment to the development and deployment of its consulting capability and its competitiveness against larger-scale consulting businesses. Keeping consultants in separate sector-based groups hindered the flexibility and critical mass that the business needed to resource projects, grow skills and provide attractive career paths. The business therefore had created a new separate consulting organization as a horizontal structure, cutting across the vertical sector-focused organization, and to which all consulting staff would belong as their prime line of reporting. Richard, the consulting director, had formed a new team to lead the formation and embedding of the consulting service line structure. The goal was to create a high-performing community of practice which would be recognized as adding tangible value to the services provided to clients and which would attract, retain and develop high-calibre consulting professionals.

It was a challenging time to embark on a reorganization of this type. Market conditions were tough: the shock to business precipitated by the financial crisis of 2008–09 had not only created a reduction in the amount of money being spent on professional services, but also a deep cynicism about their value-add. These attitudes permeated both private and public sectors in the UK, the latter as the government attempted to reduce the size of the public debt. Responding to these conditions, the business had embarked on a cost-cutting exercise which had impacted confidence and morale.

The creation of the consulting service line at this time further impacted on people's sense of value and belonging. Many people felt wrenched away from their 'spiritual home', and unclear of the nature and purpose of the entity to which they were being reassigned.

It was clear to Richard that some of the large-scale communications exercises that had historically been used to bring people on board with new changes were not going to be enough to address the morale issues among his people. He started to examine his own communications style:

> I wondered, 'How do you create a sense of belonging and a climate where they spark off each other?' So, I reflected on how I liked to be communicated with, especially as a junior consultant – the style and the content. I was also intrigued by how communication had passed over the centuries – it was through face-to-face story telling not mass technology-based communications. I felt there had to be a sense of the 'personal' for it to matter. Personal emails, hand-written cards all gave a sense that a human being was the communicator not a computer....
>
> ... I started to have smaller conversations of 15–20 people and people started to put their hands up... I started to bring people who contacted me into my network. It was ad hoc. Gradually I am building a network of like-minded individuals, starting to weave in their ideas and act on their recommendations, draw on their advice. They of course talk to their peers. If I can get more touch points... I can build an ecosystem.
>
> (Lines and Scholes-Rhodes, 2013: 176)

While there was a sense that these new communications approaches were having a positive effect, Richard was clear that he could not shift the climate of the service line on his own: he needed to enable his leadership team to join him in creating positive connections across this new and dispersed community. He decided to expand his original leadership team to include all the expertise group heads as well as the leaders of client sector groups and functional heads from finance and HR. The resulting team was big – 14 in all – not the ideal 6–8 people recommended by Katzenbach and Smith (1993):

> My focus at first was to bring together individuals who had demonstrated the ability to create connections. These individuals had to come from the broader stakeholder groups which consulting represented. I was not beholden to strict protocol on grading and title – I just formed a team around me that was right for the job. Bringing in key players as required.
>
> I was well versed in the wisdom about the ideal numbers on a team and spans of control, but it was vital to me at that stage of the service line's development that I involved people from all constituent groups within one single team. This

enabled me to create the touch points in real time by having all the key players together – it reduced the false boundaries that would have arisen from managing smaller separate teams. It also allowed us to quickly create a common language, style and approach which we could then deploy across the service line....

Having brought the team together, the next step was to enable it to become high performing.

Initial contracting, inquiry and diagnosis

Looking back, it is clear that we conducted two 'loops' of Contracting–Inquiry–Diagnosis' – within the first three steps of the Hawkins CIDCLEAR process model (Hawkins, 2017: 83) – before the coaching work with the team started in earnest. Our first contract was for Hilary to work with the team as a fellow inquirer, sharing and testing out the principles of the Touchpoint Leadership concept in collaboration with this newly formed team.

The concept and model of Touchpoint Leadership is based on the belief that leadership does not lie in the leader or the follower, but in the relationship between them, which is formed, moulded, stretched, grown and diminished at the 'Touchpoint' – the point of difference within an organization between individuals, teams and divisions. Using this lens, the most effective leaders are aware of their power to ignite positive energy or to destroy it, at every point of interaction – or touchpoint – with those they lead and lead with. These leaders see the opportunity, have the presence of mind and the agility to build bridges, spark new thought, ideas and learning; and are aware of the risks of smoothing over, squashing or alienating others at that point of connection. They know which 'touchpoints' are most crucial to business success and they build networks and teams which engender learning across those intersections.

The role of this leadership team was to spearhead a community of practice where the centre of gravity for most of its members came from their client work and their sector-based specialization. The team members would need to develop and exercise leadership influence in ways other than those based purely on authority drawn from formal position or technical expertise. In Bill Torbert's terms (2005), they would need to embrace different leadership 'action logics' from those of Expert or Achiever, and create catalytic connections across the points of intersection – or touchpoints – in the matrix, often with people more senior to them. It was clear that Richard had already started to exercise such leadership across the diffuse consulting community and his plans for expanding that connective power reflected the spirit of Touchpoint Leadership in action. We agreed that the team as a whole would benefit from viewing their own leadership in this way, applying the Touchpoint Leadership concept in their own work.

Hilary contracted to work with the team, listening to their meetings, inquiring about what she saw, sharing what she was seeing, feeling and thinking, and offering insight on how well they were creating value-adding dialogue across the different groups and interests in the business. As Richard notes: 'I wanted the coach to witness the dynamic and touchpoint in real time rather than through a second download. This was key to understanding the intricacies of the touchpoints and dynamics as they happened.' By working in this way Hilary was modelling a form of inquiry which slowed down the frenetic pace of activity, opened up space for looking at the feelings and unspoken words in the conversations that were happening, and allowed new learning and creativity to emerge (Beisser, 1970).

Listening in this way led Hilary to be curious about an apparent polarity of emotions in the team: on the one hand there was a strong sense of pride in the technological leadership and innovation within the business and excitement about its unique potential in the market; and on the other, a sense of disempowerment and confusion. On the one hand everything was fast moving and paced; on the other there was a sense of stasis. As Richard related:

> The challenge was creating an effective team which itself lacked time, and critically lacked a sense of confidence and empowerment to drive the change. In the early days the team would often see the problem as someone else's to solve – when in fact it was their own. Being drawn from disparate parts of the business with different ways of working and cultural norms only added to the initial challenge. By helping them to look at their own touchpoint connections, the intent was to help them feel empowered.

All leadership team members were client facing and held multiple roles. Leadership tasks and responsibilities got done in the 'margins of the day job' – not uncommon in service businesses – and of being focused on a number of things at one time. It was clear to us that it would not be possible to engender greater leadership power and influence within the team unless we invited the team to take time out, slow down and look at where they were currently. Unless we created space and the confidence to act, there was a danger that we would encourage new types of leadership behaviour without attending properly to the emotional challenges of their new leadership role and practical challenges of leading in this environment.

We agreed that Hilary would conduct an inquiry with each leadership team member one-to-one and share the outcome with the team on a day dedicated solely to its development.

Second contracting, inquiry and diagnosis

We contracted to undertake this second inquiry process consisting of one-to-one conversations with each of the Consulting Leadership Team members, using an open questioning approach based on the method that Annie McKee has named 'Dynamic Inquiry' (McKee and McMillen, 1992: 445–60). The intent was to be as open as possible in inquiring about the challenges facing the service line within the business, to encourage interviewees to look at the challenges both from their own perspective and through the eyes of stakeholders and to help give voice to the underlying emotional issues. We set aside some time, within these conversations, for the interviewees to provide confidential feedback for the consulting service line head on his leadership strengths and areas for development. 'The key for me as leader was to try and look down the other end of the telescope. To understand how others actually experience the leader – not how the leader believes they are being experienced.' After a thematic analysis of the data emerging from the interviews, we grouped those themes into Hawkins' five disciplines framework (Hawkins, 2017) as illustrated in Figure 4.1. Rather

Figure 4.1   The five disciplines of effective teams

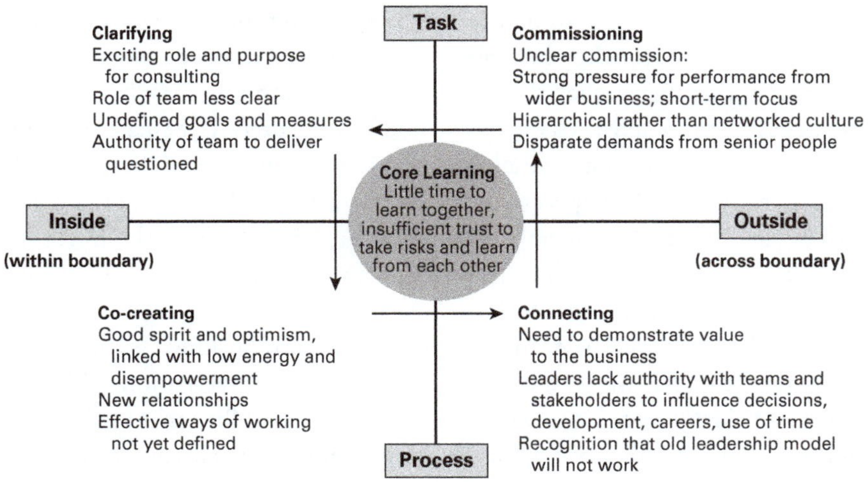

Clarifying
Exciting role and purpose
  for consulting
Role of team less clear
Undefined goals and measures
Authority of team to deliver
  questioned

Task

Commissioning
Unclear commission:
Strong pressure for performance from
  wider business; short-term focus
Hierarchical rather than networked culture
Disparate demands from senior people

Core Learning
Little time to
learn together,
insufficient trust to
take risks and learn
from each other

Inside
(within boundary)

Outside
(across boundary)

Co-creating
Good spirit and optimism,
  linked with low energy and
  disempowerment
New relationships
Effective ways of working
  not yet defined

Process

Connecting
Need to demonstrate value
  to the business
Leaders lack authority with teams and
  stakeholders to influence decisions,
  development, careers, use of time
Recognition that old leadership model
  will not work

than presenting this to the team as a *fait accompli*, the main themes and raw quotes were posted around a meeting room, and team members invited to read through them, individually and in pairs, to reflect on their meaning for them and their implications for the work of the team. They were asked:

- What in this data surprises you?
- What are you curious about and want to ask more?
- What resonates most with you?
- Which issues are most important for the team to address next, in your view?

There was a powerful sense of connection as the pairs read and discussed through the words that they had individually contributed. It felt as though this was the first time that the team had been invited openly to share their concerns about the organization structure and their misgivings about their own power. Moreover, the inquiry had shone a light onto the underlying reasons for the sense of disempowerment that Hilary had sensed earlier. Yes, there were concerns about leadership authority and style but these were secondary to a lack of clarity about what the business would hold the team accountable for delivering. Without the confidence of a clear commission with the UK board, these leaders would be unable to develop the leadership muscle to create change across the firmly ingrained sector-based organization structure.

Clarifying team objectives – and starting the work through an 'outside-in' lens

Having clarified where the work needed to start, the away day moved fast to address this gap. Richard had received input from the UK board on the targets and metrics for the year, and the team worked to define those targets for which they believed they should be held accountable and the key performance indicators against which they would be measured. The energy behind this process was tremendous; looking back, it was indicative of the ability of the team to take leadership when given the direction and the space to do so. Looking back, one of the members commented: 'This was a key highlight in the year – getting the team into second gear by agreeing its common objectives around people and capability.'

Given the need for the team to move fast in establishing its authority across the business, we wanted to ensure that each intervention with the team built clarity and focus and also enhanced the ability of members to connect – both together and with the wider community. Having developed a shared view of the commission, purpose and objectives for the team, we then moved to help members understand each other's leadership strengths and challenges (co-creating), inviting them to explore independently and then to share in small groups:

- their sense of passion in their work;
- the values they tried to live out as a leader;
- how they saw themselves living in their leadership – when they were at their best and when they were at their worst.

As they used inquiry and feedback skills to help support and challenge each other, they started to discover that they were not alone in the challenges they faced. They thus started to build greater trust between them, slowly building a team culture in which being 'less than perfect' was OK. We knew this was important, because the pressure in professional services environments to be 'the best' and 'expert' often hinders the sharing of doubts and vulnerability needed to build trust (Maister, 2003).

We then moved on to helping them view the leadership team from an 'outside-in' perspective, inviting them to put themselves in the shoes of their employees, to examine what concerns and priorities people had, and to explore what type of approaches would enable them to start to connect emotionally with this new community. The aim was to build a shared picture of the team's leadership challenge, and to help them build confidence and an initial plan of action.

The flow of this away day through the five disciplines is shown in Figure 4.2.

Figure 4.2 The five disciplines as applied in team away day

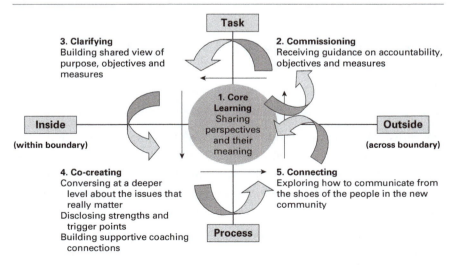

Re-contracting for sustained team coaching work

The learning from the away day precipitated demand for a more constant team coaching presence and a revised contract between the leader, the team and the coach. Developing greater clarity about the commission and purpose of the team had been helpful, but Richard recognized that more sustained coaching support was important if the team was to have a recognizable impact on the business within the next year. These leaders needed to build their own legitimacy, and that of the service line, as well as have it bestowed on them from their primary commissioner, the UK board. As Richard says: 'The major challenge was getting everyone to point in the same direction and to start to think as a team rather than a group of individuals. But there was also cynicism about whether we could achieve lasting change, and a belief that change was up to other people, not us.' Part of the work of the leader and the coach was therefore to help the team build belief in its own power to effect change where the centre of gravity for most of its members came from their client work and sector-based specialization.

Team coaching based on three levels of learning

The core purpose of the leadership team was to create a community of consulting practice, which would serve clients, attract, retain and develop great people and differentiate the company in the market. The sense of cohesion of this community would depend on the extent to which the consulting group was seen as a place where people could learn, grow, do interesting work and be successful. We therefore agreed that the work of the coach should focus on:

1 working with individual team members in developing their own leadership within the service line;

2 working with the team as a whole in building its shared leadership; and

3 helping the team to create value-adding connections with its stakeholders.

We provided a developmental framework of Touchpoint Leadership to the team to act as a guide to their personal development and for the learning of the team as a whole. Each member was invited to start a process of exploring their own leadership from the perspective of three domains (Lines and Scholes-Rhodes, 2013: 180):

• how they brought themselves into connecting leadership with others – their strengths, passions, beliefs; and how their behaviour patterns sometimes interrupted creative connection (Domain 1);

- how they could ignite learning and creativity in the moment, and enhance their presence and impact in relationship with others (Domain 2);
- how they could expand the points of connection across the consulting community and encourage learning across the organization and between the community and its external stakeholders (Domain 3).

We commenced a programme of one-to-one and team coaching in team meetings and offsite workshops, including coaching of the team leader and feedback on his leadership style in action.

Embracing the diversity in the team to broaden the connection across the business

There was a strong sense from the team that their work would benefit from them knowing each other better: some members knew each other very well from client work or shared sector-based interests, so there were subgroups and varying trust and openness between the groups. Also, a number of the team were coming into leadership for the first time, and there was varying confidence in speaking up at meetings, especially since the meetings were fairly large. We decided to use the Myers–Briggs Type Indicator (MBTI) (Myers *et al*, 1998) and Firo-B psychometrics (Schnell and Hammer, 2004) to give individual team members insight into their own style preferences and interpersonal needs and to explore the implications for their way of engaging with others, with reference to the three Touchpoint Leadership domains above. We agreed we would use these profiles as a tool for disclosure within a team offsite. Richard says: 'This was about recognizing and harnessing the diversity within the team. By understanding how people were wired we could start to create a team dynamic that played to people's different strengths rather than trying to force everyone to conform and be the same.'

There was a degree of scepticism from some members as to how useful this process would be: after all, many team members had similar backgrounds and areas of specialism and some had grown to believe that they conformed to a standard consulting 'type'. However, as team members revealed their MBTI type preferences on a room-sized type table, the richness of diversity was revealed, to surprise and curiosity. While some of the patterns on the type table explained natural allegiances and empathies, they also opened eyes to the potential for new types of interactions and contributions to the team: interactions that would help the team empathize with the views of others, and those that would ensure the closure of discussions and the practical follow-through of actions.

Expanding the learning space

One of the notable aspects of this team coaching work, from Hilary's point of view, was the active engagement of Richard in the process. It is not always the case: sometimes team leaders bring in coaches in the hope that they will bring about change in the team without the leader himself needing to change. For Richard, the challenge was to work out how he needed to change in order to enable his team to step into their own leadership: 'For me personally it was the not knowing. The sense of feeling I was not leading effectively but not having the self-awareness to know where to go next.'

One of the key dilemmas Richard faced was how much guidance and direction to give the team, versus standing back and allowing them to 'step up'. His natural style was to lead from the front, but he also wanted – and needed – his team to take more responsibility for getting this done. In trying to get the balance right he had started fluctuating his style between directing and standing back, with the result that some team members commented that he sometimes seemed very directive and at other times too hands off. This was clearly not helping them to build confidence in their contribution within the team. We started to explore how he could be present, while also allowing the space for ideas, views and creativity to flow within the team. Hilary's observation of his interaction in team meetings helped show the way to the answer: it emerged that whenever there was silence or a pause in the room, Richard felt the need to step in and help, by providing direction and answers. This, Hilary noted, was inhibiting people from offering views and learning from each other.

Richard started experimenting with creating more space in meetings, intentionally asking questions and pausing, probing, to invite contributions. It felt awkward at first – people were bemused about his intentions – and also about how to use the space created by Richard's use of silence. Two things helped here: one was Richard's disclosure about his intent in shifting his style; the other was guidance and feedback from Hilary about the ways in which dialogue flowed in the team. Naturally people had learnt to look to Richard for direction and opinion, and tended not to inquire of each other; there was also a strong tendency to express opinion rather than to seek it from others. With feedback on this dynamic and guidance on 'pull behaviours' as opposed to 'push behaviours', the conversation started to flow more freely across the team.

The big test for Richard was at the offsite meeting where the team shared their personal preferences and interpersonal needs. As indicated above, we had enjoyed a spirited morning learning about each other's type preferences and making sense of the differences and similarities within the team. Hilary had then asked each member to create a shield to represent themselves – their strengths, weaknesses, style preferences, wants and needs from the team – and these were posted on the wall before lunch so that people could browse around and look at them at lunchtime. The intent was to 'celebrate the differences' and through this to find ways to work and learn together most effectively and creatively.

When Hilary proposed, at the start of the afternoon, that each member should share out loud the highlights of their shield and then receive two appreciations and encouragements from the rest of the team, there was a tense hush – a hiatus of awkwardness. This was a challenging test for Richard, as he fought against the temptation to step in and relieve the discomfort. But he stayed silent, and gradually members of the team came forward and spoke with openness, and shared feedback with care, feeling and candour.

In retrospect he said:

> That session was a highlight for me as I really felt that we were operating on a plane. The connections were starting to form across the team and traditional boundaries were removed. Key for me personally was your feedback on my style and approach – helping me give space to the team to grow and express themselves. I also felt that we started to focus outwardly.

As others looked back on the year, they commented on this event as a key icebreaker, a turnaround, a point when the team started to be more open, connected and to work together more effectively.

One commented about the shift that he had noticed between the start of the year, when meetings were quiet and awkward, to later in the year, when debate was much more open, challenging and collaborative. Another pointed to the value of the coach acting as an authoritative counterbalance to the leader to enable him to create the space for others to step in and grow in their own leadership.

The benefit of this 'sharing of diversity' was not only evident in the way people related together, but also in the *quality* of the conversation. After the sharing of shields, in which team members shared their motivations and values, they were able to bring much more passion and energy to an exercise which defined what values and ways of working would differentiate the service line, and how they would work together to optimize the value of their time together. It was as if sharing individual passions enabled them to ignite their collective passion and to build their confidence of their mission in the business. It also helped them build the resolve needed to implement a new company-wide workforce framework in a way that would be received well by their consulting community, forming sub-teams to work together in that task. The sensitivity and effectiveness with which the team implemented this new framework were noted by the UK board. Team members also started a programme of visits to client sites to meet consulting staff in the place of their client work, attending in pairs to demonstrate shared leadership and to learn from each other in their approach and perspective.

The attention of the team had shifted from the internal focus questions of authority, purpose and legitimacy – to the job of taking practical action to build the service line and create a new community of practice.

Deepening the sense of identity and connection through stakeholder engagement

Nine months into the coaching programme the team was witnessing a drop in staff attrition and individual leaders were describing the shifts that they had been able to make in their own leadership as a result of the one-to-one coaching; gaining confidence in their ability and skill in engaging people in service-line activities and in forging new relationships of influence across the business. There was recognition from the UK board that the team had established its leadership and was demonstrating notable initiative in the way it was implementing a range of measures essential to building consulting as a home of performance and career management. Plans to develop a future consulting leaders programme were under way, with involvement of the future leaders themselves in designing the approach and format; and an intensive communications drumbeat was co-owned by the leadership team to ignite engagement of consultants in a range of practice and client-facing learning activities – the swell of people at the first client breakfast briefing exceeded the room space arranged for it.

Despite the growing confidence in the development of the community, there remained questions about the way consulting services were and should be positioned within the company's range of service offerings and products. This was a good illustration of how objectives and measures agreed on spreadsheets with the board might form only a small part of a team's real 'commission'; the real test of the board's commission would be how consulting services played a part in the key programmes of work being sold and delivered to clients, as played out by the relationships and conversations being conducted in client-facing meetings. Therefore the next stage of clarifying the commission needed to be a collaborative endeavour between the consulting leadership team and its key stakeholders.

A set of conversations was initiated with leaders in the wider business, including those responsible for wider business strategy and marketing to explore what positioning would best serve clients and the overall business. A team offsite was designed actively to engage these key stakeholders in refining and testing the thinking of the consulting team, to receive challenge and test assumptions. The result was a reinforcement of the identity of the consulting community in its role as leading the shaping of services to clients – shared with senior stakeholders, and agreed by each member of the Consulting Leadership Team.

The team was able to demonstrate its increased confidence in its role and its legitimacy within the business at an event held 13 months after its formation, in which it invited all members of the service line to come together. Previous events of this type had been poorly attended. Here the attendance was considerably higher than ever before and the leadership team, together with members from the UK board, were able stand together to communicate the synergy between consulting identity and strategy and that of the business as a whole, and connect with consulting community members in team-based activities. Attendees were able to create new connections with each other and with the range of services available to them to take to clients. Ninety per cent of attendees rated the event good or excellent and praised the opportunity to network with others in the service line. It seemed that it had genuinely started to be a place of home for a good proportion of these people.

Reflections four years on

As we looked back on the learning of the past year, we acknowledged that we had originally hoped to reach the current level of achievement earlier than has been the case. But looking back also helps us see the broader historical and systemic context of this leadership team in sharper relief. The work had started when clients were questioning the value of consulting services and when the turmoil in the business world as a whole and the organizational changes within this company had sapped the confidence within this leadership team to bring about change. Coupled with this, all the leaders held at least three different responsibilities across the service/ sector/product matrix and therefore this leadership was built from what one member described as a 'thin veneer' – a circumstance not unusual in matrix businesses which are client facing. Given all this, it was critical that the coaching work enabled the team to build its sense of legitimacy and its confidence, collectively and individually, to be able to reinforce, at a strategic level, its commission and its client-facing vision.

If we look at the development of the consulting identity with reference to the Hawkins five disciplines model, we can see an iterative process of learning within individual leaders, within the team and between the team and the wider business:

- learning how the initial commission and purpose provided clarity in the organization;
- building a greater sense of shared identity through sharing personal values and passion for the business and learning from each other within the team;
- enhancing individual confidence and skill in engaging across existing power structures through greater self and interpersonal awareness and new ways of conversing;
- connecting with consulting staff at client sites and learning how the service line was working in practice;
- learning where ambiguities and contradictions existed and re-engaging key stakeholders to refine and deepen the shared identity;
- learning how to go beyond the current sense of what is possible to build a more robust brand and service proposition.

This flow of learning within and between the five disciplines is depicted in summary in Figure 4.3.

So, looking at where the team is now in its development journey we can see:

- a leadership team that has moved from a place that felt confusing and chaotic to a working board, where people collaborate well;
- a team of leaders who have stepped up in their individual and collective confidence as Richard moves to a new role and a new leader steps into the head position;
- a set of ambitious objectives, collectively created, for taking engagement in the service line to the next level in the following year;
- a consulting community of practice that has an agreed identity and co-mission for its work with clients, where staff attrition has dropped, utilization has turned upwards, and learning and development activities increased in range and attendance, and staff were beginning to see as their professional 'home';
- a plan to run a programme for building future leadership potential recognized within the wider firm for being progressive.

Figure 4.3 Learning within and between the five disciplines

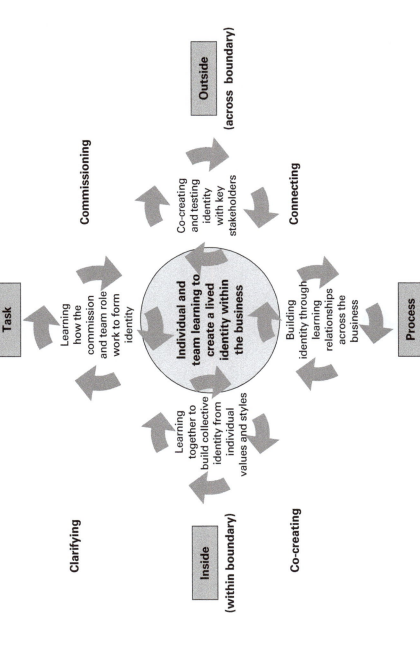

And looking forward, the team is braced for the task of demonstrating that consulting is an essential and integral role in delivering value to current and future clients, through deepening and expanding the touchpoints with other services, with company strategic initiatives, with account leaders and with clients.

Coaching the co-creating within the team

Two case studies from Canada

CATHERINE CARR AND JACQUELINE PETERS

Introduction

In this chapter, we jointly share our experiences coaching two teams through a similar team coaching process within a doctoral research project (Carr and Peters, 2012). As practitioner-researchers who were interested in exploring the experience of team coaching through the participants' lens, we each did a team coaching case study in 2011–12. We followed with a cross-case analysis to identify themes between the very different Canadian leadership teams we had chosen to work with. Catherine worked with an engagement and workforce development leadership team of six people within the British Columbia government. Jacqueline worked with a corporate finance leadership team of eight people within a multinational organization that was headquartered in Calgary, Alberta.

We used a similar team coaching process that was informed by our past team coaching experiences, the minimal literature we found on team coaching, and the broad body of knowledge about what drives team effectiveness. The process we developed is shown in Figure 5.1. The sixth step, research interviews and validation, was specific to the research but also served the team coaching approach by providing an opportunity for the individual team members to reflect on the team coaching experience and identify their key learning during the process.

Although the process was very similar, there were differences in the challenges and experiences of our two teams. We discuss our two teams separately

Figure 5.1   Overview of the team coaching process

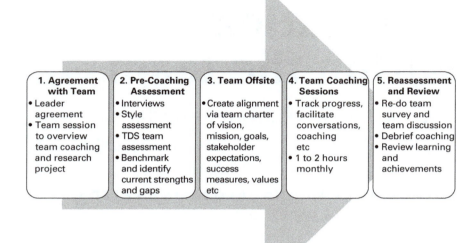

1. Agreement with Team	2. Pre-Coaching Assessment	3. Team Offsite	4. Team Coaching Sessions	5. Reassessment and Review
• Leader agreement • Team session to overview team coaching and research project	• Interviews • Style assessment • TDS team assessment • Benchmark and identify current strengths and gaps	• Create alignment via team charter of vision, mission, goals, stakeholder expectations, success measures, values etc	• Track progress, facilitate conversations, coaching etc • 1 to 2 hours monthly	• Re-do team survey and team discussion • Debrief coaching • Review learning and achievements

and share how these teams first engaged us. These case studies show how team coaching helped each team step up to what the future was requiring of them, a key question in Hawkins' five disciplines model. We include the team members' initial hopes for coaching, their goals, and what they identified as being valuable to them throughout the team coaching.

For the purposes of this case study, we particularly highlight how we coached using the clarifying and co-creating disciplines (Hawkins, 2011) to support our teams to make and sustain changes. We both assisted our teams with clarifying elements, including vision, mission, goals, values, success indicators, and working agreement protocols. The three key co-creating components that we highlight include: 1) assessments used to identify the team performance and functioning before and after the coaching; 2) a two-day team launch; and 3) an overview of ongoing team coaching over a period of 5–11 months.

Client 1: Catherine's government team

Little did I know how fortunate I was to work with the six-member engagement and workforce development team from the Ministry of Social Development in the British Columbia government. Each member of this senior leadership team skilfully leads a different business area, and supervises direct reports. The team is known for being an innovative and high-performing team with very high workplace environment scores. The task ahead was to support this exceptional team to make an even bigger impact. One team member summed it up:

> We were a top team work unit before we did team coaching and we got in the game so that is the good news... What happens if when you are on top and we keep thinking of pushing that envelope because it becomes the baseline though... you can never rest on your laurels – and we never do – it's like this is how it is and now what are we going to do? We continue to sort of push ourselves.

Coaching helped this team articulate their bigger vision and take the necessary steps to make that vision happen. They were curious and enthusiastic about how team coaching would support their next steps and were on board for where the journey might take them. The team chose an ambitious goal for their coaching based on a roll-up of their individual pre-coaching interview themes, their Team Diagnostic Assessment results (Wageman, Hackman and Lehman, 2005), and comments from their debriefing conversation: 'create a compelling senior team direction through working on a new cross-functional and innovative project that would potentially have broad impact across government'.

The Team Diagnostic Survey (TDS) is a quantitative, opinion-based assessment that collects responses from each team member about how well they think the team is functioning on key factors that have been correlated with team effectiveness.

At the team launch, the team decided to transition to a more cross-functional style of working together. They knew that connecting more with one another would foster greater learning and engagement at work and produce even greater business results. We used the term 'teaming' in the coaching in order to describe their new and more fluid way of connecting and learning at the same time that they executed their work (Edmondson, 2012). To assist them in this goal, the team completed individual DISC assessments (Extended DISC International, 2012). The Extended DISC is a popular assessment tool that is used to help team members understand how their different behavioural styles influence how they interact and communicate with one another. The DISC team profile showed them where their natural style preferences, strengths and gaps were as individuals and as a team.

Government team coaching goals and activities

The coaching goals for the initial team launch and some of the associated coaching activities are outlined in Table 5.1.

Table 5.1   Catherine's government team coaching launch agenda and outcomes (Carr and Peters, 2012)

	Goals	Activities	Team outcomes (quotes)
1	Create a reflective and open space	• Mindfulness and visualization on creating success and support to succeed	• 'I feel so much more connected'
2	Understand team effectiveness	• Conversation on team effectiveness criteria and what their team did well and could do more of	• 'The DISC helped me make sense of why I take the role I do on this team'
3	Understand each other's styles using the Disc and games	• Debrief individual and team Disc profiles, activities to complement understanding differing styles	• 'I understand you all in a different way'
4	Review and create the team charter and collaborative project	• Review of mission, vision, priorities, and new project • Discussion of their values and ways of working together	• 'I appreciate what each person does or could do to contribute to the team'
5	Identify individual learning goals that align with the team coaching goals. Explore individual goals through peer coaching	• Individual journaling and group discussion • Peer coaching demonstration, discussion and practice session using individual goals	• 'The peer coaching was great. I'd like to do more of that on our team'
6	Define next steps and closure / integration of offsite	• Action plan and review of the session	• 'I feel good about this idea of starting a new project to be coached on'

Through the coaching, this team intentionally developed a new executive career path tool that required them to work collaboratively and outside of their typical expertise areas. The team leader actively supported the coaching initiative by setting and disclosing courageous change goals for himself.

During the eight follow-up sessions, identified in Table 5.2, the team leader and another informal leader on the team stepped back more and allowed everyone else to come forward more fully to offer their unique strengths and abilities. Participation at meetings became more balanced. A comment that expressed this was: 'the last few [meetings] have just been phenomenal. We come to consensus, we hear everyone at the table.' The team did work through some conflict and challenges as they shifted their style of working together, but they used their working agreements and peer coaching to stay focused on their outward and future-facing goals. 'It's hard to get to a better place without having that conflict and working through it, rather than stuffing it in the corner.'

Table 5.2   Middle and closure session goals and activities (Carr and Peters, 2012)

Session	Goals	Activities
1	• Review DISC (Extended DISC International, 2012) styles and apply to create results • Choose project to be coached on • Create working agreements and new meeting structure to support change • Create success measures	• Mindfulness and check-in on a time 'you felt stuck but found your way through' • Process facilitation to reinforce positive changes • Team leader review of DISC with team and why this matters for business results • Discussion: What project will help your goals and performance? What is the ongoing role of coaching? How will you measure success? • Team leader facilitation of working agreements activity and create new meeting format plan to support desired change
2	• Coaching for exceptional results	• Check-in/process facilitation to reinforce positive changes • Coaching on the project: What makes your project product exceptional? How are you working differently together? What is changing? • Coaching to reinforce using the working agreements, agree on a decision-making framework and new meeting structure

(Continued)

Table 5.2   (Continued)

Session	Goals	Activities
3	• Work through conflict to solidify desired change	• Solicit team input into agenda • Process facilitation meeting for group dynamics • Explore recent conflict incident
4	• Build on strengths and create positive change	• Check in: what's going well and what needs work? • Process facilitation to reinforce positive changes • Explored Losada's (Fredrickson and Losada, 2005) framework as it relates to their team • Transfer of team coaching agenda ownership to team
5	• Embed ongoing learning structures	• Presentation by each team member on their DISC style • Facilitated review of team profile • Introduced Hawkins (2011) team huddle
6	• Cascade learning throughout the organization	• Focus on successes and harvesting the learning. • Planning for team members to do more team coaching with their own teams
7	• Create sustainability	• Focus on sustainability • Plan the closing session • Set up ongoing peer coaching
8	• Closure, review results, and plan next steps • Celebration	• Focus on TDS assessment results and celebrate team success • Team sculpting to highlight change and next steps • Discussion of sustainability and next steps for each team member and the team as a whole

One team member commented, 'I think the process of embedding what we wanted to achieve or how we wanted to be into our team meetings was both critical and eye opening. We had to actively practise the things we said we wanted, which exposed us to "walking the talk". It was a great learning experience for everyone in the team, and the changes have taken hold in how we are together.' Another team member commented on the value of coaching over time, 'because one event in and of itself may change the way you think about something but it won't actually change behaviour. Whereas that prolonged coaching through the trials and tribulations of actually trying on a different way of being in yourself and with your team – I think that is part of the process that I've noticed [that works].'

The team developed even greater trust in one another and this facilitated deeper, more authentic connections on the team where each person's needs, aspirations and strengths were honoured.

Government team coaching outcomes

Eleven months later, after a two-day team launch and eight follow-up sessions, a re-do of the Team Diagnostic Survey confirmed that the team believed they had met their goals for the team coaching and had increased their team effectiveness. They were working more cross-functionally, drawing on one another's strengths and talents. They had increased engagement in their team, and even more, across their division. Taking what they had learnt in team coaching and applying it to their own teams, they saw more innovative products coming out of their branch as a whole. They felt proud, accomplished, and more connected to each other. Mission accomplished! 'It feels like people are getting drawn in and that there is more integration happening from the visioning part of the project through to completion.'

This team continues to apply the principles learnt in the team coaching sessions and has become a strong advocate of the value of coaching in government. One team member is now certified as an executive coach and is an active proponent of coaching inside their ministry and across government. She is well qualified to speak about their team coaching process:

> What was most valuable about the team coaching process for me was that it allowed us to get to know each other on a deeper level and be able to communicate more honestly and openly and address issues quicker, understand our individual work styles better, improve and add to our team processes, and re-examine our team structure.

A summary of this government team's coaching journey is outlined in Figure 5.2.

Since the coaching was finished, members of this senior team are actively carrying out many innovative coaching projects and in doing so are modelling a coaching culture shift for the whole of government. One project

Figure 5.2   Team coaching summary for Catherine's government team

Pre-Coaching Theme Summary	Coaching Goals	Post-Coaching Theme Summary
'What happens when you are on top and we keep thinking of pushing that envelope because it becomes the baseline though… now what are we going to do? We continue to sort of push ourselves.'	1. Create a compelling senior team direction through working on a new cross-functional and innovative project 2. Shift to more participatory meetings, and develop new ways of collaborating	'We don't want to lose it. We want to continue to have meetings where we are coaching each other.' 'To have a really rich dialogue within the team… that happens very naturally now.'

example is the Employment and Assistance Worker Core Training Program. This team has transformed their traditional trainer–trainee model and moved to a coaching 'guide on the side' approach to facilitate greater learning. Another example is how they showcase the value of coaching on their blog on 'The Loop', their ministry intranet site. Staff members are invited to write in about their coaching experiences. Team coaching has been key to inspiring this team of leaders to infuse the spirit of coaching throughout their ministry.

The team requested a follow-up session nine months after the completion of the team coaching. They described continuing to feel more internally connected as a leadership team, and that they were frequently using peer support and coaching to tackle challenges. One team member expressed, 'we let others into who we are as people. We are more than just the people we are at work and you might get that with one or two colleagues, but not all at the same time. It has been a gift.'

The team's career-path tool needed some final tweaking and the team has been consumed with other priorities; however, they were resolute about launching the tool within the month. As they reflected on the value of their team coaching they realized they now needed a group supervision structure, not another project, to ensure that they offered support to one another for ongoing leadership challenges. One member commented, 'We've talked about some heartfelt things that typically wouldn't come up.' The team leader announced his pending retirement on this same day and said, 'What I want is for you to hold onto and champion what you achieved in the team coaching and continue to be strong leaders and a strong team as you go forward.'

The team had, indeed, co-created a stronger team together. Even though team members may change, it appears that the team coaching shifted the team culture and created more enduring systemic change that could hold beyond the individuals.

Client 2: Jacqueline's corporate team

The team coaching process for this corporate leadership team began as a result of a former client contacting Jacqueline about holding a team alignment offsite for her new leadership team. She was about four months into a new vice president role and had not yet established a formal management/leadership team for her small corporate financial services department. She wanted to bring the eight most senior leaders and managers of the team together to create and implement a new vision and direction for the department. As she discussed the communication and alignment issues she was encountering as the new leader of this team, Jacqueline expanded her initial offsite request to a full team coaching programme. This included pre-session assessments to benchmark the current state before the offsite, and follow-up coaching sessions to support the implementation of the team's vision, goals and agreements.

Corporate team coaching goals and activities

The initial eight team members participated in individual interviews and completed a Team Diagnostic Survey (TDS) (Wageman *et al*, 2005) prior to starting the team coaching. The TDS is a quantitative, opinion-based assessment that collects responses from each team member about how well they think the team is functioning on key factors that have been correlated with team effectiveness. The team reviewed the team summary of their input from the TDS together at an initial, two-hour 'kick off' team meeting to identify strengths, opportunities and goals for the two-day offsite. The pre-assessments highlighted a lack of alignment and a heightened sense of competitiveness among team members. They felt that for the most part, the individual contributors were smart and did what they needed to do to meet the timelines required in their deadline-focused department, but they weren't collaborating well together. They recognized that this would not serve them or the department well as they formalized their leadership team accountabilities. A comment provided by one of the team members succinctly summarized the team's pre-coaching state: 'We have competent, committed people, and interesting work in an interesting environment, but we have some dynamics/communication issues.'

As a result of the team's discussion about strengths and gaps, the team confirmed the outcomes they were seeking for the team coaching and identified how they would measure success in six months. Their high-level objectives for the team coaching were:

1 Create a compelling team purpose by defining what TEAM means for this group. (Clarifying discipline)

2 Enhance relationships with each other. (Co-creating discipline)

3 Work together more effectively as a team, internally and externally, using a team charter to guide the team's focus and behaviours (eg vision, mandate, working agreements, goals, and success measures). (Co-creating discipline)

The next step was to participate in the two-day team launch, held offsite, to support the team to have some social time together as well as work time. Two weeks before the offsite, however, the team leader talked with me about some significant changes that she wanted to make in the team. She wondered about the appropriate timing for the restructuring she was contemplating, since the team launch was nearing. I shared information about the key conditions for creating high-performing teams, reinforcing that having the right people and working within the right structure were two important pre-conditions for team effectiveness and team coaching (Wageman *et al*, 2008). The team leader decided that she needed to act quickly based on this coaching conversation with me, which was further bolstered by her concerns about the organizational structure feedback that was revealed at the team's pre-coaching assessment debrief session. She decided to restructure the department to better set up the conditions for the team to be successful and effective, which meant that the leadership team was reduced from eight members to seven.

The team leader commented on the importance of this decision after the fact:

> I do think that this type of coaching is really important if you are going to roll out changes within a group or a new direction. And that new direction goes hand in hand with coaching, and gets people working together and making changes. [It] makes it more focused and strategic.

At the two-day offsite, the team leader started the session by sharing the details of the restructured organizational chart, which identified new leadership roles and reporting relationships for some team members. I next facilitated a conversation for the team to discuss their hopes and concerns about this new structure. I could see that the changes had created a sense of insecurity and uncertainty in the team, so I aimed to encourage dialogue and disclosure in a safe way. By allowing silence and individual reflection time for team members to gather their thoughts, people started talking more honestly about what they felt. As people continued to talk, the conversation became less intense. When we finally took a break after an hour and a half of discussion that first morning, the mood in the room had shifted. There was more rapid dialogue and even some laughter in the room, instead of the long, uncomfortable silences that occurred at the beginning of the meeting.

The tone for the rest of the two-day session was lighter and livelier. There was progress as we worked through 'clarifying' the vision, mission, goals, new roles and responsibilities, working agreements, and success measures for the team. I incorporated a number of different activities to support the team's learning and dialogue. For example, we reviewed the team members' individual and team styles using the assessment tool, Insights, as a way to promote discussion and understanding of personal preferences, approaches and differences (The Insights Group Limited, 2012). We played a card game that highlighted the team's natural leaning towards competitive versus collaborative approaches, and gave them a second chance to play the game from a collaborative stance. We also used creative processes such as creating team slogans, logos, and future visioning conversations to promote new ideas and ways of interacting.

We had a conversation about working agreements and we discussed how team members would hold each other accountable to these working agreements in a constructive and respectful way, since old habits can take time to change. We discussed a strategy of offering peer coaching to one another when they ended up in a negative conversation, or were 'gossiping' about other people. I modelled a peer coaching conversation for them, suggesting a format to ask the person with concerns/issues what would help them to talk about these directly with the other person. They discussed having a frame of 'good intentions' with each other, knowing that they would occasionally transgress the agreements, but with goodwill, discipline and an agreed-upon framework for a peer coaching conversation, they were committed to develop a new way of being with each other. They captured the essence of this accountability discussion in one core working agreement: 'Hold each other accountable for breaches by identifying it directly with the person.'

Overall, the team said they felt tired but successful at the end of the offsite. They commented at the end of the session that they would not have made as much progress without the coaching support; it was instrumental for them to have the conversations and to have the safety to really delve into the 'elephants on the table'.

The team had also drafted a tangible product, their one-page team charter, which summarized all of their key agreements from the session, as shown in Table 5.3 (sanitized to protect confidentiality). This team charter became the focus for the rest of their team coaching sessions, as well as the guide for the new environment and culture that they wanted to create together as a team. (For more on team charters, see Peters and Carr, 2013, and Hawkins, 2017: 309–312)

After the offsite, team coaching sessions were held monthly to bi-monthly to support the team to progress their goals and live their working agreements. High-level details of the team coaching sessions are identified as shown in Table 5.4.

The first coaching meeting after the offsite focused on clarifying the team's success measures. The team was challenged when I asked them to identify what their many stakeholders needed from their department in the future. They made a plan to gather more information so they could build these outcomes into their success measures. This led to a further discussion about how the team could most effectively communicate regularly with their various corporate stakeholders, including the senior leadership team, the board, external partners, and other functions and business units in the organization. I asked questions to prompt and reinforce this outward focus.

As the coaching progressed, the sessions were focused on checking in with the team on their team actions, completing the team charter, maintaining alignment to the working agreements, identifying ways to enhance their effectiveness internally as a management team, and improving their external reputation, or brand, with their broader department and the organization. The team was starting to adopt a systemic approach to their work by becoming more aware of issues, opportunities and their impact outside of their department, which relates to Hawkins' Discipline 4 of Connecting.

Table 5.3

Financial leadership team charter – Fall 2011

Vision
Financial solutions that promote company growth and success.

Team Mission
We give our stakeholders the financial comfort to sustain and grow the company. We provide these financial solutions by...
(abbreviated to respect confidentiality)

Team Purpose
Provide the key leadership to the organization and our people on financial strategy.

Team Members	Team Norms	Key Goals
• Seven team members completed the team charter and six team members remained at the end of the six-month team coaching journey	• We create a safe environment to speak up • We encourage and welcome questions • We make no judgements • We resolve issues directly with good intentions; we listen 'for', not 'against' • We commit to look for successes and share them with others (big and everyday ones)	• Removed to respect confidentiality
Values (Sample) • Results • Integrity • Change • Leadership	• We educate, communicate and negotiate to balance workloads and priorities • We own our own career development plans • We respect confidentiality • We hold ourselves and each other accountable	Success Measures (Sample) • Compliance to authority levels • Increase in ratings on the annual stakeholder satisfaction survey • Development of people via 100% completion of development plans

Table 5.4   Jacqueline's corporate team coaching session agendas and outcomes

Session	Agenda	Outcomes
1	• Review progress/ successes since offsite • Review working agreements • Define success measures for the team • Confirm messages and how the team wants to 'be' for the restructure announcement to the department	• Successes identified by team members including: • Communication has been good • More positive feeling • Clarity of roles has increased • Increased positive impression of department • Greater sense of team purpose • More forward looking • More aware of branding • Approval to add new positions • Thinking more about HOW we work together
2	• Review of Actions from December meeting • Identify successes and opportunities since December • Check in on working agreements • Review of scorecard/success measures • Restructuring – reflections on how this team is modelling and leading the department • Other issues as identified by the team • Next steps	• Successes identified by team members including: • Safe environment has been created • Advising each other of deadlines consistently • Team learning about their conversations • Positives • Everyone involved • Bringing back to focus/end goal • Common understanding of significance of topics • Open to suggestions • Improvement opportunities • Don't take comments personally • Be sensitive to time invested • Communicate successes • Link back to the goal and strategy and KPIs

(*continued*)

Table 5.4   (*Continued*)

Session	Agenda	Outcomes
3	• Review of actions and progress • Review of working agreements • Review positivity research (successful team ratios on positive/negative, self/other, and inquiry/advocacy dimensions) • Decision re: Introduction of working agreements to whole department • Review the next steps for closure on the team coaching	• Agreed to roll out working agreements with slight modifications to full department • Team's working agreement successes • Feel more informed about department activities • Safe environment to speak up • Good teamwork and communication • Don't hear negatives any more • Appropriate dialogue • People are trying to work together to close gaps • Team's working agreement opportunities • Move to be with rest of team when possible • Be conscious of team commitments; align calendars • Added a new working agreement: • We don't make commitments without validating our priorities (eg Communicate re: people's workload before committing) → Education, Communication, Negotiation)
4	• Review of the TDS • Review of the team coaching journey • Successes/appreciations • Identify how to maintain the high-performance team	• TDS scores showed overall improvements • Comments about progress during coaching: • Moving in the right direction • Recovery focus • Higher functioning • Positive tone • More confident and supportive of each other • Things have improved; equitable distribution of work; emphasis on goals

One team member commented on the value of ongoing sessions, stating that:

> Follow-up sessions were important to make sure we didn't fall back to our old ways. It was helpful because... instead of just thinking about something, we actually had to do something. Our work world is so busy, we kind of just do things, and whether we follow up is iffy. [The coaching process] created follow-up.

The team coaching sessions were structured such that I co-facilitated the meeting with the team leader, and I also coached the team. I offered opportunities for the team to pause and have a 'time-out', and asked them questions to reflect on their progress and interactions during the sessions. I also supported the team to keep a focus on their end goals and outcomes, with a primary focus on the team culture that they were creating within and outside of the team. One participant commented: 'our coach was good in terms of being firm and bringing people back to what we were trying to accomplish. I have gone through lots of HR stuff and didn't find a whole lot of value. This was different; there were deliverables and timelines.'

Corporate team coaching outcomes

At the last coaching session in April 2012, the team members agreed that they had made some good progress on many of the factors assessed by the TDS between October 2011 and April 2012. In fact, there were five factors on the TDS that the team deemed to show a meaningful change, including: (1) effective work management, (2) team member relationships, (3) enabling structure, (4) well-composed team, and (5) helpful coaching. The team believed that these changes would not have occurred without the team coaching, since the team had been having difficulties for several years before the new leader joined the team, and before they started the team coaching.

Overall, as this team progressed from the pre-coaching assessment through to the final coaching session, they moved from being very internally focused on the dynamics and structure of their department to working on enhancing their impact inside and outside of the organization. They had defined success measures and were tracking their successes internally and externally, which they had not clearly done before. They also indicated in the coaching sessions that they were working more cohesively and positively with each other. In the final coaching session, the team leader summed up their progress when she said: 'We have graduated from students to teachers. We can hold ourselves and others to the working agreements and say: this is our team.'

The team members all agreed they had met their original goals for the team coaching, and indicated that they were proud of their progress. One team member commented that:

Team coaching helped a lot. You might have great individuals as participants in a team, but if they are not working as a team it doesn't mean that the sum will be greater. In order to work as a team, to do well as a team, you need to know what your roles are, how you can help, look at the success of the team, and how the team can benefit the organization.

They believed that they had achieved a higher standard for their team and department culture, to which they were holding themselves and each other more accountable. The team leader noted that their success and effectiveness were noted outside of the department as well. She said: 'Certainly the senior leadership's view of the department has been elevated [as a result of team coaching] and as soon as you see a team as more high performing, you have more faith and trust and you believe that they can accomplish more.'

A summary of this team's coaching journey is highlighted in Figure 5.3, which includes initial comments that summarize the team's starting point, the team's three coaching goals, and final comments that summarize the team's ending point after the team coaching.

Figure 5.3   Team coaching summary for Jacqueline's corporate team

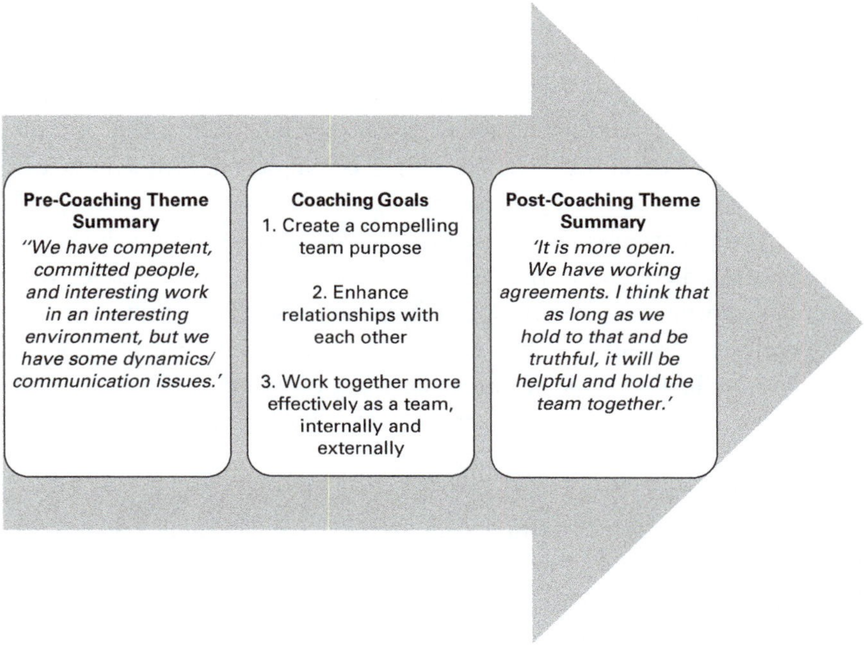

Pre-Coaching Theme Summary

"We have competent, committed people, and interesting work in an interesting environment, but we have some dynamics/ communication issues.'

Coaching Goals
1. Create a compelling team purpose

2. Enhance relationships with each other

3. Work together more effectively as a team, internally and externally

Post-Coaching Theme Summary

'It is more open. We have working agreements. I think that as long as we hold to that and be truthful, it will be helpful and hold the team together.'

Learning and recommendations

Any coaching process is only as good as the coach using it. We cannot say with any certainty that another coach using a similar process to ours would fare any better or worse than we did. The coach's influence on the team is subject to the coach's skills, manner and approach. Also, the team has an impact on the effectiveness and outcomes of the team coaching; so different teams may have experienced outcomes different from the teams in our case studies. That said, we drew on our experience, mentorship and ongoing supervision of each other, and the extensive team effectiveness literature, to guide our work.

We learnt a great deal as a result of being both the practitioners and the researchers in these two structured case studies. First, we purposefully carried out and wrote our case study findings separately so that we would not influence each other's findings or interpretations. When we did compare the results from our two teams, we were intrigued but not surprised to see our differing styles as coaches coming through in the way that we each presented our individual team case studies and their respective findings.

Catherine adopted a more fluid, solution-focused coaching approach (see Meier, 2005 and Hawkins, 2017: 322–324), while Jacqueline used a more structured and business-focused approach. In addition, the contrast in team starting points and cultures stood out to us when we read each other's accounts. Catherine's team was a much higher-performing team as identified in their higher initial TDS scores (Wageman *et al*, 2005), the positive way in which the team described themselves, and the team's reputation in the rest of the organization as a high-performing team. Jacqueline's team saw themselves as delivering on their business goals, but unlike Catherine's team, described themselves as disconnected and lacking cohesiveness. The culture of Catherine's team focused on celebration, appreciation, team successes and mutual respect. The culture of Jacqueline's team was more competitive and individualistic. Jacqueline's team also ascribed a tone of negativity to their team at the beginning of the coaching. A summary of the comparison of the pre-assessment data for the two teams is identified in Table 5.5.

Catherine coached her government team through a new project and Jacqueline coached her corporate team through a new beginning and restructuring. Catherine coached her team to define and implement a project that helped team members develop interdependency and incorporated more peer coaching/support. Jacqueline focused on coaching a team to higher performance and positivity, and an improved team brand/reputation.

Table 5.5 Comparison of TDS pre-assessment data for each case study (Carr and Peters, 2012)

(Entries in bold represent overlap between the two case studies)

	#1: Government of BC (Catherine Carr's team)	#2: Corporate Team (Jacqueline Peters' team)
TDS strengths	• **Empowered and high autonomy and respect for judgement** • Almost perfect teamwork score • Consequential work • High effort, performance strategy, and use of knowledge and skill • Well-composed team	• **Empowered (most feel this way)** • Task orientation • Highly motivated • Internal motivation • Adaptable
TDS weaknesses	• **Team norms** • **Team leader coaching** • **Organizational support** • Functioning as a real team, eg Interdependence • Compelling direction that is challenging and clear • Sharing work activities and knowledge of results • Team leader could foster good group process, in addition to other foci	• **Team norms** • **Team coaching** • **Organizational information** • Amount/quality of interaction • Development/growth opportunities • High rating on unhelpful interventions and low on interpersonal relationships

Despite the many differences between the teams' qualities and their goals, there were a number of valuable co-creating coaching components that were surprisingly similar between the teams. We had not expected to be able to see such strong commonality between our two case studies because of the obvious differences in the cultures and starting points of our teams.

Both teams found the quantitative pre- and post-coaching results from the TDS (Wageman *et al*, 2005) as strong validation for the changes they subjectively observed they had made. Table 5.6 outlines the key changes in the TDS scores for both teams. Both teams identified the two-day team launch as a key element in supporting the team changes since it provided

Table 5.6   Comparison of TDS pre- and post-assessment changes on a five-point scale (Carr and Peters, 2012)

(Entries in bold represent overlap between the two case studies)

TDS changes pre and post coaching	#1: Government of BC (Catherine Carr's team)	#2: Corporate Team (Jacqueline Peters' team)
Highest numerical increases	• **Well-composed team (4.4 to 4.7)** • Compelling direction (4.1 to 4.5) • **Enabling structure (4.3 to 4.6)** • Motivation and satisfaction (4.3 to 4.6) • **Helpful coaching (3.8 to 4.2)**	• Team member relationships (3.3 to 3.9) • **Enabling structure (3.3 to 3.9)** • **Well-composed team (3.3 to 3.8)** • Effective work management (3.1 to 3.7) • **Helpful coaching (3.1 to 4.0)**
No numerical change or decreases	• Team member relationships (4.9 to 4.7) • Supportive organization (3.9 to 3.7)	• Real work team (3.7 to 3.7) • Motivating team task (3.9 to 3.9)

focused time to build team connections and define a common path. At the launch, both teams focused on establishing working agreements and peer coaching agreements. They both created a team charter or team project to launch the coaching.

Both teams identified that ongoing team coaching was essential to integrate and sustain changes. Making the changes was not always a smooth process and the coaching helped the team stay accountable to their agreements, actions and goals. For both teams, their vision for coaching included what they needed to step up to for their team members, their desired team purpose, their clients and stakeholders, and ultimately what the future was calling forth from them (see Chapter 1).

Our key learning, once we compared the two case studies, was that having a structured approach to team coaching was highly beneficial to the team's perception of the coaching and their performance. We also noted that creating or leveraging a clearly defined new beginning for the teams was effective in creating momentum and motivation for change. Further, ensuring that the teams were clear about their own vision, purpose, goals and success measures was important for success (Hawkins's Discipline 2, Clarifying). Aligning the coaching goals to these team factors helped ensure that the team coaching sessions were focused on team performance, not just team dynamics for the sake of team dynamics.

The key challenge we encountered was around scheduling and keeping the team connected to checking in regularly via the team coaching sessions. It is too easy for teams to get so busy doing their day-to-day work that they can neglect the important check-ins about how they are working together. Also, Jacqueline's corporate team lost two members over the six months of team coaching so this shifted the dynamic twice during the coaching, and reinforced the need for the team to abide by their team charter and working agreements so that they could flex more readily when these team member changes occurred. Overall, we learnt that when team members are included in co-creating and 'owning' the team coaching, the process could be both structured as well as responsive to individual team needs.

Conclusion

We provided coaching simultaneously as we studied these two real leadership teams in their complex business settings. We worked as a team of two and provided Hawkins's seven-eyed supervision (2013) and support to each other throughout the process. As a result of our conversations, we often came to new insights and learning that we had not come up with alone. We could better distance ourselves from becoming intertwined in the dynamics of the team and kept an objective lens on what was happening and ways to best support the team. As we reflect back on our learning journey now, Peter Hawkins' words about his Discipline 1, Commissioning, stand out: 'What is the shared endeavour that the world/stakeholders are asking this team to step up to?' This question guided our work and guided our team's work.

We also believe that there are places a coach can only take a team if they have travelled there in themselves. We aspired to rise to this grand goal in our partnership with one another and through our coaching in order to serve communities at large. We particularly hope that coaches benefit from our experience and learning as much as we have benefited from the work and experience of others.

Reflections Three Years On

As we look back on these case studies from the point of view we have today, three years later, we note that the learning we had from these cases has served us well as team coaches. Our team coaching practice continues to focus on supporting our teams with clarifying the elements required for team effectiveness, including the articulation of a clear vision, mission, goals, values, success indicators and working agreement protocols. We continue to use assessments to identify the level of team performance and functioning before and after a team coaching intervention. We also include a one- or two-day team launch in our interventions, followed by one or more team coaching sessions over a period of six to 24 months to sustain results. We have learned over the years that the clarifying and co-creating disciplines are essential elements in any team coaching intervention and team coaches are well served by deliberately taking time to address these disciplines.

Coaching the connecting between a new CEO, her leadership team and the wider middle management in a UK National Health Service organization

06

JACQUI SCHOLES-RHODES AND ANGELA McNAB

Introduction

This chapter aims to demonstrate how a newly appointed CEO of a healthcare organization worked with a team coach to help redefine the focus and priorities of the leadership population – the CEO and her executive leadership team, and those making up the top 150 managers and clinicians – and facilitate the connection between them.

As team coach and team leader we are both present in the text as co-writers, providing insight into our parallel perspectives and offering a secondary account of our own development journeys as we share our reflections on the work together. Towards the end of the account we also demonstrate how the roles of coach and client have begun to shift, the CEO herself stepping into the role of coach at a crucial point in the organization's development and the team coach moving into a one-to-one role.

There is a strong theme running throughout the chapter that is defined by the CEO's driving values – her aspiration to help co-create a culture of professional equals, to enable the voice of clinical leadership to be heard, and her belief that leadership must be shared and mutually accountable.

The overall timeline is nine months, starting with Angela's arrival as the new CEO and then concluding as she herself takes on the role of team coach. The main body of the text covers the two coaching interventions, developed and delivered over four weeks. Through detailed accounts of both interventions we aim to illustrate how we engaged a significant population of leaders in exploring both their capacity for core learning and their ability to help co-define the leadership commission, and then used the outcomes from this event to help the executive team redefine its own leadership remit. The overall aim was to help connect the two groups through their shared experiences, learning and aspirations for a better future.

We document the contracting phase by first setting out what we each saw as the core challenges in the business and then sharing how we each envisaged the coaching becoming an effective intervention. Angela, the CEO of the organization, shares her thinking first as she decides to work with Jacqui as a coach, clearly drawing out her criteria for selection as:

- a relationship of trust and friendship;
- knowing when to support, and when to challenge;
- able to model the qualities of partnership needed by the leadership team.

Jacqui, in her role of coach, then shares her perspective – in many ways mirroring the insights of the CEO while at the same time beginning to develop some of the foundations for the work together.

The CIDCLEAR process framework (Hawkins, 2017) provides coherence for the work, useful both as a micro-lens to ensure the coaching is structured well and as a macro-lens to ensure the programme as a whole facilitates the vital connections between the executive team and the operational management group.

Initial contracting – the client perspective

Joining a new organization as chief executive is always a leadership challenge and one where coaching can be critical. In this instance I was entering a UK National Health Service trust which had been through particularly difficult times over a period of several years, had experienced a succession of leadership changes, a plethora of financial and service constraints and had a culture of top-down management. In addition, the organization was in the process of applying to become a Foundation Trust, which brought with it greater organizational independence, but also considerable external scrutiny, reporting demands and added pressure. The need to ensure that the first weeks and months set a positive course for the organization's future development and culture was therefore considerably heightened. As the new chief executive I was also especially sensitive to the potential symbolic importance of my first interaction with the organization and against this backdrop was keen to draw on my pre-existing coaching relationship in planning and delivering my approach.

I had previously worked with Jacqui over a 2–3-year period in a smaller NHS commissioning organization. The issues in that organization had been very different but a relationship of trust and friendship had been established. In reflecting on the decision to work together I had several things to consider:

> Jacqui knew me both as a leader and as a person. I believed that her knowledge of the 'real me' and my underlying values enabled her as coach to recognize more clearly what I was trying to achieve and what mattered. It ensured she would know practically when to intervene with support and when to challenge if I was backing off or avoiding an issue. I wanted more than anything to be authentic and so working with someone who could recognize that was crucial.

Having learnt a little about the organization, met the current interim CEO and heard about some of the actions already taken to start to form a more positive culture, I felt strongly that I needed a high-impact method of connecting with the senior and middle tiers of the organization – as well as helping them to make connections. I started to discuss the possible methodology with Jacqui, the options and the aims. Instinctively there was a strong sense that the coaching relationship should not only model the outcome I was seeking but that it should continue to model that outcome through the way we would engage with the participants in the coaching. As coach and coachee we worked together as professional equals, each contributing our experience, insight and skill. We also worked within a strong values-based framework that both advised our planning and supported the clear leadership I aimed to establish.

This all represented a parallel with my aims for the organizational intervention: to recognize the professional contribution of all staff, to establish a culture of equals and to enable leadership at every level.

I had already gathered information on the organization's culture from informal visits and conversations with the chair and some clinicians. It was clear that the 'clinical voice' had not been strong in the Trust. Many clinicians and other staff felt 'done to' and disempowered. The planned methodology had therefore to create energy and belief in those present that they could influence their own future, create service strategies in partnership and begin to have confidence to take action, knowing they would have the permission and support of the wider organization and senior leadership. More importantly, there needed to be a sense of starting to create shared leadership across the organization, where all clinicians and staff saw their own role in delivery and in influencing the Trust's future.

In determining the intervention itself, my aim was to create an initial event that would engage a significant number of staff and enable them to have a voice as well as to meet and hear from their new chief executive. The interim CEO had previously set up some local workshops to refresh the organization's values and so I was keen that the event and any subsequent work should demonstrate this values base and actively reinforce their currency without reconsidering their identification.

We both felt strongly that the event needed to go beyond the top tier and engage the 'middles' (Oshry, 1995) of the organization, a group so critical in influencing and exhibiting culture and whose messaging to frontline staff is so crucial. However, the importance of then connecting the outcome from the event into the objectives and working remit of the senior executive team was paramount. If the event was to be part of an ongoing impactful programme the senior team would have to own the outputs from this first event and translate them into a mandate for their own role. It was critical that we ensured that the outcome of the event was the 'start of something' rather than its being simply a standalone activity.

This led to the overall assignment having two stages: first a half-day event with about 100 people, including 'middles', and subsequently a day-and-a-half team coaching for the senior team.

In thinking about the format of the first event I was influenced strongly by our previous coaching work and by the history of the coaching relationship. Previous joint work had used the 'storytelling device' with good effect. In addition I had undergone my own development programme, which featured storytelling as a powerful leadership tool, and I was keen to use this personally. This choice was strongly informed by my values – I wanted to demonstrate that everyone's story and voice is equally important, I believed the stories would connect people through a shared narrative and I saw the stories as a method for learning and co-creating the 'next chapter' for the organization.

In her role as coach Jacqui enabled these aspirations and non-specific ideas to translate into a clear 'storyline event' where both personal and organizational stories would be shared.

In preparing for this first event I was very aware of the challenge for me personally. I saw that demand as twofold: I knew I wanted to open the event by telling two brief stories – things that had happened to me in my career. It felt a more genuine way of introducing myself to people rather than describing the highlights of my CV! However, I realized that to be of value they had to be stories where genuine learning or change had occurred in me. That meant that in sharing them I would be demonstrating my key value of openness but also making myself quite vulnerable.

Secondly, I would be standing up in front of around a hundred people whom I did not know and without a pre-existing relationship with the senior team. It felt much more 'my invitation' and 'my event' than anything I had done before. It added to the importance of Jacqui's presence as coach. I am not sure I would have felt so confident without a trusted colleague on hand.

The event was scheduled to take place in the first few weeks after my arrival in the role, meaning that we actually organized it before I even entered the Trust. Dates were also identified for the follow-on team coaching with the senior team, which would be the first real focused time they would have together with their new CEO. There were clear risks and opportunities around this timescale and approach and it was important that we worked together to ensure the interventions were well planned and communicated and that risks were well managed. The strength of the coaching relationship and mutual trust was crucial. We also recognized that individuals in the Trust who would normally have been working more closely on such events or programmes might feel disengaged and so as soon as I felt able, I ensured they were brought into the later planning meetings and had a role in supporting the first event.

Initial contracting – the coach perspective

It was unusual to start the contracting work before Angela had even arrived at the Trust, but I also understood why she needed to do this. Having worked with her in her previous role, we had both observed the challenges of seeking to connect an executive team's intent with the broader leadership community, and recognized the temptation to pour a tremendous amount of energy into engagement and communication that would simply have replicated the top-down culture. In this role she needed to demonstrate how she was listening to the frustrations so clearly expressed in the organization and was responding to them by connecting directly with them.

The initial brief for the work was to help co-create a sense of collective leadership across the organization – to help start the work that would turn the organization from a 'done to' culture to one that would define and own its own ambitious mandate. I understood that it was critical that the work would engender connections with the frontline, help generate positive energy, build the confidence to influence the agenda and encourage the broader leadership group to accept that it had permission to act. Above all, they needed confidence to help co-create the mandate, to see their own role in delivery and to step up into a partnership of equals.

We agreed that our own shared intent was to invite a significant group of leaders to tell their stories, to share their aspirations for the next chapter, and to help scope and prioritize the leadership commission in a way that would enable a fundamental shift in their collective performance. It was critical that our design should respect the collective need to have a 'free voice', that it should help establish an equality of vision and that it should create an opportunity to connect past and current experiences into a shared energy for their collective future.

Like Angela, I was very aware of the potential risks in the approach. As we had to do a lot of the pre-planning prior to her arrival in the role, we were unable to include the internal staff who might otherwise have been responsible for helping define the intervention. We were also inviting a large group of people to express their views and there was no way we could pre-empt the outcome. Unable to access direct input from the executive team itself, we also risked triggering a domino effect of feeling 'done to' and could well have caused them to disown the outcomes. Even worse, it could have alienated Angela just at the very moment when she needed to be fully connected with them!

It became clear that the priorities were to:

- create an opportunity for the new CEO to be 'fully present': clear in her own values, alongside them with ambition and intent, prepared to take on leadership with them;

- tap into/ignite the positive energy that had probably been dissolved by the more difficult times of the past and the succession of changes in leadership;

- signal that Angela was coming into the role with respect for 'what had gone', and to help establish a sense of connected partnership in tackling what needed to be done;

- show how she intended to work with her executive team to connect their insights, learning and specialist expertise;
- put a stake in the ground... establish a point of turnaround.

Inquiry, diagnosis and the first intervention

It's important at this stage to understand how the CIDCLEAR framework (Hawkins, 2011) provided both a micro- and macro-lens through which we developed the work. From a micro point of view, Angela and I had already begun to investigate the needs for this first event through a series of one-to-one discussions, and through her meetings and conversations with the chair, board, outgoing interim CEO and executive team members. We had also reviewed the results of a recent staff survey. We had 'tested' the diagnosis as far as we could and by now had begun to form the initial contract and were ready to run the first event.

From a macro perspective this was the first of two events, and would also represent a detailed extension of the inquiry and diagnostic stages. It would be key to defining the next stage of contracting for the executive team event.

We wanted to draw out a map of everything the organization had achieved over the last three years, encouraging the group to identify all the moments of innovation and breakthrough they had achieved. Our intention was to help them identify both the high and low spots, and in each case bring that expression of energy and emotion into the room – helping them generate a felt sense of optimism and sustain the momentum towards a new and co-defined future even as they acknowledged what had also got in the way.

We also planned to encourage them to build on what they had learnt (drawing out the core learning), ensuring they identified what it would be critical to keep – and just as importantly also let go of. We would then invite them to co-create a collage of their anticipated future through a similar approach.

In her pre-briefing to the executive team, Angela stressed the importance of developing this group of leaders as ambassadors for the changes that were needed in the Trust, critical in helping bring coherence to the cross-business activity and in enabling them to connect the Trust's work both vertically and horizontally. Listening would be absolutely key to the success of the event. Angela recognized that it would be essential that she establish trust and openness very early on, and we agreed that she would open the event by sharing the story of her own very personal journey.

We had set aside a morning for the meeting, aiming to finish around lunchtime. We couldn't have foreseen the weather – an absolutely awful rain-sodden day – but amazingly it didn't seem to affect the determination of the participants. Out of the 130 or so invited to attend, over 100 turned up. We'd set out round tables to encourage groups of people to work together, and already in the first half-hour the energy in the room had reached a high-volume buzz, many people apparently meeting and connecting for the first time.

The room was long and relatively narrow, with limited room for circulation. We had set up a table at one end on which we'd attached a long roll of paper to represent the three-year timeline. On an adjacent wall we'd attached a similar length of paper, slightly shorter, on which we would invite the group to build its collective vision of the future.

Angela opened the event by welcoming them all, expressing her absolute pleasure at seeing so many of them present, and setting out her intention and expectations for the morning. For many in the room this was the first time they had actually met their new CEO, and so these opening words were critical in establishing her reputation and impact. She was also very clear in introducing me as a coach with whom she'd already worked, and explained that my role was to listen, notice, hold the structure and ensure the process stayed on track. In this context I was present as Angela's one-to-one coach, our relationship representing the quality of partnership that Angela wanted to role-model.

As she shared the story of her own journey Angela offered clear insight into her motivation for the leadership role and her very personal vision for their collective success. Her fundamental values were clearly embodied in the way she shared the narrative, and feedback collected after the event reinforced the impact she made. She expressed a readiness to be both vulnerable and open to learning, at the same time establishing a clear leadership presence.

She then invited the whole group to share their own stories, expressing them in the form of pictures and paying attention to both the highs and lows – first with colleagues at their tables, and then after about 15 minutes transferring their images to the timeline at the end of the room. As they built up a collage of their collective experiences we invited them to identify the connections – and the disconnections – and to build them into the emerging picture.

We also invited them to build a similar collage on the blank roll of paper attached to the wall on the other side of the room, this time sharing their personal and collective vision for the coming 18 months and again making connections wherever they could. The level of listening in the room was acute.

We allowed about 30 minutes for the activity.

Angela then walked the length of the story timeline, slowly picking out the various images that represented significant milestones in the organization's recent history. She appeared to have an instinct for what mattered most to them, and the individuals who had contributed the drawings added further colour as she highlighted them and invited them to comment. The experiences were expressed with insight and energy, and as she walked along the years this extended leadership team enthusiastically shared the meaning behind the pictures. One person summed up their challenge with clear simplicity: 'We have two choices – we can either be frightened alone, or we can be excited together!'

After a short break we invited the group to work together at their tables, helping identify the actions that needed to be considered priorities for the Trust. This data would help shape the second intervention, the team coaching for Angela and her executive team, and give substance to the diagnostic that we had already begun.

A few days after the event, I reviewed the data that had emerged. It was important that we didn't make any premature judgements or assumptions that might misdirect the contracting for the team coaching work. Five clear themes were evident:

- leadership;
- commercial strength;
- quality services;
- clinical leadership;
- organizational strength.

Many members of the group had provided additional detail of the issues to be addressed, and by including the 'voices' of their service users (driven particularly by the clinical leaders in the room) had also underlined the need to ensure validation against the organization's core vision of patient-centred care. There was also collective enthusiasm for service-line events to be facilitated in a similar way, acknowledging that the timeline was a very powerful way of enabling the teams to connect by describing both the journey completed and the future they wished to co-create. Feedback on Angela's stories was very positive, with comments that illustrated how her vulnerability and humanity were beginning to promote optimism.

Continuing the diagnostic and contracting for the second event – coaching the executive team

Angela and I approached this stage of the work in two ways – as an extension of the inquiry and diagnostic that we had begun with the extended leadership group and as a clearly contracted coaching intervention that would support the development of the executive team. We agreed that it would be important to start the coaching work with a half-day reflection on the 'middles event' and an exploration of its impact on them as a leadership team.

In preparing for this second event, my role needed to clearly shift to that of team coach, with my attention grounded in the team's contract for the work. I began by arranging one-to-one phone calls with each member of the team, followed by a meeting with Angela to finalize an outline for the event. Having given such an opportunity to the 'middles' to be heard, it was even more critical that the team had an opportunity to express their own hopes and concerns for their collective leadership. I worked with a common framework of six questions:

1 What did you personally take away from the meeting?

2 Which three–four priorities do you believe we should address together as a result of the event?

3 What else does this team need to focus on?

4 What will your role be in helping enable the changes?

5 Angela talked about co-leadership. What in your view do you need to do as the executive team to really enable this?

6 If you could achieve just one outcome, what would it be?

In posing the questions I wanted to encourage each participant to explore and begin to articulate what they personally viewed as the 'work' the team needed to do. There were no 'wrong' or 'right' answers. If at any point during the conversations I felt an individual might be stepping back from collective ownership of the challenges, I helped bring their attention back to the underlying issues, hoping to catalyze an increased openness by offering a safe space in which to express some of their frustrations. I wanted to help generate an appetite for the collective resolution of the issues, putting the onus firmly back on each one of them to ensure that the day would be a success according to their terms.

Several members of the team followed up their calls with detailed e-mails containing further items to be addressed. Some offered items that appeared to be outstanding decisions that we might reasonably have expected them to be able to resolve within their own functions, but clearly felt unable to do so. It sounded like an echo of the frustrations we had already heard expressed by the larger leadership team, and seemed to offer more evidence of a restrictive culture.

There was limited commentary on how they might impact cross-organizationally but there was consistency in the areas they felt they needed to address as a matter of priority. These were:

Co-create our leadership identity from which we will rebuild our confidence.

Stay grounded in our passion for delivering good services that are sustainable because they're built on commercially sound foundations.

Join up wherever possible to co-create a coherent and clear road-map that operationalizes the strategy.

Help co-create the trust necessary to allow everyone to work freely and responsibly.

At this stage, these four themes appeared to offer a clear starting-point for the work we needed to do together, and I prepared to build our initial contracting around them. When I met Angela a few days later, she added her own input to the contract, reminding me that we should include a reference to a 'red/blue list'. This had emerged from the first event as a means of clarifying the collective priorities and so it was important that this team should respect it as a concept and maintain the language that their teams had used in describing it.

The team also wanted time to get to know each other – some had only recently joined the team – and they asked that we include this as part of the work together. Some of the telephone conversations had indicated that there might still be a risk that the executives had felt somewhat excluded from the earlier activity, and so I agreed that we should include an opportunity for them to explore and develop confidence in their leadership identities, while having both the space and permission to explore their shared leadership alongside Angela.

Second intervention – coaching the executive team

The executive team coaching event took place a week later. Although the team had already met several times in business meetings, this was the first time they had spent time together focusing on themselves as a team. We had scheduled a day and a half, with a dinner together at the end of the first evening.

With so much complexity shaping and influencing their work, it was important that we minimize any interference right from the start. Our first work together was to focus on shifting the attention in the room, inviting each member of the team to let go of whatever was drawing their attention away and allowing their focus to come into the room free of 'baggage'. Although this took longer than the writing would suggest, we were then able to begin the contracting process, starting with a 'three-way sort exercise' that helped identify what we needed to let go of, hold on to and do differently, and enabled us to commit to the behaviours and operating principles that would be necessary for our effective engagement.

With a level of clarity around the contracting, we then moved on to focus on each individual's personal hopes for the business, inviting each one to share something of themselves in the process. This was in response to their request to take time to explore how they connected as a team, and aimed to help them explore the relational space that they were co-creating (Lines and Scholes-Rhodes, 2013: 115–17). I asked each one to share three sets of images – one to illustrate how they might appear when most energized and another to illustrate what colleagues might notice when that energy was drained away. The third image was intended to help them share what mattered most to each of them.

This exercise usually takes over an hour, and in many cases will enable teams to reveal some very personal and connective insights; with this team we had a curious mix of personal revelation tempered by some cautious commentary on the significance and challenges of their roles. It may have indicated the level of trust in the group. However, what was more important at that point was that it helped bring all the voices into the room – and gave a sense of where the connections and disconnections might be.

Working with this theme of connection, I invited them to split equally into separate halves of the room – one side representing the feelings and voices of the executive team and the other side expressing the remembered voices of the 'middles'. As they stepped into their different roles the energy increased, each side both curious and passionate – and yet separated by what had become a very tangible empty space in the room. It was in this space that they needed to do most work, asking the question 'what do we need to connect in order to deliver our collective intent?' as a fundamental means of shaping their leadership role.

As we began working together on the following day, the energy in the room began to dip, and we began to lose momentum. Something had shifted overnight. The focus oscillated between seeking to engage with the four areas we'd contracted to explore, and needing to explore the team's own struggle with the past, feeling victims of the 'done to' culture and a lack of appetite in some cases for taking on the shared accountability for making the change happen:

I found that I was working hard to generate and hold the energy for them – and felt tempted to step into something I felt they were avoiding. I sensed Angela was also struggling with the temptation to step in – needing to offer her leadership but at the same time confirming that they had the space and permission to co create the collective leadership agenda. It was critical that the authority should remain within the team and that I should maintain my role as coach, supporting the team in resolving the issue for themselves, while playing a catalytic role in helping them develop their own learning process. Above all, I needed to remain alongside them and work together to explore what was emerging.

I called for a time-out and we explored the loss of energy together. They agreed that we should take more time to explore the nature of their own connections, and what they needed to do to be able to bring their individual passions and contributions into the team. Using individual shields (on which they drew their strengths and development areas), they shared more insights into who they were, and began to articulate some clarity around their roles and responsibilities. As they worked through this process, certain tensions became more obvious in the room, which they could now readily articulate. They also began to work with some of the underlying issues, facilitating the process for themselves.

We certainly didn't resolve everything, but through the time-out and re-contracting the team had realized it could begin to resolve issues together, and that Angela was actively encouraging them to learn, commit to the changes and move on.

Once they were confident that everything had been surfaced, they returned to working with the four key areas they had originally identified as their priorities. We agreed that we would develop the red/blue list together as a means of testing their commission, while also working to clarify their priorities. Their intention was, first, to ensure that the list was sufficiently comprehensive and then, second, to agree which of the items could be labelled as needing a lighter touch. It seemed important that they take the time to work out a process that they could both engage with and embed into their ongoing collective working. They took it in turns to offer items that connected to and helped build a collective list. They appeared to be trusting each other a little more and seemed much more ready to share what was on their minds.

At the end of the one and a half days they made five clear commitments to:

1 deliver on the action plan and champion a customer-focused culture;

2 focus on the critical business priorities identified by the red list;

3 resolve the current hot issues that could potentially derail the business;

4 work together according to the parameters they had agreed;

5 encourage staff to go ahead and replicate the half-day events with their teams, with the suggestion that they invite one–two members of the executive team to hear their stories.

Review of impact and action – roll-out and after

Continuing the stories

The organization achieved a considerable amount of development over the following nine months, building on both the storyline event and the executive team's coaching. The first significant action was to implement one of the key recommendations from the first intervention. Almost unanimously, those staff who had attended the first event had proposed similar events in each of their service directorates. These events enabled staff closer to the frontline to also engage in sharing and developing narrative and, perhaps even more importantly, play a key role in the co-creation of the next stage of the organization. The resulting narratives provided a valuable source of insight for the CEO and executive team, demonstrating significant differences in styles and tones and culture across the service lines. This illustrated yet again the validity and insights that such interventions can reveal – and enabled the senior teams to use the outputs gathered from all the service lines as input to the next year's organizational development plan.

Maintaining momentum

Maintaining the momentum of that commitment during a subsequent period of intense demand on the organization proved challenging. Keeping the focus on culture and behaviours was not easy and at critical points during the year there was a need to restate the objectives they shared.

This restatement was critical in developing their ability to review and learn together, and enabled them to realize that they needed to identify ways to increase their impact. They agreed to set up a staff forum and clinical cabinet, giving these groups a mandate to articulate, and hold each of them to account to, their new cultural norms – enabling everyone to develop 'compassionate management and equality of voice and influence'.

A new staff reference group was put in place, asked anonymously but frequently to rate the core cultural norms on a very simple scale: 'Is it better, the same or worse?' Using this thermometer they hope to support the focus for changing actions at all levels of the organization. That focus, supported by the new models for feedback and input, is also intended to help them hold onto the values they identified through the coaching programme: allowing core staff to influence and to take responsibility, to locally determine actions and to critically evaluate and learn from them. In short, to become the compassionate, valued, achieving group of people they aspire to be.

Ongoing learning and reflection

Reflecting on the impact of the two initial interventions, the CEO is clear that together they provided a 'powerful starting pistol' for her leadership and created a shared experience and language which was crucial for the required cultural shift. Throughout the work she recognized the potential risk in co-creating the approach with a coach from outside the organization and together we have posed the question: 'Could we have achieved a greater acceleration in the senior team's mandate if they had been given more influence in the early planning?' It's clearly difficult to judge – but the strength of the energy and the commitment to grasp the mandate was so clear in the room at the storyline event, and was then reflected in the senior team's readiness to sign up to delivery through their own team coaching, that it seems likely that this was in fact the most effective approach we could have taken.

The CEO also sees the coaching approach as having been critical in enabling her to pick up that mantle and take on the role of coach herself as she helps leads the programme of culture change. She is also realistic about the limitations of taking on the role of coach and reflects:

> When coaching or leading in teams I notice the thirst in staff for permission to work collectively to build something different. Frustratingly as CEO I am then pulled into the space of task and spread sheets and realize that without support for some powerful follow-through, changes at the ground level take longer to be realized... and when under stress we revert to our old cultural norms unless challenged and coached frequently.

Current Reflections

Having supervised team coaches for the last four years, I can now look back in 2018 and offer these three questions based on my reflections both as a supervisor and a team coach:

1 How important is it that the leader of the client organization be included in a series of joint supervision sessions with the external coach and to what extent might that accelerate their readiness to step into their own team coaching role?

2 How might a similar intervention work where the CEO is seen as overly embedded in the organizational system and the coaching has been triggered by a member of their team?

3 How can we put sufficient emphasis on developing the team's capacity to learn when other factors in the system are encouraging them to focus solely on the outcomes and increased productivity?

Coaching the team working with its core learning

07

SUE COYNE AND JUDITH NICOL

Introduction

We have worked together as systemic leadership team coaches with boards and senior leadership teams in organizations of different sizes and types across a wide range of sectors. Each of our leadership team coaching programmes begins with a team performance appraisal based around the five disciplines diagnostic (Hawkins, 2017: 324–326). In reviewing the diagnostic results for all of our clients we were interested to note that the score for core learning was consistently the lowest score of all the five disciplines at the start of their journey.

So in this chapter we focus on core learning and we will explore what happened when we coached a leadership team to increase their team learning and in the process improve their teamworking and collective leadership of the business. The team were the executive leadership team of Bruntwood, a privately owned, medium-sized company in the property sector.

We will reflect on core learning at a number of levels:

- how we integrate it into the design of our leadership team coaching programmes;
- how we model being a reflective practitioner as we deliver the programme;
- how we enable our clients to integrate reflection and learning into their modus operandi in a sustainable way;
- how we integrate core learning into our modus operandi in a sustainable way.

The Bruntwood case study

The organizational and team challenge

Looking back, the CEO of Bruntwood described the context for our work with the leadership team in early 2011 as follows:

> Bruntwood fundamentally had a good culture and set of values. It had a longstanding and loyal leadership team and the business was loyal to them in return. The team had developed informal ways of working which were often not articulated but were 'understood' as in a family that has been together for a long time and grown up together. Team members had become tolerant of each other's shortcomings and quirky ways and found ways to work around them without confronting them. There had been a series of attempts to evolve the ways of working but none of them had got any traction. As long as the business was successful it was easy to feel that there was no need to change. The burning platform of the economic downturn meant that the way the business was led needed to change. More clarity was needed around what was expected of the leadership team and around the processes supporting the business. If the team could do this work during the downturn then the business would be able to take advantage once growth returned and not repeat the mistakes of the past.

The team leader's desired outcomes for the team coaching journey were:

- personal development of individual directors (13 in total) to broaden their leadership skills to ensure they meet the future needs of the business;
- team development – more collaboration, operating in a joined-up way resulting in a joined-up organization and operating as a team so that the whole is more than the sum of the parts;
- the directors playing their part in building the new culture by living the values.

> What I want for this team is that they aspire to be business people (not just experts in their profession) to broaden their horizons, be more accepting of each other, value difference and grow. They need to develop their competence in leadership but the desire doesn't always seem to be there.
>
> (Bruntwood CEO)

Engagement and contracting

Following discussions with the CEO and chief operating officer (COO) of Bruntwood, the team coaching programme was commissioned in

March 2011. However, as we needed to ensure that all members of the team were fully engaged, we met with the whole team in April 2011 to contract with them for the journey ahead. This is part of all of our team coaching programmes and the CEO reflected that getting the buy-in of the leadership team up front was one of the factors which meant that this programme succeeded where previous programmes had failed. We built credibility with the team in this session and started to build trust. We explained what team coaching would involve, agreed appropriate confidentiality and got their agreement to take part in the initial diagnostic phase and from there to co-create the coaching journey with us. They got a clear understanding that this was not something that was going to be done to them but with them.

The inquiry, discovery and design phases

The inquiry phase in May/June 2011 consisted of each director completing the Five Disciplines Questionnaire and taking part in a one-hour face-to-face discussion with Judith or Sue. They also did a DISC assessment (a behaviour assessment tool based on the DISC theory of psychologist William Marston and developed by John Geier, 2004) followed by an individual face-to-face feedback session.

While all of the directors were open and frank during the diagnostic interviews, we realized that having open and honest conversations was not a feature of team meetings and people were leaving those meetings feeling drained and demoralized as opposed to energized. We shared the results with the CEO and COO and decided that the focus of the first team session should be on building trust and creating a climate in which people felt safe to express their views openly.

As with all of our other clients, the lowest score of 1.9 out of 5 was for core learning. There had been a lack of individual (score of 1.7 out of 5) and team development (1.7 out of 5) and the climate in meetings was not one in which people could give each other feedback in the moment (2.3 out of 5). Rather than a balance between support and challenge, there tended to be more challenge and competition between the directors. They were an action-oriented board rather than a learning board (see Kakabadse *et al*, 2013, and Chapter 14 in this book):

'The whole idea of standing back is alien, we are all too much into the detail.'

'We are very poor at feedback. There is more challenge than support and sometimes the challenge is not appropriately made.'

'In our meetings behaviour is rarely discussed and challenged.'

'We need to appreciate each other more, how talented and competent we are and what great people we are.'

How the work unfolded

1 The process

At the *first team session* in July 2011 we opened the session by introducing how we expected them to reflect and integrate their learning:

> This is not a 100-metre sprint! We will be practising a little today and then ask you to go away and practise some more. We'll review next time we meet and practise some more. Embedding learning is like exercising a new muscle at the gym; it takes time. Be kind to yourselves.

We gave each director a reflection journal and they started to use it immediately as part of the contracting for the session: 'Use your reflection diaries to note down what success would feel and look like for your today.' We used the reflection diaries throughout this first session and subsequent sessions.

At the start of the session the team generated a 'Way We Work Together' agreement comprising a set of behaviours that would enable them to work effectively together and that we would adhere to during the session. Part way through the session we introduced them to a 'TOOT' (Time Out of Time) (Oshry, 2007) in which we modelled and practised a way they could build reflection into their meetings. We explained that this is not about reviewing the content of their meetings but the process and behaviours. We asked two questions during the 'TOOT':

> 'What has been useful in the first part of the workshop?'
>
> 'Name one thing you would like to be different in the second part of the workshop.'

At the end we reviewed how they wanted to take this agreement forward into their team meetings.

We contracted with the team to send the complete and unedited diagnostic results to them all individually the following day. As part of the work on trust, we were able to do some contracting around confidentiality with regard to these results. We also explained that we wanted the team to engage with the data and specifically to prepare for stakeholder role-plays in the September session.

Right at the end of the first session we established action and review processes (see Hawkins, 2017: 98). These would become a routine for future sessions:

- a commitment to individual and team actions to embed specific learning;
- a review of what had been good about the session;
- opportunity to appreciate others for how they had behaved in the session;
- feedback to the coaching team – what worked well? What could we do differently next time?

Our aim with this was to model the importance of reviewing at the end of meetings and also to give them practice in giving appreciation and feedback.

Following the first session we had a *review meeting* with the CEO and gave him feedback on how he had showed up in the session.

Between the team coaching sessions each director had a *one-to-one coaching* session with either Sue or Judith. Our aim here was to support the individual development of each director, which would enable them start to integrate their learning from the team session in order to make the fullest contribution to the team.

The *second session* started by reviewing how people had fared with the commitments they each had publicly made as individuals and as a team in the previous session. They had been asked to e-mail us with their priorities for the team coaching journey having read the diagnostic and also to prepare for the stakeholder role plays. We then moved on to developing a common purpose for the team using a 'collective build' method (Hawkins, 2017). In the 'collective build' we asked people to complete the sentence 'the fundamental purpose of this team is...' on Post-it notes. We asked each person to do this between three and five times to get beyond their 'top of mind' responses. As people gave their responses they put their Post-it notes onto a flipchart, grouping them in clusters with similar themes. These themes were then summarized and made up the key components of their common purpose. At the end of this session we did a 'TOOT' specifically around embedding learning in the organization and getting value for money from the programme. We finished with people recording their learning from the session in their journals and also any commitments that had been made.

We circulated the actions to all team members by e-mail with the accountabilities that had been agreed.

We then started to do some work with the CEO, COO and CFO as a separate subsystem. In order for the wider team to be joined up, we realized that this smaller group needed to set the tone. We invited them to give feedback to each other as a triad and to discuss and agree their modus operandi as a threesome and as a key leadership group within the wider team. They came to an agreement about what was needed by way of consistent responses from them and also what meetings and systems were needed to support the monitoring of the business while at the same time giving team members scope to grow as individuals.

All individual team members were asked to produce personal development plans (PDP) for discussion with the COO, based both on their one-to-one coaching conversations with Judith and Sue and the emerging leadership competencies being developed by the COO.

There was then a gap from November 2011 until March 2012. The one-to-one coaching sessions were completed and the business continued to go through challenging times.

In the *third session* in March 2012 we focused on finalizing the mandate and the common purpose, plus agreeing the leadership competencies needed to achieve this. We also took the first steps towards working with the group on how to give each other feedback. We used a flipchart approach to this where each director had a sheet showing what they should stop, start and continue doing, which was filled in by the remaining members of the team. Each individual responded to their sheet by saying what they planned to focus on. Most took the feedback really well. In addition, we asked the team to consider how it celebrates success and to consider its progress since we started working with them. They drew before and after pictures that clearly illustrated the progress made. Reflecting with us in preparation for writing this chapter, the CEO recalled the before and after pictures, saying: 'An important moment was when we did the before and after pictures – the one showing the snakes and ladders board brought home to me that the key is to take two steps forward and only one back if we are to make progress.'

The *final team session* of this phase was in May 2012. The session focused on releasing the creativity and potential of the individuals and the team and giving some practical tools that could be taken back into the workplace.

We started with a 'TOOT' which by now the team were very comfortable with, which looked at where the group was now in terms of its learning about behaving like a team. We then did some work on 'comfort zones', see Figure 7.1 (White, 2008) (this is where people are doing something familiar as distinguished from their stretch/learning zones where they are developing their ability to do less familiar/new things) and on friends and enemies of learning, which enhanced their awareness about where some of the blockers might be. We introduced some content around generative dialogue, building on the work we had previously done around listening. We introduced

Figure 7.1   Comfort zones

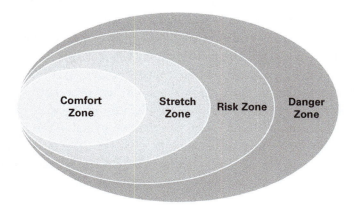

coaching skills and finished with some work on creating win/win agreements using 'the third alternative' (Covey, 2011).

We concluded with a group discussion on next steps for the team's development and agreement to do one more one-to-one coaching for each individual to help them work up their PDP.

What worked?

Once we had The Way We Work Together agreement we started every session with it, both contracting around it between ourselves and reviewing how they had done against it since the last session.

Keeping close to the CEO and constantly talking to him about his role as the leader of the team and his responsibility for the learning and how he could enable everyone else in the team to take their responsibility for their own learning and for the shared learning of the team was important. We were able to reinforce this via the one-to-one coaching sessions for the CEO and for the other members of the team. We gave clear feedback based on our own observations of them as individuals and at the team sessions.

This is a team that is very hard on itself, working in a system that was full of tough challenges, and so offering encouragement and constructive observations was very important.

Giving each individual a journal was symbolic of giving them responsibility for their own learning. There were moments of lightness, as on the second session two people had lost their books: one had the book eaten by the dog! But most people in the team had used the reflection diary and found it helpful.

This is a team that works hard and plays hard, so injecting some fun was important. Although there was initial resistance to untried new things, they role played, drew pictures, made models and did team sculptures, which were all activities that increased the energy levels of the team (for further explorations of embodied and creative techniques see Chapter 15).

Holding people to account and the team to account every time we met was powerful. The first time we did that, not only had people not carried out the commitments they had made, but they had forgotten what they were. Over time, the team got used to the fact that we would ask and learnt to follow through to a far greater extent. In fact, when we met up with them to review progress in preparation for writing this chapter we sent them all a questionnaire to fill in and without exception everyone had done so. Definite progress!

Unexpectedly, the 'TOOTs' were very powerful, although there were many raised eyebrows initially and suppressed smiles. We used the 'TOOT' as a vehicle for us to share our reflections about the group and also to have conversations with the group. We did a fishbowl with spare chairs and invited people to join our conversation. The intimacy of the circle within the circle seemed to help people express unspoken thoughts. This approach also helped the team move from action to reflection and content to process, and introduce periods of reflective learning in the midst of their busy business.

Once the leadership competencies were defined, we encouraged the CEO to push responsibility down to individuals for developing their PDPs and planning the meeting with him to explore them. This meant that there was a long pause before meetings were arranged, but when they did finally happen the quality of the thinking that individuals had done about their own development was rich and powerful. By giving them clarity around what the business expected of them and some support to raise their awareness, they were able to own their personal journeys and not wait to be told!

What didn't work?

There were times when we felt we were spending more energy on keeping the learning process going than the team was. This was not a team that had been used to making time for reflection and the demands of the day job dominated their available focus. Working by e-mail across such large numbers proved difficult, particularly when we were asking for responses that required some thinking. While team members were engaged in the sessions, we quickly lost contact with them as soon as they went outside the room.

We spent too long on trying to get to the perfect common purpose. We colluded with one of the team's patterns in relation to corporate projects, which was to get lost in process and not complete things. Getting to a working version of a 'collective endeavour' that was then refined as the team went forward would have been less draining on everyone's energy! Having reviewed this with the CEO, his view on how we could have done it differently is:

> We needed a straw man rather than trying to create the collective purpose from scratch. You could have collected information about this from individuals during the diagnostic and used it to develop the straw man. The team could have worked together then in the session to optimize this. It needs to be good enough to stand the test of time and I need to feel inspired by what is produced.

Generally the team worked better in smaller subgroups. In particular, working on abstract concepts or processes as one big group didn't work well. Using the 'collective build' technique worked well until the point that the team had to decide what to do with the output! Again the pattern of getting out of process and having to have things perfectly documented got in the way. Eventually we all declared ourselves bored of the process of trying to perfect the mandate and the common purpose and the COO did the final editing.

The team had a pattern of not completing and following through on corporate projects, which was a hard one for them to interrupt. We put too much effort in initially into trying to join things up for the team but realized that because it was a large group, they had to have a subsystem within it that would drive consistency, clarity and connection. Hence we started working with the sub-team of the CEO, COO and CFO.

There was too long between the November 2011 and March 2012 sessions. The team had momentum in November and then heavily committed diaries got in the way, culminating in too long a gap. We spent a lot of time in March 2012 'tying up loose ends' of things that had been started but not completed. We were mirroring what happened in the team and the energy levels were not as high as in the previous two sessions.

Getting the competencies agreed was like drawing teeth and became a bit of a technical exercise. This slowed down people being able to articulate their PDPs and also meant we had to stall the individual coaching as the framework was not completed.

At times there was too much content in our session due to the fact that the team had had limited leadership development prior to this programme.

The outcomes

We asked the team to rate themselves on the three core learning attributes from the Five Disciplines Questionnaire, which showed that definite progress had been made in core learning.

The results are in Table 7.1.

Table 7.1   How the team rated themselves on the three core learning attributes

	April 2011	October 2013
The team regularly and effectively attends to its own development	1.7	3.1
The team regularly and effectively attends to the development of each of its members	1.7	3.1
All team members give good real-time feedback and provide support and challenge to each other	2.3	3.1

We then asked the team to think about our Cycle of Learning model (Figure 7.2) that we had described to them and to consider what, if anything, had changed in the personal and team processes to enhance collective and individual learning.

1 Feedback, awareness, content

This is the extent to which the individuals and the team have been able to seek out, give and receive feedback, assimilate content and increase their awareness. Most of the team felt that they were now comfortable seeking out and receiving feedback one to one. Several have sought formal feedback from their own teams which they have shared with the CEO as part of their PDP. Several said they are continuing to read leadership articles and actively embrace new leadership models. The team has also done a joint session on situational leadership (Hersey, 1985), which combined with the growing awareness among them has had a powerful impact. The initial DISC profiling gave them a common language and an awareness of self and other differences which have had ongoing impact on how they interact. The team has since done a basic neuro-linguistic programming coaching course which has given them additional skills to interact with each other and with their teams.

The work we did with them exploring comfort zones (White, 2008) means they are constantly thinking about where the stretch is for them,

Figure 7.2   The Cycle of Learning model

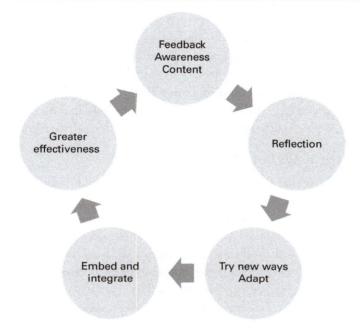

where the learning edge is. Simple tools like the stop/start/continue (Silberman, 2005) exercise (we set up a flipchart for each team member and other members wrote on the sheet what the individual should stop doing, start doing and continue doing) have remained with them and help them think about their activities day-to-day and week-to-week. The CEO said the PDP sessions he has recently run were richer than he could ever have imagined. At the recent annual company weekend, time was made for group feedback and it was hugely valuable.

Overall, the team felt that their awareness had grown but there is still scope for further development. In particular, being able to be an observer of their own behaviour in the moment is still something they want to work on.

2 Reflection

All of the individuals in the team felt there was an acceptance of the importance of reflection and an understanding of how this is key to the learning cycle. Most felt there were fewer instances of 'reacting without any thought', though they acknowledged that this is a work in progress. Most felt they reflect more on their impact with the rest of the team and with their own teams. If things don't go well, they ask themselves why. Often after a meeting, they will ask themselves how it went and what could have been done better. As part of team meetings at the beginning, people are actively asked to reflect and given time to consider things without being interrupted by others. Given the pace of the business, most find it hard to keep this reflection integrated into their day-to-day activity. The team meets in smaller functional or business-focused units and in these gatherings there is time specifically given over for reflection. The team feels that there has been considerable progress here but they need to keep actively working at it.

3 Try new ways/adapt

The team all felt that they listen more to each other and to their teams. The impact of this is that they can encourage best thinking and not rush into premature solutions or decisions. They ask more open questions, inviting exploration of possibilities. There are fewer instances of individuals dominating meetings, which means conversation is freer flowing and more thoughtful. Team members feel they are able to trust their team more as a result of greater engagement with them. The team have largely dropped preconceived ideas about each other and have re-programmed how they interact with each other. Many felt they were more aware of blind spots and were actively trying new ways of thinking and doing in response to this new-found awareness. Many talked about increased confidence to step into new roles and ways of being. Several said they felt, as a result of this, able to ask for help and not feel they had to know everything! Several talked of an increased tolerance and a feeling that constructive criticism was not taken personally, leading to greater openness and honesty among the team. The HR director said that 'whereas two years ago a project team would only have thought about WHAT needs to be done, now they think about HOW it needs to be done. This is a significant shift.'

4 Embed and integrate

This aspect felt like a work in progress to the team. Several new behaviours described above felt as though they were embedded and integrated, though interestingly the team had an awareness that they had to keep working at it. Everyone felt they had made considerable progress since the work started and that there was real forward momentum in their learning. Most felt that there was still work to do to spread the learning down the organization; this had started but needed still further energy and focus. The team felt they appeared much more united to the rest of the organization and to their stakeholders rather than being a series of individuals. Most felt that they would benefit from some external support to refresh their learning and to keep working on how to apply the learning and embed it. The HR director reflected:

> I think everyone's confidence has grown as they have taken on board the learning. My confidence has grown. We are more comfortable sitting around challenging each other, knowing it is not personal, and on the way back from meetings to our offices, quickly asking each other what we could do to make things even more powerful, how things could be done even better. If people don't want to eyeball each other and give each other feedback there are other ways to do it. People are thinking much more about their impact and how they are likely to react in advance of sessions.

5 Greater effectiveness

The feeling was that the work the team has done has resulted in greater effectiveness for itself and for the rest of the organization and its stakeholders. However, there is still work to do to help their respective teams become even more effective and in particular to make people feel supported and able to give of their best. A recent process to refinance the business demonstrated how they can present a very effective and powerful united picture to the external world. As the HR director said, 'we received great feedback on how we projected ourselves as a strong, coherent and capable team'.

The CEO reflected on how the greater effectiveness in the leadership team has impacted each of its stakeholder groups:

> *Shareholders*: 'Directors have more awareness now of the need to understand their audience. The quality of the papers the shareholders are getting from directors is better as a result.'
>
> *Team members*: 'It is a more positive environment to work in, they look forward to meetings instead of dreading them and they feel inspired.'
>
> *Staff*: 'It is early stages but there are less politics among Leadership Team members. Working in a political environment saps people's energy. Also Leadership Team members are more energized and interested and there is more engagement and involvement of their people as a result.'
>
> *Customers*: 'No question that the impacts on staff ripple through and have a positive impact on customers.'
>
> *Wider business community*: 'We have been clearer with Leadership Team members about their responsibilities here and they have taken on Board positions I used to have. Again, to be effective they have to think about their audience.'

Everyone felt that the ability for this team to have constructive challenging dialogue has had a major impact on effectiveness. In conclusion a board member reflected: 'The starting point for this work was that the team should be in a position to grow the business once economic conditions allowed. We are now absolutely in a position where we can do this. We can absolutely see the impact.'

Because the team has much more productive meetings and catch-up sessions, when they emerge into the wider business, the ripple effect is doubtless a lot more positive than previously. Because things are going well at the senior team level, the learning and development team have been able to start manager forums for the next level down, which encourage peer learning and discussion of options and challenges.

Threaded through all of this is increased clarity about individual journeys: What are we trying to do? What support do we need? How can we embed our learning in the teams below?

Key learnings

We took the opportunity with the Bruntwood CEO to develop some shared key learnings, particularly about how we might enhance our approach for the next phase of development for the Leadership Team. A key area of focus in our discussion was greater integration with HR to embed and integrate the learning between sessions:

> We introduced Sarah from HR into the process towards the end. She worked with the directors on how they work with their teams. The work you did positioned them so they were ready to work with her. We could have set this resource up from the beginning and used it during the whole of the programme to help get things embedded.

The Bruntwood Board has identified growth opportunities for the business going forward and the leaders themselves need to grow in order to continue to meet the growing requirements of the business: 'If we are to continue to grow and get the most out of our people we need to continue on this journey.'

Given that the team currently rate themselves at just over 3 out of 5 for core learning, the CEO asserts: 'My ambition is to get to between 4 and 5 in a year's time. A lot of things need to happen to make that possible.'

Our learning

The learning of the team is only going to be maximized if we as a coaching team of two were also learning. Therefore we built reflection and development into our own process. We identified that a learning edge for us both was being able to learn in the moment and adapt our process/approach there and then, as well as giving feedback to the team in the moment. We supported each other in this and by the end of this programme it had become almost second nature.

We reflected together regularly during the programme and also had regular supervision to ensure we were being as effective as possible.

Some of our key learnings are:

- To build greater collaboration with HR/team leader into the design to support integration between team sessions. We could also do more to support this by offering shadow coaching or observation of her work with the next-level teams, to give feedback in the moment.
- Not to introduce skills/content that is too far in advance of the current level of leadership capability.
- One-to-one coaching is key as leaders are not self-aware enough at the start to do their own reflection in between team sessions.
- There is a pace to the coaching programme that fits with the team. It will establish its own rhythm and it is better not to force the pace. The pace changes throughout the journey. Phase one is more pacy and has more process; the team then settles into the journey and it can go slower while integrating learning. There needs to be sufficient pace and frequency to ensure the energy behind it doesn't dwindle away.
- It is often better to work with a real business issue rather than use an abstract exercise – this is like learning on the job, so it more relevant to the day to day and easier to integrate.

Conclusion: 'We have had an incredible journey'

This was the collective conclusion of the Bruntwood team. We would conclude that if you really want to embed learning:

- It doesn't happen overnight.
- It doesn't happen in one intervention.
- It doesn't happen just at a collective level, but needs to happen at an individual level as well.
- Attention to how the learning will be embedded and integrated is the red thread that runs through the design and delivery of the whole coaching programme if it is to be sustainable and have impact.

In assessing whether a team is ready for team coaching, paying attention to their attitude to learning is key. Some useful questions to ask as team coach are:

- Do they have a development mindset?
- Does the organization have the capacity and capability to support them in embedding the learning?
- Are they ready to collaborate and work with the coaching team on their learning journey rather than expecting the coaches to do it for them?

If the answer to these questions is not yes, the team will end dissatisfied with the process and blame the coaching team for the failure.

In order for this to be successful you need a senior champion for the programme – ideally the team leader, who understands about making the sort of changes that are required.

Continuing to learn and grow is the only way a Leadership Team can ensure it stays fit for purpose and relevant in the long term. Organizations in which we have worked where the leaders haven't grown at the same or a faster pace than the organization have found they have a capability gap which is impossible to fill quickly.

Reflections Three Years On

We re-contacted the CEO of Bruntwood and asked for an update on the team that was the subject of our case study.

We asked him if the team was 3/5 three years ago on reflecting and integrating the learning into how they operate where are they now?

He replied:

> You could say that we are 5/7 now... we've certainly developed, however, the demands on the senior team have also evolved significantly too. Overall though I am happier with where we are. One of the main catalysts for driving this change has been our widening the Leadership team to our top 90 then using this group, particularly the younger ones, to drive the evolution of the leadership model of the business. We have organized this group as a nimble Team of Teams, rather than a fixed hierarchy. The group of 90 is governed by its Leadership 'Board' of 30 people, with a tight corporate board of five steering the agenda for the Leadership 'Board'. Our colleague strategy continues to be driven by creating an environment of autonomy for all, one where everyone feels that they are moving forward, learning new skills and deepening the engagement of everyone with our purpose of making our great city regions greater.

Bruntwood continues to have an innovative approach to leadership and creating a positive learning environment for all continues to be at the heart of the culture.

We also met together and reflected on our board and team coaching work over the last three years. We realized that our experiences of how these teams have worked with their core learning have a lot of common threads.

We concluded that learning and embedding the learning remains possibly the greatest challenge for leadership teams and boards. We feel that this is partly due to increasing 'overload' issues and the demands to do 'more and deliver higher quality, with less'. Also, there is ever more focus on value for money and cost reduction, which means that partners and suppliers are bought on 'how cheaply' they can do something. In terms of team/board coaching this can mean that making the intervention sustainable by helping to embed the learning is 'costed out' of the intervention. We see little sign that this will change in the immediate future.

As a consequence, this can lead to a tick box mentality rather than a focus on making sure the interventions are truly making a difference by way of increased learning resulting in things being done differently and better.

The overload issue can mean that the headspace that is required for people to try new approaches and behaviours is not there. In order to keep delivering at pace it is easier to keep doing what you have always done and focus on 'business as usual'.

Working with a team coach over a period of time starts to create the habit of reflecting, identifying what needs to change and then embedding that change. However, we have noticed that many teams are not creating the time for ongoing team coaching. They are instead just having team events, rather than engaging in full action learning cycles of reflecting on what is happening, creating new collaborative meaning, planning new experiments and then reflecting and learning from how these succeeded and failed in action.

As a result of the above, boards, leadership teams and execs are spending more and more time in Covey Quadrant 1 (on things that are important and urgent) and not enough time on Quadrant 2 (important but not urgent) which is where reflection and embedding learning sit.

Only where there is a burning platform, or a crisis do we see organizations really thinking hard about commissioning high-quality and therefore higher-cost interventions likely to produce lasting change, as they have no choice at this point: the alternative is not a risk they can take.

So in the midst of this 'pressured' environment what is the key to teams identifying their core learning and integrating it so that they continue to grow, develop and improve in order to better meet the future needs of their organizations?

It comes down to the team or board leader. The leader is vitally important in setting the tone with regard to attitudes towards learning, as is evidenced by the quote from the CEO of Bruntwood. Where he or she is prepared to role model the importance of reflection and learning and to integrate reflective practices into the team's modus operandi, it is more likely that the team or board will have a growth mindset and be committed to embedding change in a sustainable way. We are finding that where our work begins with the CEO or leader of the team, it is more likely that he or she can role model and champion the change that is needed of the rest of the team, due to a greater personal understanding and commitment.

Team coaching as part of organizational transformation

A case study of Finnair

DAVID JARRETT

Introduction

Often leadership teams of large companies turn to team coaching when they know they need to lead a major organizational transformation. In these cases the team coaching has several distinct but interconnected areas:

- The team jointly clarifying, developing and owning the transformation process (Clarifying discipline).
- Discovering how they need to operate as a team to lead this change process (Co-creating discipline).
- How they need to live and role model the values and behaviours that the company will need to be successful with the transformation (Connecting discipline).
- Building the trust and cohesion necessary to deal with the turbulence caused by the transformation process (Co-creating discipline).
- Increasing their collective capacity to communicate the transformation process, engage staff and other critical stakeholders and win commitment to the change (Connecting discipline).
- In addition, the team need to check they have the right remit from their board, shareholders and stakeholders to undertake the transformation (Commissioning discipline) and be constantly learning throughout the process (Core Learning discipline).

Figure 8.1   The Triangle of Integrated Change

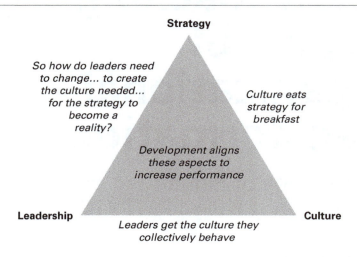

At Bath Consultancy Group this has been the most common environment in which to apply systemic team coaching. The systemic view is deeply connected to our wider organizational development work carried out over the past 25 years, which integrates the strategic challenge, culture change and leadership development (Figure 8.1). As the rate of change increases in nearly all sectors, organizations have to constantly adapt and develop new strategies. The challenge then becomes how to embed these strategies within the company. We often use the phrase first coined by Peter Drucker, 'Culture eats strategy for breakfast!', for new strategies call for new cultural responses, and this involves changes in behaviour, engagement and ways of thinking. Changing the culture is always much harder than changing the strategy.

We also use another memorable one-line statement to describe the link along the bottom of this triangle: 'Leaders get the culture they collectively behave.' Leadership teams cannot deliver successful change unless they are able to look at themselves and see how their way of behaving and engaging influences the climate and culture of the rest of the organization. Developing a new culture in the wider organization begins with the leadership team learning how to 'be the change they want to see'.

So often we have come across leadership teams who have gone away and developed both a new organizational strategy and core values for their organization and then returned to communicate these to the unsuspecting members of the organization. For successful organizational change the leadership team needs to find ways of sharing the challenges and co-creating the change with the wider leadership of the organization, while modelling the new culture it wants to create.

A way of focusing the collective team mind is to ask the following questions:

- If the existing culture has worked perfectly to get us here, what does it include that will stop us from implementing the new strategy?
- If the behaviour of this leadership team has contributed to that culture through behaviours and decisions, which behaviours do the team need to stop, continue, and most importantly start doing? (see Hawkins, 2017: 310–311)
- How will we bring about this change and make it visible to our people?
- How do we as a team start and sustain the journey as individual team members working apart?

A period of challenge and change in organizations presents a great opportunity for accelerated leadership development. Often we find that leadership development needs to begin by developing the leadership team within the organization, through systemic team coaching that addresses how they engage together and then with the wider organization.

In this chapter we will describe one of many such processes we have been involved with, working in partnership with the CEO, executive team and wider leadership of Finnair. Other examples are published elsewhere, such as: the work with Ernst & Young UK (Hawkins and Wright, 2009), British Aerospace (Hawkins and Smith, 2013: 113–15) or the BBC (Hawkins and Smith, 2013: 104). More examples can be found on the Bath Consultancy Group website (**www.bathconsultancygroup.com**).

The context

Finnair is one of the world's longest continuously operating airlines. It flies today to around 60 countries, carries over seven million passengers a year, has a turnover of €2,400 million and employs about 6,000 people. As a national carrier of Finland it has weathered many storms that have ended many other European airlines. It has been an iconic business in Finland, regularly receiving comment as one the preferred companies to work for or join as a graduate. The leadership team was responsible for a portfolio of activities from air travel to catering, and from maintenance to tour operators.

This helped create an integrated business which to some extent insulated the company from external shocks.

Early in 2000 the European air traffic market was opened to new competitors, and from 2006 the cost pressures on Finnair were becoming unsustainable, as increasing oil prices and reducing fares, driven by low-cost competitors such as Blue and Norwegian, were creating the perfect storm and eating away at the profitability of the business. Losses were funded by the Finnish people through government support.

In 2010 a new CEO was appointed with an agenda to return the business to profit. By mid-2011 a few new appointments had been completed and a renewed executive board (leadership team) had been formed. The need for business transformation was then determined and scaled in terms of cost savings, process changes and investments needed. The strategy was in place to be the leading airline in the Nordic region and in the top three for all transit traffic between Europe and Asia. This long-haul aspect of the business was vital to revenues and profits; European short-haul required significantly lower costs and support from higher passenger numbers on the long-haul schedule.

The strategic challenge

The culture of Finnair had been built up over a number of years in largely public ownership (56 per cent owned by the government of Finland). This had contributed to an organization that had not changed as quickly as the market and with possible resistance to the necessary changes identified in pricing, service and cost management. Indeed, there was a view among managers that the culture had tended over the past 10 years to maintain the status quo and now Finnair faced a cliff face of change – and could managers really be expected to make that happen given that past experience? One way this culture manifested itself was that managers appeared to delegate decisions upwards for the leadership team to run the business. They said: 'We are too busy and do not have the time to do this work on leadership and team building stuff!'

The new team was a mix of new appointments and experienced Finnair leaders. The two different subgroups had different perspectives on the approach to the scale and pace of change required. The CEO saw leadership as a key capability, and believed a change in leadership approach was essential for the company to succeed, though this was not a widely shared view in his leadership team. In addition, the business was made up of about 10 business units or functions with different views and needs about leadership.

At the initial inquiry stage of the team coaching process we used the CIDCLEAR process model (Hawkins, 2017: 83–97), but we decided it was important to get a wider view and carry out a deeper inquiry from within the organization.

A deeper inquiry

At this stage the HR and development leads in Finnair were leading the drive to ensure that the organization spent time on essential leadership and culture, with the strong support of the CEO. However, the leadership team as a whole did not share this belief. With the assistance of the HR and L&D leads, we spent some weeks talking to about 20 key influencers two to three levels below the leadership team to explore (or disprove) the link between leadership and the change agenda.

One of the challenges as a team coach is finding an appropriate way for each client system to view the existing cultures and to specify the cultures they wish to move towards. One technique we used at Finnair was to break the culture down into 'layers' (Figure 8.2).

We then took the following quotes and placed them into the model to create a picture of the current alignment. We then created a session to discuss

Figure 8.2   The five levels of culture

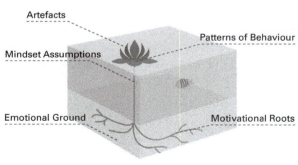

The five levels of culture model shown here can be really useful as a way of analysing cultural alignment, especially in an acquisition. Our work with culture allows teams to identify cultural elements at five levels as shown here.

Artefacts

Mindset Assumptions

Patterns of Behaviour

Emotional Ground

Motivational Roots

We often work with teams who are merging and we use this to identify cultural patterns of behaviour, based on their mindset and their assumptions about each other. Emotional Ground is also a key element which shifts over time and surfaces the unspoken feelings which may drive behaviour and which can vary in teams and across functions. Motivational Roots relates to original founder aspirations and to why people join and stay with an organization.

The purpose of this process is to check alignment of levels and draw out how they are shifting and changing in a function or team. Changes cannot be made at the behavioural levels without addressing lower levels.

how these would need to change and how we would work to shift them. The outcomes informed the design of the leadership team development and the work with the next two levels of leadership:

Our leadership ideal is a quick fix-expert manager

'That person is quick, thinks at speed – gives opinion/answer almost immediately, wow!'

'You can't really expect people to follow you if you don't know how the landing gear works – can you?'

'People value experts who solve problems – so leaders do that automatically.'

'Managing is a dominant activity rather than leading – perhaps roles require it?'

'We have a strong habit to seek out, stay with and talk to people from our own function/type.'

'Typical interventions – inform, prescribe, closed question and their own answers and lengthy options.'

Feedback

'Not sure feedback is really helpful – takes a lot of time which we don't have.'

'Our "Leadership Attributes" are in fact a perfect description of a feedback-rich environment.' (see below)

Addressing emotions not part of our current leadership model

'Managers are worried about how to motivate people – and how to do that differently according to where their people are on the change curve.'

'Managers are not expressing their feelings or using emotion as part of leading people.'

'Little evidence of managers making interventions that included: support statements, feelings, confronting, asking why something was happening, or inquiring how the person was going to respond to their challenge.'

'Many leaders and managers avoided conflict when it was live in the moment. They also found passive resistance so very hard to address.'

Interestingly, the leadership attributes had been agreed by the leadership team before we arrived and the attributes were in direct opposition to the nature of leadership we encountered in the culture. There was 'a rift between the rhetoric and the reality' (Hawkins and Smith, 2013). In the long run these leadership attributes, which some would term leadership values, would provide a very good framework for developing the new leadership culture and the team worked well with this. So while the 'rift' existed, the cultural challenge was to begin to change behaviours, not to define attributes that 'matched' the existing culture.

The leadership attributes were:

goal-oriented: fact-based, bearing responsibility;

fair: clear, consistent;

encouraging: accessible, support-giving, inspiring;

developing: visionary, creativity-promoting;

caring: communicative, listening, open and easily approachable.

This process enabled us to raise the dilemmas with the leadership team – that they sensed they knew what was needed, that is, behaviours that would role-model the attributes – because the leadership attributes would be an excellent counter to shift some key elements of the existing culture. When we discussed this with the team, the response included comments such as: 'We are not sure if leadership development would help but certainly it should not need to start with us! Surely the managers need training if this is what they are saying?'

The deciding moment was during the first leadership team meeting we attended, as presenters not coaches. We showed the data and talked through the linkages between leadership and results. We talked about how the culture would kill the strategy and in fact was already doing so based on the quotes. We proposed that the team went first in developing their leadership.

The CEO asked how we knew this was right; we stated that all the data provided by their people, not our interpretation, called out for leadership of people. The skill set in the team was largely managing by expertise. The journey through the change curve (Kübler-Ross and Kessler, 2005) would require the team to lead their people into uncertainty, facing some difficult emotions, and then to encourage them upwards towards the vision and future success. We gently suggested that as a team that was embarking on a new level of organization change, which they had not done before, they could not expect already to have the capability to succeed or the ability to judge the right approach. So by confounding the 'we know the answer' mindset we replaced it with the offer to help them see that they were not playing with all the leadership cards. To encourage them, we stated that other leadership teams had been where they were now and had succeeded using similar approaches.

As a result, led by the CEO and HR director, there was a highly qualified decision – we would have one day, a night and a morning with the team to see what happened! I guess you want an airline to have a degree of carefulness!

Approach: developing the senior team

As a result of this 'decision', the leadership team agreed to start the leadership development process and if the impact was proven with the team, they would consider how to involve all the 120 senior leaders in all businesses of the group.

Given our knowledge of the existing culture, that the data-driven expert types needed to start with some data about themselves as leaders, and also knowing that feedback was not an everyday occurrence, we started with a visible action to show the team and the organization that the intent was serious and different – 360° feedback. Using a standard, externally available tool designed to explore leadership attributes, each leader received data from subordinates and peers. This was debriefed personally for the team of 10 and we set the expectation that they would be sharing the data with each other. These data also informed the content and approach of a two-day leadership development workshop.

The day/night/morning event was designed, agreed in outline with the CEO and HR director, but not owned by the team. This may not have been ideal and might have been an issue had the team not experienced an 'aha' moment early on.

Picture the scene: in the woods of Finland, near a lake, midsummer, in a wooden cottage, cramped space. Each team member has talked though the headlines of their feedback, made the understandable explanations and agreements – and then came one of those silent moments. Out of the stillness, one voice haltingly apologizes to the team for failing in his view to deliver what was needed and for putting the airline in this situation!

What is interesting about such situations in a team is that the relationship between team members moves in an instant. As a coach there are no real techniques, plans or methods to ensure that the real emotions, concerns and fears get voiced, yet they do – if the right enabling conditions have been established. It was delightful to be able to show to the team that the way they responded was more in line with their leadership attributes than anything we had seen to date. So they could do it, just perhaps, without thinking – something about the leaders' 'being' and using their humanity, not brains.

Another seminal moment was when we showed the team the change curve (a model new to some) and asked them to come up to the flipchart and say where they were themselves at that moment. The highest impact was made by one team member saying that he was not even on the page but way below, off the bottom of the flipchart, as he felt so concerned about how people were not taking the cost issue seriously. He put this big issue on the table: 'This is how I feel about the team... you are not taking the cost problem seriously at all – it will kill us and yet I feel I am the only one acting as if it matters.' This simple model produced a moment of high emotion from one of the least expressive members of the team, which changed the tone of the event.

This is a discussion as a team that can only be held using leadership capacity and human openness. I recall that another person said, 'I felt slightly optimistic having heard the team's responses'; however, it was clear that there was a lot of work to do to create a team capable of performing at the level that the organizational challenges would demand.

Continuing the team session in the morning, we felt that the team would benefit from getting a shared view about how to perform – what they would need to be doing, what score they needed to get. So we used the High Performing Team Questionnaire (Hawkins, 2017: 301–304). This specifies three topics within each of the five disciplines.

A simple tool for the team was to score themselves individually against the key determinants of team performance, and then share the scores publicly. The variances are as interesting as the high or low scores. The data were confidential to the team and as a form of contracting into the coaching process, they are very valuable. The next question was to ask what the team wanted to address first and so we moved from workshop to team coaching, enabling the team to make their own informed choices.

In designing a team intervention that was integral to organizational change it was necessary to build in 'real work' (business agenda topics that would otherwise be carried out in the monthly team meeting) and use that context to highlight team dynamics and capability issues. Agreeing the topics with the CEO in advance also increased the relevance and application of the techniques and leadership, live in the room. Picking the difficult topics also enables the coach to add value directly by helping the team succeed where they feared they would fail. On this occasion we used the pressure of upcoming communication meetings with unions and staff as that catalyst. Rather than following our own coaching path, we listened to the team and their immediate issues.

The approaches taken in such situations are always enlightening about how the team really works. In this case we could anticipate from the inquiry stage that communication to staff would take on a flavour of leaders as expert. Very helpfully, the communications director was a recent joiner and therefore not bound by the culture as much. So as we explored the messages needed we also rehearsed different leadership modes. It is not appropriate to tell the details of the interactions other than to say that the team realized what 'communication in the style of our leadership attributes' looked and sounded like. The individuals were also freed up to express themselves – much easier than trying to bring a script to life. The approach worked and they later reported that the discussions had proceeded much better than expected, with a better rapport and understanding of each other's views.

In this short day the leadership team had proven to themselves that 'leadership development' would help them specifically, that their changes would allow wider change to occur. 'So what is the shift in me, which will shift this team, shift our managers and therefore move the whole business?' sums up the evening discussion.

Table 8.1 lists the specific behaviours they wanted to try to do more of as a team. To explain the Feedback approach: this was to build a new habit at the end of each meeting or process to ask just two questions – What Went Well (WWW) and Even Better If (EBI). This is a habit we use at Bath Consultancy Group for our internal and external work. It was pleasing to be able to role-model it with them throughout our relationship and to see them adopt it themselves.

Table 8.1 Finnair leadership habits

Know your business:	Delegate:
• Start with your numbers • Define the target • Show the outcome/profit	• Enforce decision making at the lowest level • Encourage risk taking – it's ok to fail! • More team decisions – share, involve, openly discuss and develop new solutions together!

(Continued)

Table 8.1   *(Continued)*

Demand delivery of results – celebrate when you get them	**Listen:** • Practise active listening • Ask more! • How do you feel?
Feedback habit – WWW and EBI	**Encourage:** • Foster positive conflict • Encourage creative ideas and experiments

Take decisions – take responsibility to:

- give us more profit
- add value to the customer
- help us beat the competitors

On the following morning the team captured their reflections as follows and then decided to set about the 'cost problem' out of which a whole flow of energy and initiatives were agreed and initiated.

Approach: creating hub, spoke and wheel

The culture of the organization was rather focused on the leader as expert. Decisions would go up to the most experienced person, who would demonstrate their value by making the right call really quickly and telling the others exactly what to do. As a customer of Finnair, that has a degree of comfort to it. As a coach of leaders, it is a frightening prospect.

In the culture, and perhaps it is part of the Finnish CEO role, the team was there to advise the CEO, and the CEO then took the decision. This is also linked to Barry Oshry's views (*Seeing Systems*, 1995) of the systemic pattern that 'Tops' get anxious about the amount they are responsible for and about 'sucking up more responsibility', then they feel overwhelmed and split up different responsibilities, which creates silos, with the CEO as the only point of integration.

In all models of high-performing teams that I have seen, silos are not included as being desirable. The team did have functional responsibilities – maintenance, catering, pricing and so on; however, organizational change is always in my experience between the functions. For example, how does a full-service airline compete with no-frills or even zero-frills operators? Do we make more money or less money if we cut unprofitable routes?

Figure 8.3   From 'hub and spoke' to team as an integrated wheel

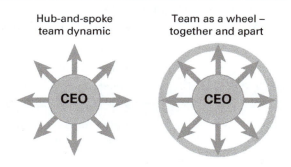

We worked with the team on the live dynamics in the meetings, in particular to help them disrupt the silos, non-delegation, 'same-old' solutions (see new behaviours in Table 8.1). The CEO does need to provide the hub (Figure 8.3), the spokes do need to be connected to that person – what makes the wheel go round is the way the team joins up, outside; when the CEO is not there, if you like.

What we did was simply to call the moments when the hub or spoke was taking more airtime and to substitute it for discussions about how we are feeling and what is going on between us, and then asking 'why is this issue one for the CEO to decide'? In time, the team created informal meetings to address what mattered and the pace picked up between meetings.

Approach: developing the wider leadership group to help lead the transformation

While the leadership team was continuing its development directly in its meetings and one-to-ones, the next 120 leaders were invited to participate in a similar leadership development process. This was designed to create a common leadership approach and to shift the overall leadership culture, with the leadership team members sponsoring and actively attending.

Over 100 leaders were involved in the process, including 360° feedback, a two-day workshop and learning group coaching sessions. In March 2012, the process completed with 120 people meeting with the leadership team at a leadership summit event, designed to share new leadership experiences, successes and learning.

The link to team coaching was that to effect organizational change, the 'changes in leadership behaviour, which create the culture, to enable the strategy to succeed' needed to be carried through all the leadership teams that report to the top leadership team. At Finnair we were able to design and implement a two-day programme with learning group follow-ups. The design took the steps shown in Table 8.2, using the overall organization change as the frame.

Table 8.2   Two-day programme

Day 1 Flow	Day 2 Flow
Why is leadership so important – especially now?	**How to lead performance –** feedback
But it is not easy – adaptive, personal change	**Changing my leadership 2 –** learning group
Let's help each other – coaching, learning group set up, share 360° feedback and development needs	**Leading a high-performing team**
	Changing my leadership 3 – learning group
Changing my leadership interventions	**Inspiring** – rehearse messages and
Apply to your real situations – learning group session, what am I deciding to do differently?	vision, apply storytelling techniques to communicate to our people

The work the attendees did was essentially a coaching structure in groups of 24. Each session had one of the leadership team attending, including the CEO. They would join in the sessions and demonstrate that they too were working to shift their leadership. This live role-modelling was so much more impactful than the message. It meant we could practise the new attributes live in the room, such as upwards feedback, enabling managers to see that they have most of the answers and could take decisions themselves, to share how the change is personal, painful and emotional. The speed of the change was set by the ability of the leaders to help people notice their feelings so they come to terms with the fact that their mindsets and long-held assumptions needed refreshing, to enable people to become high performing again.

The design used learning groups so that these more personal feelings had the space to be explored with colleagues (often from different functions). So the design created moments of cathartic release, where emotions or feelings were voiced and the team could notice how that empowered people to act.

Team coaching is a practical art, carried out in the moment; breakthroughs occur when coach and team feel discomfort, even risk. Leveraging that to an organization transformation requires that the same 'frisson' is replicated in the 'call to leadership' (ie the development programme) and in turn by the leaders with their teams and one-to-one discussions.

So, to reframe the coaching question to an organization setting we asked: 'What is the discomforting change the leadership team needs to experience, that will trigger the leaders to hold the discomforting conversations with their teams, that will create the change needed to deliver the strategy?'

Notably, in Finnair the organization built on the programme and completed the full cycle of development so that changes were embedded in the business. Equally important was the work carried out by the Finnair HR team to implement all the processes in a joined-up way. This included 360° feedback, performance measurement, succession and talent processes, reward mechanisms and mentoring. It meant that the individuals could see how the leadership attributes had become a series of golden threads that explained what was expected of them.

The leadership team of course then had a challenge. How to live up to the standards they had set their reports and teams? At this stage, about a year into the process, the leadership team began a process of personal coaching and also intact team coaching for their own teams. The journey was therefore replicated. The managers were invited to participate in a programme that made the same content relevant to their situation and also had learning-group arrangements to enable personal discussions.

Over the two-year process, therefore, a very joined-up and tight process had been completed (Figure 8.4).

So, in the words of their own people, this was what the Finnair leadership team had put in place:

Figure 8.4   Full-circle development in two years

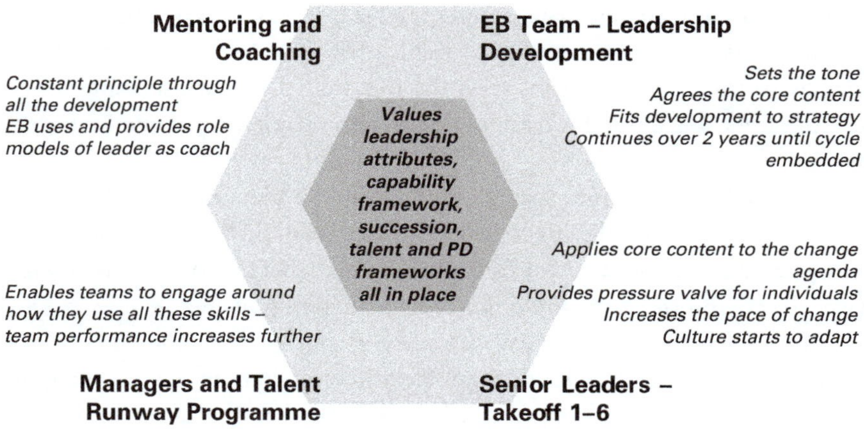

Mentoring and Coaching

Constant principle through all the development
EB uses and provides role models of leader as coach

Enables teams to engage around how they use all these skills – team performance increases further

EB Team – Leadership Development

Sets the tone
Agrees the core content
Fits development to strategy
Continues over 2 years until cycle embedded

Values leadership attributes, capability framework, succession, talent and PD frameworks all in place

Applies core content to the change agenda
Provides pressure valve for individuals
Increases the pace of change
Culture starts to adapt

Managers and Talent Runway Programme

Senior Leaders – Takeoff 1–6

'When this amount of top management people are gathered together under [the] same topic, we share the same challenges in everyday life and had the possibility to learn from each other.'

'A more unified leadership style and clearly communicated attributes within Finnair.'

'We get closer to a common view on leadership so the mutual trust in the organization has a higher likelihood of growing.'

'The holistic approach to problem solutions will increase sustainable profitability of Finnair.'

But then time for hard hats – the culture fights back!

A sensitive but important part of this team development story concerns how the team faced some serious and significant public and political challenges. Whether this really was the culture fighting back – just as the Drucker quote famously predicts – may be academic, but what was very real was the feeling of a team coping with the internal and now external pressures.

There was a story in the public domain saying that the press, public and politicians alleged they had found inappropriate behaviours on behalf of the board in granting the CEO a flat in Helsinki. The employees and unions were outraged to hear that some executives had been granted 'stay bonuses' by the board at a time when their colleagues were being made redundant owing to the need for savings. A new board was appointed and also a new chairperson in due course.

We are not commenting upon the issues here, but what may be instructive was how these forces impacted on the leadership team as far as a coach could observe. I would focus on three dynamics:

1 We had discussed as a team that at some stage we should expect a reaction to all the change – they were moving extremely quickly and putting a great strain on friends, colleagues and union relationships. We discussed how they would mobilize the team to operate the functions while focusing on communications and relations.

2 We began to invite more of the next-level leadership into the leadership team meetings. In particular, the transformation programme was to be led by someone who was not actually in the leadership team. This was counter to 'everything goes to the CEO' and iconic of the request that the

teams run the business. All the leadership team's time could be, and at times was, focused on relationships.

3 The leadership team, as a wheel, operated together without the CEO; at times, this had the impact of creating a team-apart mentality, which speeded up implementation through the teams.

As a result, the organization continued to pursue the vision, the cost management and revenue enhancement decisions were made and implemented, and the managers took up their right to lead. In a situation where the external pressures could perhaps have led to an understandable slowing down or even to halting the changes, the leadership found its strength and, not without difficulty, pushed on and achieved what they set out to do.

There was one event where the team coaching and leadership work combined at a critical moment. It might be instructive to explore whether team coaches can provide a voice for organization issues that otherwise are stifled by the old culture.

The design of the leadership development included a leadership summit. This was a single day attended by all the 120 leaders and the whole leadership team, designed to show everyone the power of the 120, what they were each doing differently in their leadership and the resulting impact. Usually this is a great approach at the end of a programme of multiple groups, one where people learn from each other and agree how they will continue the journey together.

This event coincided with public announcements on television and in the media about the questions being asked.

The issues from a team coach point of view included:

- How would the situation help or hinder the development agenda?
- Would the situation be raised in the learning event anyway? What is the best way to address or incorporate that energy?
- If one sees this as a change curve, where would the participants be, and therefore what would they need?
- What intervention styles were needed?

The team coaching to this event followed the CIDCLEAR process in microcosm:

- Contract with the CEO, leadership team and HR leadership – on how to utilize the dynamics.
- Ask a subset of participants what is happening for them. This highlighted that they were actually making more changes happen and would like that recognized.

- Design a process that was 'real', ie acknowledged how people felt, and let them speak.

- Contract with the participants to find out what they wanted.

- Listen in the room to how the CEO feels. Each of the executive board members also voiced their feelings. We encouraged the detractors to speak up – those who felt let down or were ashamed – they had the microphone and spoke to their experience.

- Explore what was actually happening, not just what we heard in rumours. Firstly, are we making change happen and are there any good news stories?

  - This worked incredibly well because the 120 leaders spoke to what they were achieving anyway, the results they were getting, and it was obvious that they were as a group really succeeding, saving money, increasing loading, changing practices.

- Action was discussed concerning whether they wanted to let the situation get in the way of the probably successful journey that they were on – one of the most difficult transformations of a business in Finland.

- Review was a mix of ways they would support each other by continuing some learning groups; they agreed to roll out the leadership development to their managers and to embed the new development processes.

In the evening, during a dinner to enable reflections and chat to occur, the CEO spoke for a few minutes to simply thank the leaders. Other leadership team members added their views, and a few voices spoke from the floor. In my view, the collective leadership of the organization was formed, in adversity which may have helped, and the results show what that group of people achieved for themselves with help from the coaching and leadership development.

Outcomes

It is clear that the leaders worked really hard to turn around a worsening financial situation, which in their 2012 business results showed the impact of two years' work (see Table 8.3). This was continued into 2013 by the new CEO and much of the same leadership team.

Table 8.3 Finnair reported financial results

	2003	2004	2005	2006	2007	2008	2009	2010	2011	2012	2013
Turnover (€m)	1,558	1,683	1,871	1,990	2,181	2,256	1,838	2,023	2,257	2,449	2,400
Profits (EBT) (€m)	−22	31	88	−15	139	−62	−125	−33	−111.5	16.5	10.1
Number of employees (average)	9,981	9,522	9,447	9,598	9,480	9,595	8,797	7,578	7,467	6,784	5,859
Number of passengers (m)	6.8	8.1	8.5	8.8	8.7	8.3	7.4	7.1	8.0	8.8	9.2
Passenger load factor (%)	69.6	71.2	72.6	75.2	75.5	75.2	75.9	76.5	73.3	77.6	79.5
Number of aircraft (at year end)	59	69	69	72	62	65	68	63	65	60	70

Some outcomes to highlight:

1 For four years prior to the work the net loss was on average about €80m; after the transformation process, for the next two years there was a profit of about €14m – almost a €100m transformation.

2 The company is now in a wonderful new building, a confident celebration of the design and perseverance of the employees in Finnair who are once again attracting the attention of the nation for all the right reasons.

3 The culture is forward facing; for example, the new building is called the House of Travel and Transportation (or 'HOTT') and there is no HQ from which leadership is dispensed.

It is important to emphasize that while results look good for now, legacy carriers in Europe continue to struggle. The economic growth in 2014 across Europe is predicted to remain low, projected to strengthen to only 1 per cent in 2014 and 1.4 per cent in 2015 (World Economic and Financial Surveys, World Economic Outlook (WEO) Update, Is the Tide Rising?, January 2014), so there continues to be a lot of hard work ahead in order for the leadership team to maintain the profitability they have achieved.

Conclusions

Much has been written about the difficulty in linking coaching and team coaching interventions to financial results, calculating a return on investment and how the linkages are at best tenuous (Grant, 2012). However, we would argue, supported by the evidence and the views of the client, that without three significant changes, the organizational transformation at Finnair would not have been possible. These are:

1 the leadership team moving from a hub and spoke team to a wheel of greater shared leadership and responsibility;

2 the leadership team members moving from being expert managers who had to have all the answers to leaders radically delegating challenges to teams lower in the business;

3 the team developing some collective resilience, loyalty and trust, necessary to withstand the attacks on the leadership from staff, unions and press and stay committed to the long-term change journey.

Leadership team coaching is a key element of organizational development and transformation. It seems implausible to think that the leadership team can remain the same when an organization is undertaking a major organizational transformation. Of course, CEOs can and do coach their own teams through times of change (see Hawkins, 2017: chapter 12) and may not need external team coaching support.

The key is to set leadership team coaching in the wider systemic context of where the organization is in the community it serves; how it performs for its clients, employees, unions, suppliers and owner(s); the rate of change the strategy demands of processes, structure and behaviour; the nature of the culture and leadership culture.

Being a team coach is necessary rather than just facilitating team workshops. As a team coach in such a transformation process it is useful to combine team workshops with live process consultancy in regular team meetings, individual coaching of the key players and what we term 'tow-path coaching' or 'kerb-side coaching' where the coach is present alongside the team at key moments in their leadership of the change. As much work can be done in a 10-minute Time-Out during an important meeting as can be achieved in a week of offsite development. The executives respond well to being 'called' on behaviours in the moment – otherwise the habits of senior leaders are so strong as to be invisible.

Making systemic team coaching relevant to a difficult situation is both easier, because there is 'a burning platform', and harder, because, under pressure, leaders can become more defensive and revert to old patterns of reaction. Therefore my final thought is that the coach seems to have the most impact near the boundary of the relationship, where they are also vulnerable and having to work in the moment with uncertainty and risk – feeling comfortable often means low impact.

We were only the catalyst in the process; the wonderful people in Finnair are the ones whom we applaud.

Reflections 4 years on

The business flourishes. The organization has moved into new offices, had new planes delivered and more SE Asia routes have opened. The profitability has continued, and the organization continues to take great strides forward. The leadership team is significantly different with many key roles changing including those of the CEO, CFO and HRD.

Reflecting on this case four years later, in practice there are four learnings that I have taken from this experience, which have greatly influenced my work with leadership teams since then:

- I continue to be struck by the need to be 'relaxed' about being on the edge of relationship when intervening with a team, neither in the team or outside it, neither accepted or rejected.

- Inviting discomfort in oneself and the team, and making that feeling somehow OK, continues to appear for me as a necessary part of the process. The more comfortable sessions seem to add less momentum and produce less change.

- Our ability to 'call out' is so important to a team when we notice conflict, 'loaded moments', patterns of behaviour or thinking, important moments the team is ignoring, or positive progress the team need to celebrate.

- In the case of Finnair the ability to help was impacted by working at multiple levels on leadership, performance and talent. This challenged the 'lone-coach' model of team coaching. I realized that to be transformative we need a team around us!

Team coaching for organizational learning and innovation   09

A case study of an Australian pharmaceutical subsidiary

PADRAIG O'SULLIVAN AND CAROLE FIELD

This case study describes how the Australian affiliate of a multinational pharmaceutical company developed a strong discipline of organization learning which enabled them to become more innovative, foster high engagement scores and win prestigious awards. It was achieved through building processes to accommodate sustained learning even when key leadership personnel were regularly changing.

Background

When David took over the reins as Managing Director for Australia/New Zealand (ANZ) he said: 'While the business is not broken, there are plenty of areas that need to be fixed.' The organization had a proud history both locally and internationally. Prior to separating its pharmaceutical division from medical divisions and then re-branding in 2013, it leaned upon its heritage as being one of the oldest global pharmaceutical organizations, which has grown to employ over 21,000 people in over 170 countries.

The coaching relationship with David started during his previous role in one of the organization's medical divisions. The relationship was then extended to support his 'onboarding' (the process of transitioning into a new role and/or organization) to the role of managing director in the pharmaceutical division. Over time, the one-to-one coaching relationship extended into a team coaching engagement for his collective leadership team and also included individual coaching for team members. This was done in parallel with the team coaching. Initially, a team of four coaches was involved. The individual coaches and coaching relationships changed over time as the needs of the organization changed and as leaders were promoted to international roles.

First insight that learning was being missed

At an initial leadership team offsite meeting where the team was discussing the core purpose and functionality of the team, one brave team member asked a question. The question itself, while relatively simple, shocked the room! The conversation went something like this:

Leadership team member: 'Now that we are discussing what this team is supposed to be doing, can I ask a question? When we meet every month as part of that other operational meeting, I am not sure what I am supposed to be doing in that meeting. I don't actually understand the figures and so I just stay quiet.'

Everyone in the room: [Silence...]

Team leader: 'I think I might have misunderstood you. Did you say you don't know what we are talking about in that meeting we have every month?'

Leadership team member: 'That's right. I don't understand what the meeting is actually about.'

Another team member: 'Now that you bring that up, can I say neither do I understand that meeting and what I am supposed to be doing in it?'

Everyone in the room: [More silence...!]

Team leader: Breathes slowly....

'Firstly, can I say thank you for your honestly and courage. Many executives would not have been that open.

Secondly, can I say that as the leader in the organization I am taking responsibility for not have onboarded you both fully into your leadership roles in the organization and on this leadership team.

Thirdly, (addressing the CFO) can you take responsibility in ensuring everyone in this room fully understands the numbers, ratios and questions for deliberation before the next one of those meetings?

Lastly, can I ask why has it taken so long for someone to raise this need?'

As coaches, we found the level of honesty of those leaders refreshing. Many times in organizations, senior leaders hide their lack of knowledge and understanding for fear they might get caught out and then look stupid. Of course, it is this very fear that prevents learning taking place.

Our experience is that the learning time needed to arrive at a level of competency for a new executive in a leadership team takes between 9 and 11 months. If there is a lack of understanding on what that person needs to know and how they go about learning that knowledge, the speed to competency is elongated. Given that the leadership team members are the highest paid in that organization, this makes little sense.

When David asked the question 'why has it taken so long for someone to raise this need?' a great conversation ensued about how learning in the organization happened or did not happen. Experiences from other organizations were shared. The coaches in the room shared best practice. The outcome of the deliberations was a commitment to ensure that the whole organization focused on learning becoming one of the leadership team's key priorities.

Key questions that guided the team

In the conversation the coaches helped to frame three key questions which guided the discussions and further decisions:

1 How could the onboarding of new leaders to this leadership team and to the organization as a whole be optimized?

2 How can the collective speed to competency in leadership be increased?

3 How can learning across the organization be captured and shared across the organization?

The leadership worked through these questions to develop plans and programmes that addressed their learning needs. These were implemented and over time a range of successes was experienced. Their plans were targeted at both a leadership team level and an organizational level.

Core learning actions at the leadership team level

The team agreed to meet once per quarter to discuss and reflect on how they were functioning and developing as a team, its progress, the way the team worked and how it needed to improve. Over time, these quarterly meetings ranged from a 2–3-hour session to all-day sessions. They usually involved the external coach.

The leadership team put into place an action relating to their fortnightly Business As Usual (BAU) meetings, involving a quick, end-of-meeting reflection on how well they had performed in that meeting.

Over time, this quick reflection raised questions and concerns and also nipped some potential issues in the bud, such as making sure that all voices were heard and 'group think' did not prevail. As new members joined the team, they expressed positive feedback about the end-of-meeting reflection. One leader who joined from another affiliate commented that the fortnightly and quarterly team review process meant that he settled into the team's routines faster than he had elsewhere.

Individual coaching for leadership team members was running in parallel to the team coaching processes. Coachees actively sought feedback and peer input as part of the coaching process. Many of the members actively engaged in sharing learnings from their coaching with colleagues.

Coaches also encouraged the leaders to do more peer sharing and collaborative working. Over time, it became common for leadership team members to actively seek input regarding broader business challenges from colleagues who were previously not consulted about functional concerns. The team was beginning to move from a hub and spoke team to a wheel of greater shared leadership (Hawkins, 2017: chapter 10; Chapter 12 by David Jarrett in this book).

The overall outcome was that the active process of being open to asking, reflecting and integrating became part of the natural operating style.

Key initial changes at the organization level

An active process for the induction and integration of new people into the organization and their role was developed to go beyond the existing programmes which really only demonstrated 'the basics' to a new person. Each new hire into the leadership team was buddied up with an existing team member to learn the 'un-saids' (the informal cultural patterns and unwritten rules) in order to make them overtly 'said'. They spent time understanding the processes of how the team worked, the history of the team development and the conversations they had in order to get to this place of success. The rules of engagement were clearly articulated and the expected behaviours of a leader in the team and in the organization were outlined.

Each new leader hired also spent time with an external coach to understand the history of the team development from an outside perspective. The overall process accelerated the learning and 'onboarding' of the new leaders into their role but also becoming a leader in the organization. The team developed an understanding of 'co-leadership', which meant that they were collectively responsible for the success of the organization. This included collective responsibilities for ensuring that everyone understood their role, their responsibilities and how to make things happen. The style of collaborative leadership remained after the original leaders departed.

The second wave of change relating to core learning was in an organizational-wide 'Rising Star' programme. This was a leadership development programme aimed at direct reports to the leadership team who showed promise and were considered to have high potential for being a future leader. They were also key influencers across the organization.

Each programme was co-facilitated by a leadership team member and an external coach. Having the leadership team present in each programme ensured that they cascaded learnings down to other levels below the senior leadership team and led by example. The leaders, in opening each session, stressed the critical importance of organizational learning if the organization was to achieve its strategic aims. Concepts such as vulnerability as a leader were discussed and developed. The notion that not understanding something was normal, but avoiding learning about it was fatal, was fostered.

A feedback mechanism was introduced to share learnings from the previous month, irrespective of how major or minor they might seem. These were recorded with the intention of creating a hard copy of organizational learnings on a quarterly basis. A narrative stemming from learnings of the leadership team was created in the organization, with specific phrases used to describe aspiring behaviours and, indeed, unwelcome behaviours.

Given the pivotal role that the ANZ affiliate played across the Asian region, learnings from the local experiences were shared with regional colleagues through the Singapore office. Some programmes that originated in the Australian office were later rolled out in affiliate offices across Asia.

The challenge of being successful in an Asian context

The organization continued to grow. Owing to the success of the leadership team and the overall contribution of the Australian affiliate to the Asian region, the Sydney-based team was considered to be a source of talent for regional and global positions. Over a 24-month period, of the original 11 team members 7 were promoted to regional or global positions.

While these promotions were evidence of a great success story, it potentially was draining the tacit knowledge that led to the successful turnaround of the business. How should the organization both promote great people into senior positions and retain the capabilities and capacities knowledge that had been developed in the original business over the previous years? This was challenging for the next-stage leadership team.

A more robust talent management and succession planning process was cultivated to ensure that the learnings of one generation of the leadership team were transferred to the next. But then came the next challenge when David, the managing director and team leader, was promoted to a global position in the United States.

Resetting the bar

His successor was promoted from within. Katherine had been hired by David a year earlier and was earmarked as a potential successor. Her strong industry experience with another multinational corporation, coupled with her commercial nous, made her an attractive candidate. Given that David was moving overseas with the organization, he was able to hand over in such a way that there was a smooth transition.

All new leaders want to understand their business and go about building the organization with their personal stamp on it. Katherine recognized that David and the leadership team had built strong foundations but work was still to be done. She broadened the range of external coaches and experts to assist in the next phase of the journey.

Over a series of leadership team meetings, led by Katherine, the team re-clarified (Hawkins, 2017: Discipline 2) and confirmed the purpose of the leadership team, its core objectives and priorities. This included a focus on innovation for the organization.

Focus on innovation

In this phase of the leadership journey for the organization, a focus on innovation became more important and prominent. Traditionally the pharmaceutical industry is product led when it comes to innovation. The pipeline of products can be many years. Insourcing products through licensing deals can also take a long time and may be a struggle within the local government regulatory frameworks if new products have not been pre-approved to sell in that country.

The local leadership team decided to look at innovation from a number of perspectives, beyond product innovation. The team was facilitated to address a number of key questions:

- How best to serve customers?
- How the current customer meetings took place and how to improve them?
- What external relationships could be formed that would add value to the customer relationship?

A range of other questions were raised and answered.

Cross-functional teams were set up to engage with core questions, work up potential ideas and development strategies. These were all shared. Decision criteria were set to evaluate ideas and strategies as they were developed. As with all kinds of innovation, not every idea was successful but the learnings from these sessions were shared.

Continued use of external coaching and other experts

When David commenced the leadership team journey he realized that he needed external support and hired the authors to assist in the process. Initially a team of four coaches worked on the project. Over time, the need for coaching fluctuated and therefore so did the number of coaches. Individual coaching continued for specific needs and outcomes. Over time, this fluctuated depending on needs.

When Katherine took over the reins she continued the use of external coaches and other related experts. Matching specific expertise to specific needs became more prominent and appropriate. As an example, team coaching for the team as an entity decreased but on occasions an external team coach was asked to facilitate a leadership team discussion on particular topics such as engagement scores. Other specific interventions included using coaching for 'onboarding' new expatriate leaders to Australia, 'New Leader Assimilation' sessions for new functional leads, functional team offsites when deliberating how to cascade down organizational strategies and content sessions such as innovation skills.

Both leaders recognized that for a leadership team to transform itself, using expertise on a regular basis was important. The temptation during belt-tightening times is to do away with external support. This can often be a short-term strategy that saves initial costs but slows down the transformation.

Top 30 award for most innovative organizations in Australia

Business Review Weekly (BRW) is the premier business magazine in Australia. It covers all business areas, such as leadership, innovation, technology and gadgets, politics and the financial and commercial markets. It also hosts a number of lists such as the Top 500 companies in Australia, the Top 75 fastest-growing companies, the young rich list and the Top 30 most innovative companies.

In 2012 this organization was recognized as one of the most innovative companies in Australia. According to Kate Mills from BRW magazine in December 2012:

> Although this list focuses on the end point of innovation – the product or process that came from the innovation – the 30 companies all displayed an understanding of the culture and processes required to support innovation. Whether it was a weekly ideas meeting, or building innovation into key performance requirements, or giving out awards, each of the Top 30 had something in place to foster innovation. They also understood that driving innovation has to come from the top and were able to show how senior leaders were involved.

Innovation specialist and competition judge, Dr Amantha Imber, commented at the time: 'Innovation starts on the inside. The Top 30 companies (listed as finalists) don't necessarily see innovation as bringing something new to the market.' She said that, instead, what they had in common was that 'their leaders took it seriously, they didn't just pay lip service to the concept of innovation. They were investing resources in building the right culture.'

Dr Imber suggests that innovation rarely bubbles up from the bottom of the organization. 'The senior team needs to unite in driving innovation and setting the tone. It's also vital to embrace different points of view,' she commented in an interview to BRW magazine in 2012.

Receiving an award such as the 'BRW Top 30 Most Innovative Companies' award is an amazing achievement by any standard. To achieve that in the pharmaceutical industry, against obvious contenders from software development companies and other industries with fewer barriers to disruptive innovation, is even more striking. There is little doubt that the organization was recognized for many reasons, among them the internal culture built up over time, which fostered teamworking, openness and challenge, which in turn allowed for ongoing learning to blossom and experiences to be shared openly and easily.

Engagement scores that reflect a strong culture

The consulting group Great Places to Work is an international organization in its 21st year of operation, and is one of the world's foremost authorities on workplaces globally. Its lists of 'Great Places to Work' span more than 45 countries on six continents, including regional lists for both Europe and Latin America.

This pharmaceutical organization was listed in the top 50 organizations that were great places to work in Australia in 2012. This is an external award and is strong recognition of its journey.

Highlighting the impact of the leadership team's efforts, the Australian affiliate was shown to outperform its benchmark organizations by an average of 10 points on all the key drivers of engagement. This has been something the team has been actively working towards.

What is marked about this outcome and the team, though, is that the team is not content with the scores. Demonstrating its ongoing commitment to learning, innovation and achievement, it is actively engaging in a process to understand where the areas of potential improvement still sit, identify the root causes of the issues and develop strategies and plans to improve the situation.

Inputs to the process have been gathered from all the relevant stakeholder groups and again demonstrate the commitment to listen, be curious and look for learning. While there is recognition that the areas for improvement are now relatively small, it is making the small ongoing calibrations to fine-tune performance that facilitates the journey from good to great.

Reflections and conclusions

As two of the external coaching experts who have worked with a range of leaders in this organization over six years, it has been our privilege to watch this organization move from being 'not broken but in need of being fixed' to one that is dynamic, innovative, engaging and continuing to build upon its historical successes. In reflecting on the experience, there are a number of considerations relevant to this case study which will be relevant in other organizations.

1 Who has the courage to challenge the status quo?

Leaders who want to maintain their historical success with little eye to the future will eventually lead the organization to a slow demise. The ultimate leader and the leadership team in an organization need to have the courage to challenge themselves to learn, push, and strive beyond what might be expected. Sometimes these are intrinsic drivers. Occasionally the leaders borrow this confidence from elsewhere.

2 Have clear and transparent priorities that link to an overall 3–5-year strategy

It is very tempting to continue to do 'Business As Usual' and get caught up in the reactive tendencies of busy organizations rather than taking time to create the future (Parker, 1990). The various leadership teams took time to really clarify and be transparent about the organization's strategic aims and the core priorities needed to deliver on that strategic promise (Hawkins, 2017: Discipline 2).

Leaders have a delicate job balancing the competing demands of global, regional and local stakeholders. There was, and is, a real challenge in maintaining focus when noisy competitive voices demand attention.

3 Set up cross-functional teams to execute on priorities

Cross-functional teams or brand teams are led or sponsored by the directors but heavily involve middle-level leaders to execute on the core priorities. The ability to involve key stakeholders and influencers in the organization accelerates ability to execute. It also demonstrates shared ownership by all parties in the organization in the performance of the business. From a sustainability perspective, involving levels one to three layers below that of the executive also improves the learning experience down the organization. This removes risk of project failure if or when senior leaders get promoted out of Australia.

The sound practice and good intentions with which cross-functional teams are established are not enough to ensure that they actually deliver what is required of them. Ensuring that there are appropriate systems, processes and coaching in place to support effective cross-functional team performance would have been a complement to this programme.

4 Get out of the way!

Many senior leaders feel the need to ensure project success by getting heavily involved in all manner of details. Both Katherine and David commented on the need to set clear direction and then to leave execution up to the players involved. At times, this may mean that execution did not happen as fast/as well/as exactly as they might have wanted or how they felt they could have done it themselves. However, in many examples execution happened much better than expected and with surprising outcomes.

5 Develop criteria to assess innovative ideas and suggestions

Most organizations that strive to become a learning organization or an innovative organization overlook the basic requirement of answering two fundamental questions:

a What does innovation mean around here?

b By what criteria will we recognize and evaluate successful innovation?

Successful organizations in this regard have a leadership team that drives the vision and tone for both learning and innovation. They not only ask and answer these questions but make sure that this is effectively communicated to all others in the organization so that there is a clear, shared understanding.

While the need for this capacity was understood at the initiation of the programme, there was not a clear process or practice in place. This did emerge over time but there would be significant benefit in ensuring that this was established at the outset.

6 Create processes that are not individual leader dependent

Many Australian organizations that are affiliates of multinational companies suffer from the challenge of having the managing director and other leadership team members receiving promotions and leaving for overseas assignments, typically into either regional Asian or global roles.

While this is of course a good thing and fits with the career aspirations of many Australian executives, it often leaves holes in the organization's local leadership capability, stalls performance and disrupts momentum, and many worthwhile projects fall over. Creating systemic processes that outlive any individual leader is essential for organizational learning to become a discipline rather than an event.

7 Creating organizational learning across the organization

Learning what works, what was tried, what did not work and why leads to better outcomes for the organization over time. The organizational learning culture is developed by allowing mistakes to be seen as both 'innovation normalities' and perfectly fine as long as they are within the agreed frameworks for risk and everyone learns from them so that avoidable error is not repeated. Developing an overall sense that vulnerability is upheld within the organizational structures allows for greater sharing to take place.

Practical applications were seen in the leadership team taking time to reflect on their meeting effectiveness. Encouraging the sharing of this learning through the organization would fast-track the creation of the learning environment.

8 Tailor outcome-focused coaching for individual needs

Coaching, whether provided by internal or external coaches, needs to be tailored to the individual leadership challenges, the outcomes needed by the organization and the individual's learning needs (Hawkins, 2012). This sounds basic and relatively obvious. However, we noticed how clear David, Katherine and many others on the leadership team have been when organizing coaching assignments for themselves or their direct reports. Coaching within this organization is seen as a tool to develop a leader so that they can fulfil their strategic outputs and clearly defined goals, not as an end point in itself.

9 Use external coaches to increase organizational speed

In every market downturn, organizations naturally cut back on non-discretionary spending. Learning organizations recognize that no matter how good they are, they will never have all the expertise they need in all areas at all times. Utilizing the services of coaches and experts in particular areas can often speed up the overall learning so that the speed to competency in leader effectiveness is maximized. This is particularly true when hiring new functional heads at director level, for example sales director or CFO, into an organization that is high performing.

A team can only go as fast as its slowest team member. Slowing down the leadership team of functional departments to the level of the new hire is not an option worth considering.

10 Re-clarify, reset and recalibrate on a regular basis

Every fitness-related goal involves a regular check-in with progress and a resetting or recalibrating of the outcomes. Leadership teams are no different. Setting 3–5-year strategic outcomes with annual priorities is essential. Taking time to recalibrate the team on what it is working on and resetting how the team needs to work together accelerates the chances of success. This is no truer than when changes in the leadership team occur and members get promoted or leave for elsewhere. The team needs to take time to quickly check in and potentially start again.

This organization is a living demonstration of the excellent performance outcomes that can be achieved through team coaching developing and sustaining a practice of core learning. Investing in the individual and group skills and practices that create core learning enables growth and sustainability at the individual, team and organizational levels.

Inter-team coaching 10

From team coaching to organizational transformation at Yeovil Hospital Foundation Trust

PETER HAWKINS AND GAVIN BOYLE (CEO of Royal Derby Hospital, previously CEO of Yeovil District Hospital)

Introduction

It was a beautiful summer's day and I (Peter) got a call from the HR director of a district general hospital about 40 miles from where I lived. She invited me down to visit her and her chief executive as they wanted help with some team coaching of the senior team. The following week I went and had separate meetings with both of them, curious to hear about their challenges.

The CEO told me how they had just undertaken a major review of the structure of the hospital and had made three important changes:

1 They had recognized that the organizational structure had been too fragmented and siloed. They had recently restructured the 10 clinical directorates into 3 larger clinical divisions, each led by a medical divisional director who would stay clinically active but have 1.5 days to lead their division, supported by a full-time general manager and a divisional chief nurse.

2 They had widened the senior leadership team operating immediately below the board of directors to increase the impact of clinical leadership at this level, and so in addition to the current medical director and director of nursing, the three new clinical divisional directors were also included.

3 Each of these clinical divisions' senior teams would also have a finance and HR lead working for them, devolved from the central functions but still with a dotted professional reporting line to the central function.

The HR director also told me how they were a young executive team, most of whom were in their first board-level executive role; all seeking to assert themselves within the team and establish their relationships with their peers. Also, there was an imbalance of experience between the well-established non-executive directors and the relatively inexperienced executives. Board relationships had yet to fully mature and the board was yet to operate in a fully unitary way.

They asked me whether I would start by working with the board, the new leadership team comprising the executives and the divisional directors, and also the divisional management teams themselves.

This sounded like potentially five pieces of team coaching, but I was wary. At these first meetings I asked several key questions, as follows.

1 What did the CEO, the executive team and the hospital want to achieve? What was their aspiration?

It was clear that the CEO wanted to be successful in this, his first job as a hospital CEO, but he was also ambitious for the hospital. He recognized that smaller rural district hospitals were potentially 'an endangered species' given the pressures of increasing sub-specialization making it difficult for smaller hospitals to maintain a comprehensive and sustainable range of services, together with the general challenge facing the whole of the NHS to do more at higher quality while simultaneously making large savings. These challenges were potentially easier to meet in larger urban hospitals benefiting from economies of scale. As we talked he became excited and said he would like to create a new flagship model for smaller rural district general hospitals that others could learn from, or follow a model where the hospital was successful in all its effective connections: vertically within the local health economy, upstream with all the primary healthcare doctors and practices, downstream with community services and social care, and also horizontally across the region, forging a greater range of partnerships with other hospital providers to develop sustainable ways of retaining a range of hospital services in South Somerset and North Dorset. I told him how exciting this sounded and said that if I were to work with them then part of the contract would need to include that he and I would write a joint paper in two years on how this had been achieved. This chapter is part of the fulfilling of that contract.

2 How were they going to avoid moving from 10 smaller silos into 3 larger silos?

The first answer I received was that the integration would happen by the three divisional directors all being on the newly enlarged executive team, but they would not be members of the unitary board. This caused me some concern, as with 1.5 days a week to provide leadership of their clinical division and its clinical specialities, their own divisional team and sit on the hospital executive team, I could not see how they could be the major connecting points between the three clinical divisions and also between their division and the central functional departments, such as strategy, HR, finance, IT and estates.

3 What would success from this work together look like?

A range of objectives for the hospital began to emerge from this inquiry:

a The need to meet the many government-set targets on treatment times; delivering contracted services and activity; financial savings; improving quality, for example reducing mortality rates; efficiency improvements, for example reducing length of stay, increasing productivity; and so on.

b Improve the patient experience, for example against the national Friends and Family Test (the number of patients who would recommend the hospital to their family and friends).

c Become sustainable and valued by the local community.

d Become a model rural district general hospital that others would want to learn from.

I then asked about what needed to shift in the leadership for the hospital to be successful. Both the CEO and the HR director were clear that the hospital objectives could not be achieved without the executives moving from being overly 'operational', constantly pulled down into fighting fires and managing crises, to having more of their time focused on creating the future and working with the external stakeholders.

4 How would we need to work together to avoid the team coaching being a series of discrete siloed projects?

I also pointed out that at this stage I could not create a contract or a proposal for even the first piece of team coaching, as for that I would need a contract with the whole team, but I would be willing to undertake some inquiry and diagnosis and then meet for a half-day workshop with the whole team to discover whether we could create a joint inquiry and diagnosis and agree a way of working together. This they agreed to, and so a few weeks later I went and had a series of individual meetings with each of the team members, followed by a half-day contracting workshop. In addition to meeting each executive, I asked them to fill in two questionnaires: the High Performing Team Questionnaire (see Hawkins,2017:275–79) and Descriptor Analysis (see Hawkins 2017: 305–307).

What struck me was that, unlike the CEO, who had a strong aspiration for the hospital's future, the other members of the executive team were more focused on the sheer challenge of achieving the necessary short-term objectives, both those set by the NHS centrally and those agreed by the board in the strategic plan. Their focus was much more immediate and operational and they felt individually pressurized to prove their ability, under the scrutiny microscope of the CEO and the non-executive directors. The rest of the team did not feel like a supportive resource but rather fellow strugglers focused on their individual targets. The board seemed a long way from being a 'unitary board', which was its supposed form, and rather a place where young first-time executive directors had to prove their worth in front of much older experienced business people. It became clear that to ensure a successful organizational transformation, team coaching of this leadership team would not be sufficient, for it would be necessary to shift several inter-team relationships. These included:

a the relationship between the non-executives and executives on the board and between the board and the hospital leadership team;

b between the three new clinical divisions, so that they were able to resolve issues directly between them, to avoid a move from 10 small silos to 3 larger ones with inter-divisional issues delegated upwards and so pulling the executive back into resolving operational issues and therefore lacking the time to focus more on the future and the external;

c the relationship between the executive team and the three clinical divisional teams. I was interested in what was going to change the systemic pattern of the clinical services not taking full ownership of their

Figure 10.1   The five disciplines of high-performing teams: exec scores –
October 2010 current scores out of 5 with target scores in
brackets

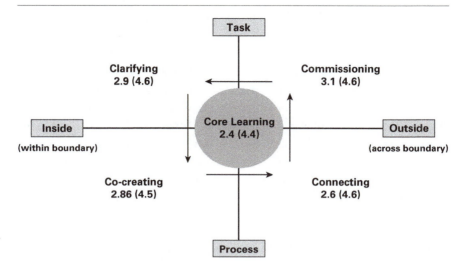

operational challenges and delegating difficult issues upwards, and the executive team not trusting the clinical divisions and diving down to fix operational crises.

From the High Performing Questionnaire results (see Figure 10.1) it was clear that the team had challenges in how they worked together and how they connected with their wider stakeholders; they had particularly low scores in 'Core Learning', with a learning style that was based on constant fire-fighting with little space for reflection on the deeper patterns they were all caught up in.

From the Descriptor Analysis the team was very self-aware that they needed to move away from being functional, isolated and disjointed and become more corporate, aligned, decisive, responsive and future focused. I wondered if they were aware of what such a journey and transformational change would entail.

At my first meeting with the whole executive team together, I showed them the patterns that had emerged from both the questionnaires and my interviews with them. I pointed out that this was what they were saying about their own team and how it needed to develop, and not my views as an outsider. The team worked in pairs making sense of the data and deciding what they needed to do as a team in response for the team to move forward.

I then said to them that I thought there was a bigger challenge beyond how they improved their functioning as a leadership team. I showed them my map of the inter-team relationships (see Figure 10.2) and said that my professional judgement was that even if I did very good team development with the executive team, the board and the three new clinical directorate teams, we would collectively fail to shift the deeper organizational systemic dynamics that lay not in the parts but in the connections. I spontaneously used a phrase that has subsequently become part of my intervention vocabulary: 'A reorganization is too costly a disruption to waste. The only way to get a return on your investment is to utilize the unsettlement to consciously evolve the underlying culture to one more in alignment with the future needs.' The simple map was a powerful way of reframing the focus and the team immediately realized the importance of addressing the inter-team relationships.

The hospital had developed a very effective frontline programme based on a set of clear values for improving patient care and recognizing the contribution of hospital staff, called iCARE, which stood for:

Figure 10.2   Foundation trust – 5 key teams – 6 critical relationships

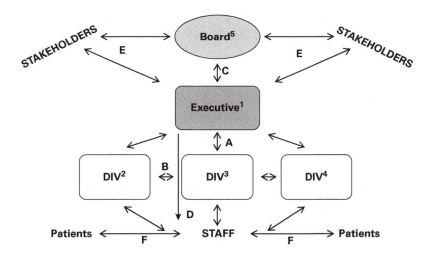

'i'   for individual, recognizing each patient as an individual but also that every staff member had a unique and individual part to play;

'C'   for Communication;

'A'   for Attitude;

'R'   for Respect;

'E'   for Environment.

I will communicate effectively with my colleagues, patients, and visitors to enable them to carry out their work to the best of their abilities, be involved in decisions about the care we are providing, and make the most of our services.

I will have a positive attitude toward my work and others, always focused on improving the experience of the patient.

I will respect patients, carers and colleagues at all times, valuing their beliefs and wishes and always taking these account during my work.

I will help to create an environment which is conducive to good care and recovery, and in which people feel safe and comfortable.

This gave voice to an inherently positive culture that existed within the hospital, and articulating it was intended to foster that culture and build a positive cycle of reinforcement. The iCARE programme had engaged a lot of frontline staff and was felt to be influencing an improvement in patient care and experience as well as staff morale. However, for this to be fully successful it would need to be matched by a parallel top-down culture change from the executives and the board and a horizontal culture change in the relationships between the divisions themselves and also the corporate functions.

To deepen this understanding I asked them to consider the proposition that to shift how the frontline staff engaged with patients, they needed to shift the relationship between the non-executives and the executives. My contention was that because the executives felt judged and overly scrutinized by the non-executives on their operational performance, this drove them to become increasingly focused on operational matters and on ensuring that they had fixed all the operational issues in their functional area that they could, in order to avoid being challenged at the board, despite the unintended consequences this might have on other parts of the system managed by their colleagues, or on long-term sustainable change. In addition, this 'siloed' behaviour among the executives did not build confidence with the non-executives and so led to further detailed scrutiny and challenge driving an unintended behavioural cycle.

One consequence of this was that the next tier of management felt both less trusted and less responsible for managing their own areas, and had adopted the attitude that it was the hospital executives' responsibility to fix the problems. This lack of trust and taking personal responsibility potentially then rippled down to frontline management and staff.

After having explored and developed these propositions, the team then engaged in multi-stakeholder contracting (see Hawkins, 2017: 93–94). We displayed flipcharts, each linked to a different stakeholder group, and invited the team members to step into the shoes of this particular stakeholder and define from that perspective what success would look like from the team coaching. The stakeholder groups included:

- patients and their families;
- the staff;
- the board and governors of the hospital;
- the wider community of health and social care providers and commissioners;
- themselves as the team.

All team members displayed their responses on Post-it notes on each of the flipcharts. The team then worked in pairs, clustering the Post-it notes and deciding the main three or four themes for a particular perspective. Then as a pair they stepped into the shoes of that stakeholder group and told the rest of the team what they were looking for from the team coaching and the difference they expected to see as a result. This provided the data to agree with the team the outcome objectives for the team and inter-team coaching and enabled them to make a few initial agreements about the process of working together. This echoes the principles laid out in Chapter 1 of this book: that the contracting is 'triangulated', with the focus beginning not on what does the team need from the team coach, but what do the team and team coach need to achieve together to be in service of the wider stakeholders of the team.

The inter-team launch of the clinical divisional teams

Based on what had emerged from the inquiry, diagnostics and executive team contracting workshop, it was decided to launch the new structure, with three new clinical divisional teams, by having a large workshop for these three new teams, the hospital executive team and the collection of central functions. This happened on the first day of the new structure going live.

Each of the five groups was seated around its own table and was coached through a series of team-building steps:

- Agreeing their *commission*.
- *Clarifying* their mission, including:
  - team purpose;
  - strategy;

- core values;
- vision for what they wanted to achieve in the next two years.
- Deciding how they wanted to work together (*co-creating*), including:
  - protocols for teamworking;
  - green card behaviours, which they wanted to encourage in each other;
  - red card behaviours, which they wanted to discourage in each other.
- Agreeing their key stakeholders and how they would connect with them.

The workshop then moved from parallel team coaching to inter-team coaching, by first asking each team to present their agreements to the other teams and then receive feedback on what the other teams appreciated seeing in their plans and what further developments they would request from the team.

The teams then re-gathered to digest this feedback and prepare the next stage, where they told each of the other teams:

- what they would offer this team to help it achieve its team goals;
- what they would request from it to help in achieving their own team goals.

This naturally led to some live inter-team contracting, both across the system between clinical directorate teams and between clinical directorate teams and the core functions, and also vertically between the teams and the hospital executive.

This launch event ensured a clear and energetic launch of the new structure and everybody realizing that the reorganization provided an opportunity to collectively develop the culture and rewire the relationships in the senior parts of the system.

The board development

Soon after the launch event we also held a board development event. The initial inquiry and diagnosis had indicated that there was a dynamic that was not only holding back the board from becoming a fully unitary board, but also was negatively impacting on the hospital system and its performance. This was the dynamic where the executives individually took reports, papers or proposals to the board, non-executives then scrutinized and critiqued these, executives then felt criticized and became defensive and then non-executives became impatient and more critical, doubting the ability of some of the executives. I (Peter) wanted to test out this hypothesis by discovering how the board and the hospital were seen from the perspective of the non-executives.

The board members were asked to fill in the High Performing Board Questionnaire (see Hawkins, 2017: 274–79) and I also had one-to one interviews with each of them.

The interviews and questionnaire confirmed the dynamic mentioned above, with the non-executives mainly commenting on the performance of individual executives, the defensiveness of some and the absence of challenge between them. Clearly this needed addressing, along with the emerging pattern that while many executives were in operational fire-fighting mode, the non-executives were mainly focused on scrutiny and oversight of individual problem areas and there was limited sense of vision of where they wanted to take the hospital.

The CEO's vision and aspirations did not seem to be fully owned across the board. Having made inquiries in the larger NHS, I became confident that small district hospitals were likely to be under threat unless they were delivering outstanding service to their locality, with high levels of clinical excellence, patient satisfaction and staff engagement. Running hard to stand still was not going to be a recipe for long-term sustainable success. I became interested in some of the limiting beliefs that were holding the board back from leading the hospital into the future and in what was preventing the CEO from getting his vision more widely owned. I explored these with him and we embarked on a short series of individual coaching sessions which focused on how he could develop how he led his executive team from being a 'hub and spoke' team, dependent on him resolving issues one to one with his executives, and often acting as a go-between and mediator between conflicting executives, to a shared leadership team. We also explored how he could better engage the board in more future-focused strategy creation.

The possible limiting beliefs that the CEO and I explored included:

- pedalling harder to struggle to meet targets set by the government and the central NHS, which was limiting a sense of ownership of the strategy and strategic objectives;

- reputational risk – the board members were mindful of the often hostile media environment within which the NHS functions and were concerned to avoid any potential risk to the good reputation that the hospital had developed and their role in this;

- seeing neighbouring hospitals solely as rivals and competitors rather than potential partners for mutually beneficial collaboration.

At the board event

The board development event was a whole-day offsite meeting and, as with the executive team, it began by presenting the themes that had emerged from both the interviews and the questionnaires. This led to a facilitated dialogue between the executives and non-executives that included what they valued about the role the other subgroup played, what they found difficult and what they would like to see different. As coach, I asked what needed to happen differently in the space between the two subgroups for the board to become more truly 'unitary'. This led to the board deciding to restructure its agendas, adopting what I later termed the three-gear approach (see Figure 10.3): that is, having the first section of time for board scrutiny of performance, the second time period for strategic discussion and dialogue on issues of strategy, and the final section for decision making. In the first period the non-executives clearly need to hold the executives to account, whereas in the second section where the whole board are co-strategizing it is important that they are engaging as equals, each bringing their independent thinking to bear and bringing in perspectives from the wide range of stakeholders that form the wider system. In the final section they also engage as equals, taking equal and several responsibility for the decisions the board makes. Creating this three-act meeting structure allowed the board to move between different ways of thinking and relating to each other, as well as ensuring that more time was given to future and outside focus.

Following the board event, the CEO and the strategy director created a strategy map which showed the range of interconnecting strategy issues that

Figure 10.3   Introducing the three gears

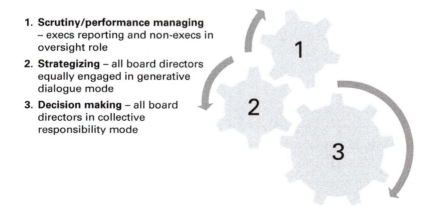

1. **Scrutiny/performance managing** – execs reporting and non-execs in oversight role
2. **Strategizing** – all board directors equally engaged in generative dialogue mode
3. **Decision making** – all board directors in collective responsibility mode

needed addressing and all board papers showed not only what strategy area was being addressed but how it connected to other areas of strategy. This led to board members feeling they had a much greater grasp of the whole system, rather than battling through an enormous agenda of separated issues.

Also, as a result of seeing how low they had all scored the board on the discipline of 'core learning', they collectively decided that they needed to build greater reflection time into their meetings. They introduced a meeting 'review' to take a live sounding on how the board meeting went and the effectiveness of their collective contribution.

Possibly the biggest breakthrough in the board event was when the board were debating the trouble they were having meeting the financial targets set by the National Health Service to make 4.5 per cent savings annually. As the team coach, I challenged them on how they seemed stuck chasing a target set for them and asked why they did not set a much larger savings target so that they had an investment fund to develop their own services and operations. Somehow this galvanized the board into taking charge of their own future and shifted their focus from being centred on how to avoid failure to how they can create success.

Connecting with the wider system

One of the major outcomes from the board development event was a collective recognition that the board needs to spend a greater percentage of its time focusing externally and on the future. This led to the board deciding on a major refresh of the strategy and in particular a concerted and deliberate 'partnering' strategy aimed at developing a range of relationships. Gavin writes:

> We established regular Chair/CEO meetings with counterparts in neighbouring Trusts, also set up a regular non-executive director meeting between ourselves and Taunton, the nearest larger district hospital. A practical benefit of this was greater trust and beginning to see each other as potential partners rather than competitors and this underpinned the establishment of a joint venture to build new pathology laboratories with a private sector third partner, which would not only lower the costs of pathology tests for both hospitals but also generate income through selling its services to other hospitals and GP practices.

Another realization, which many individual board members had but which had not yet become adopted into the collective discourse of the board, was that many of the hospital challenges could not be resolved within the boundaries of the hospital operations. A good example of this was that the hospital's figures on length of stay for patients who had suffered a stroke were much higher than the national average, despite focused attempts to improve the service within the hospital. Making a quantum step in improving this performance area could only be achieved by collaboration with the whole community of GPs in both preventive work and early diagnosis, and improvement of social care to ensure that there were alternatives for discharge for those who were not well enough to return home. The board began to think about how they could be proactive in partnering with other bodies to ensure greater nursing home and social care in the locality as well as how to improve their joint working with the primary care community.

One of my colleagues, Peter Binns, then worked with the strategy director on coaching the relationship between the hospital and its wider health community, identifying issues that neither the hospital nor the primary care community could solve by itself, but which together they could successfully collaborate on to resolve. So often, inter-agency meetings become transactional negotiations with two-way criticism. Partnership and effective collaboration are only achieved if both parties recognize a compelling challenge that neither party can resolve by itself, but which all parties recognize they are essential to addressing (see Hawkins, 2017: chapter 7).

Further work with the executive team

Following the board meeting I continued to coach the executive, both through individual meetings with Gavin, the CEO, and the occasional meetings with the wider team. One of the processes the team found most helpful was critical reflection on a systemic process to which they had all been party, but which had not been as effective as they both needed and wanted it to be. By collectively mapping out the process and seeing the pattern of what happened over time within teams and between teams, the executive could move from either blaming individuals or teams, or rushing into fix the problem themselves, into systemic organizational learning and deciding how to orchestrate and build better organizational processes.

Some teams are stuck

One of the realizations that came from the critical reflection dialogues of the executive team was that the divisional teams performed very differently to each other and two of the three teams were really struggling to step up to the new challenges and responsibility that they now had. It was decided that they should choose what team development support they had, which in retrospect was a mistake, as when they became flooded with urgent operational issues they found it very hard to step back and focus on their development, or ask for help. The teams' performance was critically dependent on the working relationship between the clinical director, who in 1.5 days a week needed to provide the leadership, the general manager and the chief nursing officer.

Again in retrospect, these teams needed greater joint training in how to operate as a leadership team, their different roles and their collective focus. Without the clinical director taking clear and strong leadership, they failed to get the clinical buy-in from the other consultants who were major role models in the culture of the hospital. However, if the clinical director tried to manage everything in just 1.5 days a week, they were doomed to fail or become 'burnt out'. They needed to build a strong working team and rely upon them to manage. In later work, both Peter and Gavin have adopted the analogy of the clinical director being like the executive chair of the division, with the general manager as the managing director and the chief nurse as the chief operating officer. The analogy does not completely work, but it helps the team to realize that they all need to take independent and joined-up leadership.

It also became clear that many issues that were inter-divisional were being delegated upwards to the executive to resolve. The CEO recognized through coaching that several hours of his week were taken up with being referee, mediator or go-between between the different divisions or the divisions and the central functions, or indeed between the different central functions. We explored together how he could set a challenge and architect some enabling processes that would effectively change this pattern. He challenged the three clinical directors to work out between them what were the most important areas that needed addressing that required more than one division. Once they had developed this prioritized list, he then asked what forum they needed to create to address these and who needed to be at the meeting and how it needed to be structured. The clinical directors set up a monthly forum, which also involved their general manager, chief nursing officers and several clinical leads. One of the clinical directors took the initial lead for chairing the meetings and ensuring follow-up and this forum reported back to the executive on what issues they were addressing and how they were resolving them.

The follow-up

Nine months on from the initial event which launched the new structure, we asked the executive team, the three clinical division teams and the group of central function heads to fill in High Performing Team Questionnaires both on their own team and also on how they saw the other teams.

Figure 10.4   The five disciplines of high-performing teams: executive scores and scores by four other teams (July 2011)

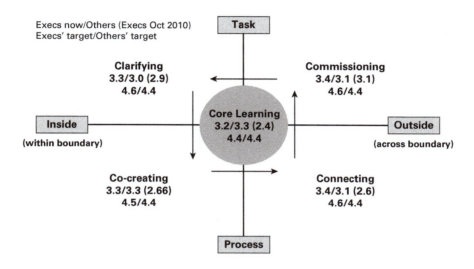

This was then shared with the teams at an offsite event. With the executive team we had scores pre the team and inter-team coaching as a baseline and there were two pieces of good news. The team consistently scored themselves higher than they had nine months previously. Secondly, the other teams scored them higher than they had scored themselves originally. However, the other teams had scored the executive team lower than the executive team had scored themselves now, suggesting that there was lag in how the improvements were being seen externally (see Figure 10.4).

The scores for the clinical divisions were, as expected, very variable and for two divisions were quite confrontative. They had to face the fact that not only had the executive team indicated in their scores that they were under-performing, but so had their peer teams in the other divisions and central functions. This became a wake-up call that could not be ignored or brushed aside and led to both internal changes in both teams' members and ways of operating in these two divisions.

There was also a follow-up session with the board a year after the original workshop with the board, at which the board was facilitated in sharing the areas in which they believed they had made significant progress and areas that required further development. The board was confident that not only did they see the process of their own meetings and functioning as having greatly improved, but they also viewed the executive much more positively.

As the external coach, I was struck by the greater participation of all board members, non-executive and executive alike, on all issues and not just on those where they had specific responsibility or expertise. This may also have been affected by the appointment of a new chairman of the board, the previous chairman having come to the end of their second period of office. The board reported that both the selection and induction of the new chair and the speed with which they were able to step into leadership had been greatly assisted by the board coaching.

Reflections and conclusions

A year and a half after this work began, the chief executive had accepted a new job as CEO of a larger hospital elsewhere in the country (Chesterfield). Peter provided some transitional coaching for the finance director, who became acting CEO, and then completed his work.

Gavin writes of the learning he took with him from this period of transformation at Yeovil District Hospital into his new role:

> The key learning for me was the value of adopting a consistent coaching approach with each of the different layers within the new structure from the Board through to the divisional leadership teams. The time spent co-creating the new arrangements and particularly the relationships between the different groups was critical. A clear understanding of each element's role and responsibilities to other parts of the structure was essential. With hindsight one area we could have paid greater attention to was the level of personal development support offered to the new divisional directors and indeed their wider teams. A number of individuals were taking on new and challenging roles at this level and although support was given, on reflection this could have been more.

Peter's reflections are that most of the literature, models, research and teaching on systemic team coaching focus nearly entirely on the team as a distinct entity and pay scant attention to how to provide inter-team coaching between: the leadership team and the board; the leadership team and the teams that report to it; the horizontal relationship between those teams; and between the leadership team and the wider stakeholder groupings. My belief is that the whole field of inter-team coaching will become increasingly important and that this will require a new creative blend of team coaching and organizational development. This will also require drawing on the new thinking and research on partnership working (Pittinsky, 2009; Hawkins, 2017), collaboration (Williams, 2010), networks (Katzenbach, 2012) and intergroup dynamics (Moss-Kanter, 2011; Hawkins, 2017).

Since carrying out this work with Yeovil District Hospital, I have successfully adopted a similar approach to working with two other district hospitals, a health education regional body and two commercial companies. However, I believe we are still only in the foothills of discovering what this approach of inter-team coaching can deliver and how best to practise it.

Postscript 2014

Peter Wyman, the current Chair at Yeovil District Hospital, added that over the subsequent two years, building on the foundations laid by Gavin, the management has developed into an extremely effective group. The board functions as a cohesive unit able to concentrate on strategy and on the big issues, individual executive directors have the confidence and expertise to carry out their responsibilities efficiently and effectively, and the next tier of management is increasingly empowered and able to carry out their role having bought in to the goals and values of the Trust.

Update: from inter-team coaching to 'team of team coaching' to 'eco-systemic team coaching'

Since working with this inter-team approach at Yeovil District Hospital, Gavin went on to be Chief Executive of Chesterfield Royal Hospital. He invited Peter (supported by Alison Hogan co-author of Chapter 14) to also use this approach of coaching multiple teams that were leading various aspects of the hospital at the same time and thus coaching the relationships between them. Gavin has since gone on to be Chief executive of the Royal Derby Hospital as well as Chair of the NHS East Midlands leadership body.

Peter and Alison further developed this work over several years with North Bristol Hospitals Trust, helping to integrate two hospitals (Frenchay and Southmead) into one organization with a large brand-new hospital.

There has been a growing recognition that the major challenges of hospitals cannot be resolve within the hospital walls, and that hospital organizations need to become orchestrators of the wider regional health eco-system, from self-care in the home and the work of the general practices in the community, right through to the social care back in the community that is necessary to enable many old people to leave hospital safely. The approach of inter-team coaching has itself transformed, and become a 'team of teams' approach (see next chapter), where the goal is to build as an effective collaborative partnership between teams, as team coaching does within teams.

The demands on the Health Service globally are growing exponentially for not only is the world's population still growing at a fast pace but the number of people over 85, who are the biggest users of the health facilities, is growing much, much faster.

For the Health Services throughout the world to cope with the growing demands, partnership working will become more and more essential. That is, partnership between frontline agencies, between GPs and hospitals, between hospitals and social care and between patients and health practitioners, with individuals and their families becoming more active participants in their own health management. Increasingly we are adapting team coaching, not only to a team of teams approach, but to an 'eco-systemic team coaching' (Hawkins 2017: 185–217); an approach that works with all the health agencies across a local region, including patient groups and the voluntary sector, to create effective partnership responses.

Developing an effective 'team of teams' approach in Comair

BARBARA WALSH, DANNY TUCKWOOD (METACO), ERIK VENTER (CEO), GERALDINE WELBY-COOKE (HEAD OF OD), TRACEY MCCREADIE (MANAGER OF SERVICE DELIVERY, OPS) AND JUSTIN DELL (MANAGER OF GROUND OPS) (ALL IN COMAIR), PETER HAWKINS (METACO, SUPERVISOR)

Introduction

This chapter tells the story of working with a complex airline business in South Africa, not only providing systemic team coaching to a range of key internal teams but also coaching the connections and relationship between the teams. This approach builds on the eco-systemic approach to team coaching (Hawkins, 2017: 185–217) and in particular developing a culture of a 'team of teams' (Hawkins, 2017: 196). It is also influenced by General McCrystal's book *Team of Teams* (McCrystal et al, 2015), which describes an approach to fundamentally shifting the culture of military operations in post-war Iraq. The chapter is also written by a 'team of teams'!

The case study shows how organizational development, individual coaching, leadership development and systemic team coaching can be integrated to dynamically develop the collective leadership across a complex organization.

Background and context

Erik Venter, CEO of Comair, describes the context for a different approach to leadership development in their rapidly changing environment:

Comair has operated in the Southern African aviation market for 71 years and has achieved an operating profit for every year to date. Its key to success has been its organization culture and the consequential ability to attract and retain excellent talent, resulting in a significant pool of experience and institutional memory. However, there has been almost no growth in the South African domestic airline revenue pool since 2008, and consequently Comair's growth in profits has been derived from growing market share, improving operating efficiency and pursuing ancillary revenue streams. More recently Comair has actively grown and marketed some of its insourced airline services to third parties as a means of diversification and creating new growth streams. These include crew training, catering, travel services and airline lounges.

Delivering all the above has however come at the cost of increased complexity and therefore the need for significant digital transformation of the business. This in turn has driven the integration of business processes and data management, which has created greater interdependence between departments and the need for ongoing change to the delivery methodologies as well as leadership style. Fundamentally the departmental silos needed to be removed and the management structures and styles need to evolve to reflect a new way of working along functional rather than departmental lines.

However, there are many line management functions that still require traditional departmental structures to work, and therefore the achievement of working on functional lines currently takes the form of greater teamwork within and between departments, and leadership training has had to adapt to facilitate this teamwork approach.

Airlines, by nature, are very operationally focused with documented procedures and compliance checklists for the majority of functions. The development and maintenance of specialized operating procedures by departments typically exacerbates the silo symptoms as well as developing managers with a relatively narrow and short-term focus. Leadership training of 10 years ago therefore focused largely on introducing managers to other aspects of the business while training them on leading people within their silos. This was done in the typical classroom environment where everyone received generic training, as most staff fitted into broad, generic categories.

Rapid changes to the way we do business has created a different demand on managers and the need for a different skill set and a different way of training. Not only do managers now need to have a detailed understanding of their dependence on other departments, but they also have to deal with a faster pace of delivery, more complex governance and legislation, a deeper understanding of technology solutions, understanding of the strategic direction being taken by business partners, new specialized roles within their structures, and the roles of new specialized departments within the organization to assist them in the delivery of their objectives. Partnering, cross-departmental teamwork and strategic direction are now critical compliments to daily operational delivery.

The managers within Comair are all at different levels of competence within these new requirements, and so for the sake of specific competencies, training has become more modular and tailored to the individual, while in parallel using a systemic team coaching approach to develop the recognition of interdependence and the need for partnering.

This remains an iterative process of identifying the needs of the organization, assessing the skills that are evolving and attempting to fill the gap with the most appropriate forms of development, while the business and its environment continue to change – like fixing an aircraft engine while flying at 30,000 feet!

In South Africa (perhaps greater than in more developed parts of the world), we have additional complexities. There is a desperate shortage of skilled people, and competent specialists are extremely difficult to source. Comair goes to extraordinary lengths to engage the right people and it is crucial that they are able to motivate and retain this key talent. At the same time, with advances in automation, the skills requirements of average employees are increasing in complexity. Furthermore, the strong political influence on the environment in which the business operates demands strong relational abilities, creative thinking and adaptability at all levels.

The OD context for systemic team coaching

Geraldine Welby-Cooke, Comair's Head of Organizational Development, describes the context for systemic team coaching as follows:

*Today, our leadership approach has evolved to prepare for the future of our business, focusing on a number of factors targeting specific individual **and** team leadership development needs. These needs are being addressed through rigorous leadership assessment coupled with individual* *development planning, team and individual coaching, online learning and education around talent management utilizing simulations.*

We are focusing on equipping our leaders to L.E.A.D., that is:

- *Lead to Inspire;*
- *Embrace Change;*
- *Aim for Solutions;*
- *Drive Results.*

This must be done through focusing on how they show up as leaders and as a collective leadership team. Our focus is reflected in Figure 11.1 (adapted from Hawkins and Smith, 2013).

Figure 11.1   How do you 'show up' as a leader?

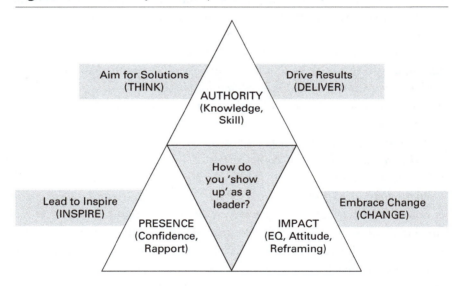

Starting team coaching in Comair Limited

Metaco was contracted to work with Comair's HR leadership team. At that time the HR leadership team was disconnected and needed to align as one HR team to provide an integrated service to the business. After an intensive scoping process, a multifaceted eight-month programme was implemented in late 2016.

As the team engaged in activities generated in their team and individual coaching, other parts of the business started to notice the changes. They were inspired by what they observed and expressed interest in undertaking a similar process.

Geraldine adds:

At the same time, we were designing the next phase of our leadership programme and realized that if we were to be successful, we needed to develop leadership as a whole rather than focusing on individual leaders. To enable whole teams to take on the role of leadership, adapting swiftly to the demands of stakeholders, staying focused on 'what is in the best interests of Comair' and collaborating across silos to achieve collective objectives. The answer was systemic team coaching which inextricably connected leaders with purpose and meaning.

Three operations teams wished to improve their respective internal team dynamics, and simultaneously improve the collaboration between their teams and with other stakeholders. Their ability to partner closely with each other, holding the strategic vision of Comair as top of mind over individual achievement, is important for the reputation and success of the airline.

The operational context of these teams required a different approach to that of the HR team, with flexibility around engagement and operational demands. This case study illustrates the eco-systemic approach taken to a systemic team coaching programme which is still currently underway.

The operations teams

The three teams are diverse in their structure:

- *Service delivery* is a large team of thirteen individuals. Besides Tracey (the team manager), the team consists of airport managers, cabin services managers and a special services manager. Their aim is to ensure a seamless experience for passengers from check-in at the airport, through boarding the aircraft, onboard services and collection of luggage at their destination airport.

- *Ground operations* is a small team. Besides Justin, there are three ramp managers who supervise and coordinate the activities of ground services in the loading and unloading of cargo and baggage at all the airports Comair serves. They also supervise the cleaning crews, loading of catering, and any special requirements (such as wheelchairs). They work towards tight deadlines.

- *Flight operations* is structured differently. The flight operations manager reports to the chief pilot. She manages a team of ten supervisors across two divisions: operations control and irregular operations. They handle flight scheduling in conjunction with commercial operations, maintaining information on the status of inbound and outbound flights and providing planning, oversight, and support when problems occur. The team works under a great deal of pressure, especially when flights are delayed or cancelled due to technical issues, bad weather and the like.

Process framework overview

A comprehensive process of consultation with team leadership and key stakeholders was used to understand the challenges the team faced, and the organization's unique cultural and operational dynamics before contracting with the team sponsor and team leaders.

A multifaceted team coaching programme was proposed, including a team 360, a two-day workshop on communication skills to set a platform for the work to follow, a two-day team launch workshop, individual coaching and inter-team coaching. Monthly review meetings with the team leaders and OD manager allow for discussion on progress and co-design of the next team coaching workshops together with bi-monthly meetings with the sponsor to discuss the impact of the team coaching on operations. Regular meetings were also scheduled with the CEO to discuss the various partnership activities taking place in Comair.

This is described in more detail in the following sections.

The activity

Scoping the project

In this case, the scoping consisted of three parts:

- Individual interviews with the leaders of service delivery, ground operations and flight operations respectively to establish perceptions of their teams' strengths, challenges and areas for development.
- A joint interview with the three team leaders together to learn more about their challenges, the current status and expectations for further cohesion and collaboration between the teams, and any other desired outcomes from the team coaching.

- An interview with Martin Louw (Executive Director, Flight Operations) as the teams' sponsor and Erik Venter (Comair's CEO), with the team leaders present, to understand their expectations of the three teams independently and collectively, and what they would like the team coaching to achieve.

Tracey McCreadie, Service Delivery Manager, describes the situation prior to commencing coaching as follows:

> At the start of our journey we identified that our team was operating under the following conditions:
>
> - The team culture was that of a victim mentality.
> - There was very little connection within the team, with pockets of alliances and support.
> - The team had little understanding of its primary stakeholders and their needs, challenges and mandates nor awareness of inter-business systems and the impact they have on these systems.
> - The team dealt with conflict in a defensive manner, playing the blame game.
> - Team members were extremely inwardly focused with little learning.
> - There were high levels of drama and they were not solution-focused.

Similar sentiments were expressed by the other leaders. The flight operations manager added that her team of supervisors relied heavily on her (she was reasonably new to the role) and she needed them to see themselves as leaders, become more comfortable with taking responsibility, collaborative decision making, and being accountable to each other.

The team leaders agreed that each of them had tended to focus on optimizing their own team's output rather than considering the impact of their actions on other teams, which in turn can have a knock-on impact on other stakeholders such as passengers. They agreed that holding a higher perspective on the performance of Comair rather than their own team was necessary to align them to a common objective.

The sponsor and the CEO added to the above areas of development:

- The teams need to see themselves as one team of teams. Team members should not be confined to their job descriptions but rather look to what is needed in the situation. Team leaders have to be seen as being on the same page and drive this down into their teams and into other parts of the organization in order to deliver a consistently high level of service to customers. The teams pull together very well when there is a crisis. They need to perform like this on a daily basis.

- Where individual performance is lagging, this needs to improve to deliver consistent and high levels of service.

- Know what the other teams are doing – each team is part of the orchestra and contributing to the whole. Be proactive rather than reactive. Anticipate and collaboratively fix things before they become a problem. Get others on board to assist, ask for and offer help.

- Continually strive to exceed rather than just meet targets such as on-time performance and safety. Build margins for when unavoidable situations occur.

- Rather than blame, pick up the ball and be part of the solution. Eliminate 'CYA' (cover your arse) emails, see other points of view and offer help and assistance. See the bigger picture and accept decisions made as being in the best interests of the airline, even if it may negatively impact you/ your team at the time. Trust the positive intent of others, avoid drama and find out how you/your team can add value.

- Team members need to be changeable and ready. They should be able to balance the necessary compliance with appropriate discretion, initiative and innovative thinking.

- Bring people on board. Engagement of staff at the lower levels and contractors needs to increase through collaboration, communication, cross-functional learning and growth, flexibility and support.

Creating the foundation: Advanced Communication Skills

With a clear mandate to bring the 3 teams into closer alignment, the first task was to help the team members create a common language to aid communication and cross-functional cooperation. This took the form of a joint two-day offsite workshop using an action learning approach (Revans, 1982) to the concepts of the NLP communication model (Bandler and Grinder, 1975), adapted to the contexts of leadership and management.

From the outset, we wanted to mix things up and so all the small group experiential activities were conducted with a range of participants across the functional teams. The atmosphere was cautiously positive and participative.

The first real shift occurred when we conducted an exercise in listening skills where all the participants rated their listening as being much higher than was evidenced in the results. This caused a lot of laughter and contributed immensely to bringing people together.

This was further reinforced when we conducted small group exercises in questioning as a way of leading through seeking clarity and understanding. The predominant mode of leadership being utilized at that time was that of command and control with the team leaders being responsible for making decisions and issuing instructions (which were even termed openly as 'Directives').

Tracey, described it as:

> For me as the leader of the team, my greatest challenge was moving from full-on team participant and driver, often making the majority of decisions, to that of empowering and conducting the team in their activities and decision making.

The participants struggled to adapt to a new mode of questioning but were supported by the others in their groups and this assistance also helped to bring individuals closer together.

To make the workshop more than an academic exercise, the last afternoon was devoted to a 'real-play'. The team leaders were asked to devise a 'nightmare scenario' day for the operation. Key roles were allocated to individuals with no prior experience (eg one of the ground operations managers played the role of the maintenance manager). Those not allocated to specific roles became observers with a mandate to focus on the interactions and communication.

As the scenario unfolded, additional problems were introduced to increase the pressure. The team leaders took roles as members of the executive and interjected to increase the pressure further. At certain points, we suspended the activity and had the participants listen in as we led a discussion with the observer group, looking for their thoughts and suggestions to improve the role players' communication.

It was interesting to observe how the nature of the conversations changed over the course of the afternoon, becoming far more collaborative and solution-orientated. Subsequent feedback from participants indicated that this exercise was a fundamental turning point for them in understanding the systemic nature of their roles. These activities were vital in establishing a foundational framework and common vocabulary for the teams to engage in value-creating conversations.

Team Panorama 360°

A revised online version of the High Performing Team Questionnaire (Hawkins, 2017) was developed and completed by team members, direct reports as well as key internal and external stakeholders identified by the team leader. The results were compiled and aggregated to inform the team launch workshop for each team.

Team Launch workshops

A two-day workshop was held with each team using a common framework. This involved knowledge transfer as well as small group activities. The key themes emphasized were around the shift needed by the team and individuals to embrace the complexity of the 21st-century business environment through:

- changing to an 'Outside-In, Future-back and Whole to Parts' approach with a focus on the connections between individuals, teams and organizations;
- understanding each other at a deeper, more humanistic level; and
- removing the drama from the workplace.

By having the work completed predominately in small groups that were frequently reorganized, the teams developed a greater awareness of their team mates. They started to experience the value of collective thinking as team members utilized their new listening and questioning skills.

The key outputs from the workshop included a set of team commitments on behaviours and a process of using virtual red and green cards to give feedback, which allowed team members to hold each other to account for these commitments. The document was subsequently laminated and brought to their team meetings and each team coaching session.

It was interesting for the coaches to note the range of reactions to the workshops. As Tracey, described it:

> With any change, there is a certain amount of discomfort in the discovery phase. We all as individuals had the best intentions, however once aware of our behaviour, there were different reactions within the team to the process we needed to follow. These moved from frustration in not understanding how to change, resistance from team members who felt isolated in the process and not asking for help, to discovery, enlightenment, surprise and delight.

Justin Dell, Ground Operations Manager, observes:

> The first response of most team members was 'Is this just another course that we will forget in the foreseeable future?' To our amazement, it was quite the contrary... The team has embraced the coaching experience with open arms and they have really put what they have learnt into perspective within their personal lives and also within their teams, ultimately changing the dynamic and drive within their teams. There is a hunger that was created within the team to perform

better every day, which is ongoing and rolling over into other members within Comair – seeking bigger results, looking at the future and not just the short term.

Team coaching

Amongst the areas highlighted for improvement were:

- Creation of a greater sense of purpose through clarification of the goals for the individual teams as well as those of the other operations teams, which enabled a greater appreciation of how they individually and collectively contribute to the organization's strategic intent.
- Creating the space and time for individual and team reflective practice.
- Understanding that the ability to perform depends on the quality of collaboration with key stakeholders, setting an example and supporting functional team members to cross-collaborate both within respective teams and beyond.
- Broader interaction and engagement between the respective teams to help create a cohesive operations team that is 'more than the sum of its parts'.
- Developing the team member's direct reports to understand the common goals and their role in achieving these, both through their own work as well as through collaboration and knowledge sharing with their colleagues in the wider operations environment and with other stakeholders.

Team coaching sessions integrated a multifaceted approach, which allowed the teams to co-create their respective team charters and address the Listening, Exploring, Action and Review elements of the CID-CLEAR model over a period of 7–8 months, whilst moving across the elements of the 5 Disciplines model. Core learning is included with each session.

Ongoing activities included:

- key stakeholder mapping with an introduction to and appreciation of systemic thinking in relation to the stakeholder environment;
- finding out what the key stakeholders needed from the team;
- development of a timeline of progress to date and visioning the future with specific time-based activities to achieve collective goals;
- development of a strategic narrative for the team that could be shared across departmental and organizational boundaries as well as at all levels within the function;
- reframing conflict and establishing tools for dealing effectively with tensions.

From the mid-point onwards, the team coaching content for each of the teams diverged as they started to work on the key priority areas for their specific needs, with reflection facilitated by the team coaches to highlight how the team had operated during the meeting to help them to identify new areas that the team could work on in their normal meetings.

Some of the coaching involved the team coaches attending team meetings to observe/facilitate live meetings. This allowed the team coaches to challenge the thinking within the team and provide in-the-moment feedback as well as contributing ideas and supporting the team in achieving increasingly higher levels of engagement, partnership and delivery.

From our observations in the team coaching as well as supervision of individual coaching as the programme went on, significant changes in attitudes and behaviours were being reported amongst team members. Team members were visibly connecting at a much deeper level, collaborating to find solutions to issues and they reported a greater sense of cohesion. They had made significant shifts in their efforts to present a unified face to the organization, although these internal changes took significantly longer to register fully with the wider organization.

Some behaviours, possibly indicative of the organizational culture, were still being evidenced, such as reticence to give in-the-moment feedback on unhelpful behaviours upwards to team leaders and across teams. Given the highly time-pressured nature of the business, the teams were struggling to find space and time for more reflective practice. The team sessions have started to develop into a space for this to take place.

The team coaching programme will conclude with a reflection session with the team as well as 360° interviews with key internal stakeholders to evidence changes that have been observed.

Individual coaching

All team members embarked on a contemporaneous individual coaching programme including: tripartite contracting and outcome setting with the individual and their team leader; mid-term and close out reviews; together with supporting books, journals and other reading materials.

The coaching allowed individuals to identify specific areas of personal development, which would supplement and support the team coaching initiative.

As Justin, described it:

The coaching experience has taught me to look within myself for answers, and that it is also ok to ask junior members in the team for help when I don't know – teaching me to become more humble. I have also learnt to take a 'pause' at times and to understand and to listen to what staff are really asking by learning to train my ear.

Although some individuals initially expressed their discomfort at the challenging nature of the conversations, the majority of participants engaged well in the coaching conversations once they became more familiar with the nature of coaching. However, the issues brought to individual coaching were, in many cases, performance- and task-oriented rather than more personal and inter-personal developmental areas.

The importance of integrating and aligning individual development with team development from an OD perspective is articulated by Geraldine:

> We acknowledge that we need strong leaders as well as strong leadership as the one cannot work in isolation to the other. We are developing a system and all parts are connected. Working on the collective level, you will still need to address individual development needs and when working with an individual leader, the system around the individual also needs to be addressed.
>
> Developing leaders in isolation is like rehabilitating a drug addict and then putting them back into the same environment where the addiction first developed having no consideration that the behaviour is linked to the environment around the individual. Whilst this is not the most positive example, it does demonstrate that leadership cannot be developed in a vacuum; there is much more power in development when it is linked to the whole system and not just isolated parts of it.

Early emerging organizational themes

The use of thematic supervision with the individual coaches as well as supervision of the team coaches allowed organizational themes to emerge.

There was a lack of clarity in the broader organization as to the teams' roles and responsibilities. This similarly applied to the teams' perceptions of other departments and divisions. Teams were often referred to by the team leader's name rather than the specific function.

Given the growth of the business, people found it difficult to keep track of who worked where. When attending meetings often not everyone knew all of those present – or endeavoured to introduce themselves. In addition, not all e-mail signatures utilized in internal communications carried job titles. This led to departments tending to do their own thing, without understanding who or what was impacted by their actions.

In some cases, individuals were waiting for authority to take decisions or for others to respond rather than being empowered to take the initiative and make decisions for themselves – even though this was encouraged by their managers.

Elements of historical culture remained, expressed as a fear of speaking out in case of reprisal, anecdotal story-making and frames of mind about the ability to challenge hierarchical structures. Managing upwards was perceived as a challenge.

Team of teams (inter-team coaching)

Part of the purpose of the team coaching was for the three teams to shift the relationships they had with each other and explore the issues that required their effective collaboration with each other. They were making good progress as a result of their respective team coaching sessions, and so we decided to stretch them further. We proposed a 'Team of Teams' workshop, which would include all leadership teams within Comair who had been exposed to team coaching including the Exco, the initial HR team, the food directions (catering) team and a combined standards and training team.

The workshop took place offsite in late November 2017, five months into the team coaching programme for the operations teams. The facilitation was led by Peter Hawkins, Metaco's supervisor, assisted by Barbara and Danny. Between the seven teams there were approximately 60 participants, and the workshop was scheduled for 4 hours. Associate coaches providing individual coaching with the various Comair team members attended as observers.

Each team had their own table and flipchart. Peter began by asking them to draw two metaphorical pictures, the first of their team a year ago and the second of their team today. He then asked them to describe their team purpose and strategic priorities and team KPIs for 2018. They presented this back to the other teams and received feedback, appreciation and encouragement.

For the second part of the process the teams were asked to prepare their needs of the other teams present and to articulate what they would offer. This was presented as:

- To be really successful what we need from (team name) is…
- What we offer (team name) is…

These were presented with dialogue between the relevant teams. Finally, taking the focus back into the wider group, they were requested to identify three things they need to do to increase collaboration as a team of teams. The commitments made were summarized into the one-page diagram and distributed to the teams.

All three of the operations teams reflected that they had found the expanded session very useful for connecting and stated their appreciation for the willingness of the other teams to engage fully in the process – even though most had not advanced as far in their respective coaching programmes. They were particularly appreciative of the Exco for their willingness to participate alongside them and felt that at this workshop they felt the unity of being 'one Comair team'.

A second inter-team coaching event is planned for later in the programme. Geraldine concludes:

The inter-team coaching was a new and valuable experience. It provided the opportunity for teams to more formally share who they are and where they see themselves going. It furthermore enabled them to receive 'real time feedback' from their stakeholders in the room on what they could improve and what they were doing well. Commitments were made and, if followed through, will really change the landscape of how they connect with each other.

Future 'moments of connection' will become easier to create if more platforms for conversation are put in place... I see really value in this for business to develop strategy at all levels through stakeholder engagement and alignment. More importantly, it will create a platform for sustainable change.

Progress made

Tracey describes the progress made in her team, and by herself personally:

Whilst we still have a lot to learn as a team, particularly about becoming more strategic and the need to ingrain a culture of continual learnings, we can however already start measuring our success by feedback that we have received from stakeholders and the quality of the task output we are seeing. Trust is clearly evident, and the team are using the tools provided at the Advanced Communications workshop that has created a common language. And the most pleasant surprise in this experience is the amount of fun we are having as a team...!

On a personal level the benefit has been immense. This experience has been inspirational with exciting light bulb moments and new exciting discoveries about how I think and how to expand the way I think, how I create my reality with the words I use, changing my perspective on learnings and rediscovering the ability to imagine. I also learnt that I want to rescue people and how I enable poor outcomes from this behaviour and thus how to filter and use this ability in a more productive manner. I feel more empowered and in control and am delighted about the avenues that have opened for me to grow and keep growing.

Justin adds:

> The experience has brought a lot more cohesion within our department and we are working a lot more unaided and getting on with the job – a lot less micro managing is happening. We as a unit are now closer than ever as we had to learn to become vulnerable in front of each other, pushing the boundaries of things we didn't like seeing and hearing and owning our mistakes.
>
> The managers are excited to put what they have learnt into practice and I've heard them on several occasions asking for help – putting the ball back into the employee's court for answers and creating better team dynamics and interaction. There are continuous ongoing practices that we share with our teams and roll out our learnings with them so that they too may profit out of this experience that we have been given.
>
> There is also better relationship building with other stakeholders within the business – a lot less playing the man and actually getting the job done now, which is ongoing and rolling over into other areas within Comair...
>
> I can confidently say that this experience has strengthened my team, created more awareness, better communication with stakeholders, more confidence, seeking learning opportunities, looking to the future, more drive.

Geraldine, from the OD perspective observes:

> Wow! Previously the teams in operations were working in silos and either not having important conversations or having conversations that were not necessarily supporting the best interests of Comair. I have seen radical changes in how the operations managers relate to each other as well as to their stakeholders. Dialogue has opened up and they are finding ways to co-create solutions. They are stepping up in how they lead their teams, how they ensure their teams are connected to each other and how they are achieving their broader objectives.

Taking a broader perspective, Erik Venter, CEO, comments:

> The initial observation of the team coaching is that participants have become more connected on a personal level and more understanding of each other's work challenges. This has facilitated better joint problem solving, more consideration and less passing of blame. Participants are also more open to challenging conversations without immediately feeling threatened.
>
> As with most leadership development (and amidst the surrounding changes) the outcomes and the return on investment of team coaching are not explicitly quantifiable but will definitely contribute positively towards the evolution of the leadership culture within Comair.

Comair's talent management strategy

Geraldine explains:

Comair's talent strategy is focused on 'building its own' given that there is a real shortage of skills in South Africa and this issue is compounded when you are looking for talent in aviation, which consists only of a handful of companies in South Africa. Building our own skills is not necessarily the only or most significant factor that differentiates us from our competitors, but it is an important one...

We cannot build skills in the absence of good-quality leadership teams who know what our business stands for, where it is heading and have the ability to nurture talent.

The actions of our **collective leadership** shape our culture. For 71 years having the right skills coupled with a unique culture has enabled us to grow from strength to strength. Team coaching is enabling us now, as a growing business, to really refine our culture even further into one where we can drive enterprise-wide performance through collaboration in an era where change is the norm and continuous evolution is required to stay ahead of the game.

Frankly speaking, we are changing mind-sets, eradicating silo thinking, whilst still keeping the essence of what makes us Comair.

OD perspective on team coaching at Comair

Geraldine continues:

My personal experience of the HR team coaching process coupled with individual coaching was phenomenal. It created a platform for the unsaid in the team to be spoken and for us to really focus on what we needed to deliver to our stakeholders. I almost do not recognize the state we used to be in as a team a year ago compared to how we function today. Yes, there always will be room for improvement, but we are in a much better place today than we were when we first started.

As the OD sponsor, I hear positive sentiment on the changes the participating teams are experiencing and from their stakeholders. The consequence is that a new language is being developed around how people need to work together to achieve outcomes. Furthermore, participants observe the difference in their own mindsets compared to those who have not yet embarked on the journey.

As co-coach with Barbara to another Comair team, it has been valuable to watch them open up their minds to new ways of thinking about the possibilities of what they could achieve as a business. It was interesting to see how they grappled with defining a future state as individuals, and then the magic happened when they worked together, and a new level of thinking came out from the team. That is what we want, no that is what we *need* to thrive as a business!

Reflection and learning

Standing back from this very intensive work with a complex, growing organization, we reflect on the key themes and learnings through integrating eco-systemic and systemic team coaching along with individual coaching and personal development into an integrated programme to achieve remarkable change.

- Team coaching is not restricted to sessions with the coaches, and it happens when the team are together and when they are apart.

- The three team leaders now see themselves as a team and have commenced regular meetings between themselves, inviting other key internal peers to join them. This is a move away from attachment to their functional teams to form a new identity as an integrated Comair operations senior management team.

- There has been a move away from assumption and blame, in favour of fact finding and co-created solutions. As a result, their collective performance is improved, and the regular crises which are commonplace in this industry are addressed faster and more effectively, therefore supporting the key 'On Time Performance' objective.

- All three teams have expressed how much they have enjoyed the team coaching. Although it has been a challenging journey they have put their hearts into learning and making significant changes. It has been rewarding to hear of the impact as they began to partner with their own team members and with other teams. A focus is now being placed on supporting them as they develop their functional teams to do likewise.

- Individual coaching of team members contributed significantly to the rapid change in attitudes and behaviours. We consistently notice how much faster change at the team level happens when individuals are concurrently working with their own coaches in alignment with team objectives.

- The Advanced Communication Skills workshop prior to commencement of team coaching is valuable. We find that learning the basics of how to communicate effectively provides a solid platform for beginning the team coaching work. Systemic team coaching is not always coaching, rather a multifaceted approach, co-created with the team, that addresses what is needed at the time, and both structured and 'in the moment'.

- It has been extremely valuable having open access to the CEO, Erik Venter, who is supportive of the process and actively partners with us through giving valuable feedback and suggestions for improvement.

- Partnering across different roles of leadership, at various levels and across different parts of the business in our work with Comair has provided valuable learning. Key to this has been keeping the strategic vision as top of mind, whilst developing a true appreciation for the business, what makes it special, and the challenges it faces and will face going forward. The doors are always open for us to meet with any internal stakeholder, at any level, on any topic. The ability to have honest co-challenging conversations, whether engaging with the CEO, the head of OD or senior managers and their management teams has enabled us to truly think and work systemically and eco-systemically.

- The complexity of the environment in which Comair operates, the changing structure of the organization and the variety of sub-cultures that exist have enabled us to develop our skills in systemic complexity thinking and adaptability. We have learnt not to take anything at face value, but rather to take time to explore non-apparent linkages between seemingly unrelated factors, which has uncovered some interesting awareness for all involved.

Empowering the 12 next generation of team leaders in fast-moving startups

SHANNON ARVIZU

Introduction

- What does systemic team coaching look like in a fast-moving startup environment?

- How is team coaching approached by a new generation of leaders committed to purposeful work and personal growth? What are the critical few behaviours that startup leaders need to enable their teams to operate at peak performance?

- How can systemic team coaching enable startups to leap ahead of their competition and embrace agility in the face of an uncertain future?

These are the questions I address as a sociologist and team performance coach who lives and works in San Francisco, one of the world's largest tech hubs.

Within the San Francisco Bay Area, there are over 6,000 startups, with 2,781 in Seed Stage, 1,140 in Series A, 557 in Series B, and 308 in Series C (Source: Angel List). Those that 'make it' eventually get acquired or become publicly traded organizations.

In this world, every startup is in a race against itself (by continuously improving prior performance), and in a race against its competitors to prove market viability and secure the next round of investment to scale its impact. While very few companies make it to the acquisition or IPO stage, it doesn't stop visionaries from trying. There is a prevailing ethos that anything is possible and worth risking if it leads to solving problems in a new way and generating greater value for the world. It's a vibrant culture driven by passion, technological expertise and a desire for impact.

At the same time, there is a lack of know-how about what it takes to help individuals and teams stay committed over the long term. Startups spend a significant amount of time and resources to recruit the talent they need. Once this talent is brought into the organization, there are very few resources dedicated to their development. High turnover and burnout are common. According to Culture Amp's benchmark data of 'new tech' companies in 2017, only 58 per cent of startup employees see themselves working at their current company in two years' time.

My premise is that team coaching, in tandem with next-generation leadership development for managers and executives, is the missing link needed to help early stage companies become resilient in the face of constant change. My firm, Epic Teams, equips managers and teams in fast-growing tech companies with collaborative leadership skills to drive performance, engagement and growth.

Case study

This is a case study of a transformative journey with a leading San Francisco-based startup that took the leap into systemic team coaching development. It is a snapshot of a team development engagement with Lever, a recruiting software startup, over the course of nine months (from March 2017 to December 2017).

Because of its young stage and fast-moving environment, Lever needed an emergent and adaptive approach to team coaching. Rather than start by working with Lever's teams right away, we needed first to build the capacity of its leaders. Along the way, we also helped craft its performance development system and we were instrumental in shaping its team-based approach to engagement.

The company history

Lever was founded in 2012 to 'tackle the most strategic challenge that companies face: how to recruit and grow their teams'. Lever's software helps companies post job descriptions, collect applications, conduct interviews and analyse job candidates in a way that decreases bias and enables collaboration in hiring decisions. Its product is particularly known for its intuitive and UX-friendly approach to make sourcing and recruiting easier.

Lever's CEO, Sarah Nahm, is a driven 32-year-old who graduated from Stanford's Design School and was a former speechwriter at Google for Marissa Mayer. She later worked on Google's marketing team, which was responsible for launching the Chrome browser.

At the beginning of our engagement, the company was deep in fundraising mode for its Series C round of $40 million. It was also transitioning from an 80-person company to a 155-person company in the span of a few months.

Eighty-two percent of Lever's workforce, and 100 per cent of its founder team is made up of those in the millennial generation (those born between 1978 and 2000). Research on the workplace beliefs and attitudes of members of this generation indicate that they have a markedly distinct desire for growth and development (Gallup, 2017) and a need for purposeful work within an empowering environment (Hawkins, 2017b).

The desire for purposeful work within an empowering environment is evident in the organic development of Lever's culture. Within the first few years of existence, Lever had built a strong reputation for its commitment to diversity and inclusion (having been one of the first companies of its size to hit 50:50 gender parity in Silicon Valley). Currently, the company's board is 40 per cent female, women occupy 43 per cent of technical roles, and the company overall is 40 per cent nonwhite.

Lever's commitment to diversity and inclusion was initially driven not by its executive team, but by its team members. One of Lever's earliest engineers, Rachael Stedman, gave a presentation on diversity and inclusion and what it was like to be a female engineer in a predominantly male industry. That moment was a turning point for the organization. It sparked vibrant discussions and informed product decisions about how to eliminate bias in the onboarding process and foster the recruitment of candidates from diverse backgrounds.

Concurrent with the beginning of our engagement, the company also hired its first VP of People Operations, Mike Bailen. Bailen is a seasoned, 34-year-old HR professional. Prior to Lever, he led recruiting efforts at Eventbrite and held recruiting and HR roles at Zappos. When asked about what drew him to join the Lever team, Bailen replied:

> What I found with Lever was that we share the same fundamental beliefs. We both believe that engaged and diverse teams that work in psychologically safe

environments will outperform organizations that don't have the same ingredients. While Lever already had the makeup of a diverse team and instilled inclusion as part of their core identity, there wasn't a lot of structure to build this engaged and exciting culture for the long term. Because they were already the leader in the recruiting technology space, in my opinion, and were well regarded for their culture, one can only imagine what they could accomplish if they had the tools, the communication frameworks, the coaching, the guidance and the people programmes to propel them further. So that was the main draw to coming on board with the company.

Why focus on frontline management?

In a startup with limited resources, it is key to direct development in a targeted way – but where to start? Sarah Nahm speaks about the company's position at the beginning of the leadership development work:

> When we started this work, a whole bunch of things were very different at Lever. We had not hired very many managers from the outside and we had not promoted very many people into management from the inside. We didn't have a vision of how we wanted to scale teams and if anything, we felt quite a lot of peril that in that scaling we would lose a lot of what we had already built up.

Both Nahm and Bailen agreed that the most immediate challenge for the company was the development of its new middle-management and a structure for the continued performance, engagement, and growth of its people.

To understand the thinking behind this decision, Bailen remarks:

> I think back to this saying I picked up from Duran Duyon, who used to run L&D at Eventbrite. He said, 'For successful organizations, all roads run through great leaders.'
>
> At Lever, we now had this management layer that influences the direction of all of our employees and determines whether our organization is successful. We needed to transform this layer into a high-powered leadership group that could be our competitive advantage.
>
> And because many of these leaders were stepping into management for the very first time, it was critical to establish a philosophical alignment around what the role means. We needed to give managers the tools to think of themselves as people developers, not as somebody's boss. We wanted them to understand what makes themselves and their direct reports tick. We wanted them to

motivate employees to fire on all cylinders and have a growth mindset to improve in their role.

And, obviously, a big part of an employee's engagement is a result of their relationship with their manager. More than ever, employees want to gain skills, learn new things, and be developed. If they can't find it within your organization, they are going to go somewhere else. So that's why we started with the management layer.

Cultivating the next generation of team leaders

Given the charge to create a pilot development experience for a high-powered leadership group, how might we design it so that today's millennial managers increase their effectiveness in the most transformative way possible?

To design this experience for organizational impact, it is important to make the distinction between leader development and leadership development (Hawkins, 2017b: 27). Leader development is focused on a person's capacity to be effective in a leadership role. This particular conception has influenced the design of most conventional leadership development programs to date. These programs typically involve removing individual leaders from their work context and sending them on one-day to multiweek programmes to learn new models, tools and techniques. There may be an assessment of individual leadership competencies and perhaps a series of one-to-one coaching sessions to develop skills and behaviours with outside expert help over the course of a short period of time.

Leadership development, as defined in our work, is 'the actualization of self and others towards an extraordinary mission'. We are less focused on developing the individual for success in a role and more focused on developing an individual's capacity to grow oneself and others – particularly within a team context.

The methodological approach we take to leadership development is rooted primarily in: 1) behavioural sciences, 2) positive psychology and 3) team performance. From these fields, we recognize that the most effective form of behaviour change happens with live, face-to-face interactions in a group setting. We also acknowledge that change happens most readily when we utilize our collective strengths and focus on what is working well. Last, we transfer team coaching skills to managers so that they can facilitate their team's capacity to produce value for the organization and its stakeholders.

Our goal in the design of the pilot program for Lever, called the Leadership Accelerator, was to empower mid-level managers to move through the journey from team manager to team coach over the course of six months (Hawkins, 2017a: Chapter 12). Hawkins describes this as:

- team manager (focus on managing the team members);
- team leader (focus on collective goals);
- team orchestrator (focus on internal and external connecting);
- teach coach (focus on developing the team capacities).

Because the organization had not yet implemented any development to date, Lever decided to focus first on developing its managers independently of their teams. The thinking behind this approach is that managers could practise with each other and implement the tools and techniques that they felt would be most beneficial to their teams.

To ensure successful behavioural adoption for Lever's leaders, we utilized training modalities for today's workplace, including:

- peer group learning sessions and peer coaching;
- personalized coaching on specific growth areas, as identified by close colleagues;
- relevant exercises to apply to real work.

The content of the programme focused on three core behavioural strategies. They included:

- **Own your growth:** This module included segments related to personal growth planning, social and emotional intelligence, productivity habits, and work–life balance.
- **Develop your people:** This module included segments to coach direct reports in growth conversations and spot coaching.
- **Empower your team:** This module focused on foundational team development activities (team charter, team KPIs, and action-planning sprints).

We detail the experiences and the concurrent evolution of leadership within Lever in the following sections.

Own your growth

The first month of the Leadership Accelerator focused on behaviours related to 'owning one's growth'. Our premise is that to coach individuals and teams well, managers need to become familiar with their creative and reactive tendencies and have the skills to minimize reactive tendencies when needed. This premise is also substantiated by the research on emotional intelligence in the workplace (Brackett et al, 2011).

The notion of taking accountability for one's growth, and recognizing that leadership is a journey of self-discovery, is also espoused by Lever's CEO. Nahm says:

> I don't think Lever will ever reach a scale where that is not the hardest thing about being a leader. When it comes to personal challenges and growth edges, you sometimes see ugly things about yourself and you have to face them on a daily basis. When I became CEO, I had to do this [personal] work at the same time when we were doing a million other things. Thankfully, a lot of people invested in me and were honest with me. These people, especially my co-founders, taught me in those early years that I was too focused on right vs wrong, that I wasn't good at listening, and that we (as executives) weren't supposed to make all the decisions. And we all need to have co-founders at Lever, people who are committed enough to help each other through the difficult and deeply personal journey of leadership.

To facilitate this level of self-awareness amongst leaders, we introduced the Mental Saboteur framework, based on positive psychology research and encapsulated through the work of Chamine (2012). From the Mental Saboteurs assessment, leaders developed personal growth plans that focused on specific ways to overcome the most prevalent mental patterns that derail their abilities to be good leaders at work. They received in-depth one-to-one coaching sessions to explore these tendencies in a safe and personalized context. We also brought this concept into the peer learning sessions and equipped managers with peer coaching skills to be of support to one another when sabotaging thoughts and behaviours come up in the course of the everyday workplace setting.

In this module, we also introduced the notion of 'growth edges' for managers to further their exploration of personal development. Growth edges are those areas of improvement that make the biggest difference to one's personal development *and* one's team. This concept derives from the work of Kegan and Lahey (2016). To uncover these growth edges, we asked managers to solicit 360° feedback in face-to-face settings with at least three people who worked closely with them. Examples of growth edges selected by managers include overcoming sabotaging thoughts or behaviours, building their competence or skill set in a particular domain, finding a greater level of work–life balance or implementing more effective productivity and workflow habits.

Develop your people

The second and third months of the Leadership Accelerator focused on developing coaching skills within a one-to-one context. To create an empowered and responsive workforce, leaders need to adopt a performance coaching mindset. They cannot expect to personally direct and influence everything that their team needs to do in a given workday – especially in a fast-moving environment. As Hawkins (2017b: 23) writes:

> Leaders are increasingly recognizing that they cannot be the main point of integration and decision making in the company. They need to radically delegate and wean the other leaders from being dependent on them. They also need to encourage and even insist that leaders and managers at all levels can solve issues and conflicts directly across the organization, rather than up the hierarchy.

To do this well, it's important that managers know how to create shared expectations and a strong culture of accountability, while also inspiring and motivating action.

Traditionally, managers have relied upon rewards, such as role status and financial compensation, to inspire action. These actions were typically evaluated annually and, when positively perceived, resulted in a promotion or pay increase. This approach is no longer as effective as it may have been with previous generations. As such, companies big and small are replacing the conventional performance management system with what is now termed a 'performance development system' (Gallup, 2017). This system is based on frequent feedback interactions that develop direct reports in an iterative, upward fashion and results in improved performance outcomes and career development.

Most managers, unfortunately, do not innately know how to do this well. And, while there is now a plethora of technology tools designed to assist managers in this endeavour, it's important to recognize that this is a behavioural competency that requires significant face-to-face interaction and practice in order to do well.

To equip managers to powerfully develop direct reports, we introduced two coaching skill sets: developmental coaching for quarterly conversations related to career development and 'laser coaching' for real-time problem solving. In the peer learning sessions, managers peer coached each other using personal growth plans and practised laser coaching in a variety of real-life situations to help direct reports increase their competency and commitment to goals in 10 minutes or less.

In thinking about the importance of cultivating one's craft as people developers with peer managers, Bailen says:

> You can't just say, 'Here are some frameworks and a couple of tools. Now go use them with your direct reports.' You need to learn and grow yourself as a leader before you can do this for the team. It's about identifying your saboteurs, getting comfortable with the communication frameworks, and practising with peers in a safe environment that's really critical.

Empower your team

The third module focused on developing basic competencies in team coaching. We introduced a team charter tool (Hawkins, 2017; Peters and Carr, 2014) and started practising with the ways managers could use it to identify areas of growth and improvement for their teams.

At this point in the pilot programme, however, managers told us that they were unsure about their role in using these tools.

Mike Bailen explains:

> Once we were a few months into the programme, there was this realization that the managers were hungry to bring these concepts and tools into their teams. Some were more eager to bring these tools back to their team than others (and there's a variety of factors there), but in general there was confusion around 'Is this a mandated thing? Should we all be doing this? I have this cool tool called the team charter – should I use it? Should I not? I don't know what Lever's expectations are.'
>
> There was an aha moment here. The managers wanted to use the tools – they just didn't know when or how. That's when we knew it was time to bring it to the team level and bring it into the business.
>
> At that point, the executive team and the people team officially sponsored these tools and said to the managers 'This is your role as a leader.' We moved out of the 'pilot stage' and made it a 'team programme' to put these tools and frameworks in action.

At this moment in the development journey, Lever also ran its first engagement survey (using the Culture Amp platform). In terms of overall engagement, Lever's workforce scored the organization at 2 points above comparable technology companies (with an engagement score of 74 per cent). Upon digging deeper into the data and viewing the side-by-side 'team heatmap' of different engagement dimensions, it was clear that there were important areas for managers to focus on as part of their development as team coaches.

We designed a company-wide team coaching initiative (called the Team Accelerator) that included the introduction and implementation of customized coaching tools for the organization. Those tools included a company-sponsored team charter (Lever's Team Impact Plans) and an action-learning tool (Lever's Team Impact Calibrations) to plan, design and iterate on team behaviours. The company also designed a personal growth plan (Lever's Individual Impact Plans) for use by team members to plan personal performance, engagement and growth, and to document the outcomes of developmental coaching conversations with managers.

In total, we worked with eight teams simultaneously across the organization over the course of five months. The Team Accelerator included monthly team coaching sessions (Lever's Team Calibration meetings), as well as monthly manager check-ins and manager trainings on how to use the new tools.

The design elements we implemented for the company-wide programme are similar to what Hawkins terms the '3 new principles for creating continuous leadership learning' (Hawkins, 2017b: 33–5).

Those principles include:

1 **Align leadership development to organizational development.**
   As an organization, Lever wanted to increase its engagement scores while also developing the leadership capacity of its managers for improved team and individual performance outcomes. To meet this aim, we equipped managers with team performance coaching skills within the context of real work.

2 **Make it less about theory and more about fast-forward rehearsals and action-prototyping.**
   In the team coaching sessions, we introduced new ways of interacting and relating to one another that are rooted in the science of behaviour change, positive psychology and team performance. With each new practice, we shared a nominal amount of background about why these practices could be helpful and jumped immediately into rehearsal. After experimenting with these practices, we asked teams to reflect on their usefulness to help them accomplish real work and the contexts in which they could be helpful. For those practices found useful, we then asked for

specific team commitments on when they wanted to put them into place and who would be responsible for their implementation. Lastly, when we met again as a team, we asked teams to reflect on the implementation of the practice and how it might be improved moving forward. In this way, teams were intimately involved in the design of their action-planning cycles and developed improved abilities to reflect, learn and iterate as a group.

Along the way, the team coach met independently with the team leader to help him/her reflect on the process, as well as to transfer the adoption of behaviours and approaches to collective leadership. The role of the team coach in this context was to model distributed leadership practices with the manager – not to replace the manager. To ensure the actual transfer of team coaching skills, managers were asked to lead the sessions near the end of the engagement (with preparation, supervision and feedback with the team coach).

3 Create new rituals and habits that cultivate an exploratory mindset.

This last principle speaks to the need for continuous leadership development that cultivates an 'improvisational exploratory mindset' through embracing 'our other ways of knowing beyond the rational mind (EQ, somatic awareness, etc.)' (Hawkins, 2017b: 35). We began each team coaching session with an improv warm-up activity to help team members enter into a creative mindset. We often stood up from our chairs when engaged in activities and moved around the room to keep the energy up. We also began and ended sessions with empowering music.

Perhaps the most impactful way we encouraged an exploratory mindset, however, was simply by inviting teams to meet face to face without the use of phones or laptops. As a *de rigueur* practice for team coaching sessions, this element was quite provocative for a tech startup (and, admittedly, was sometimes met with resistance by a few team members who 'needed to respond to something urgent').

To foster rich discussions and generate novel solutions, teams need adequate mental space for high-quality thinking (Kline, 2015). Meeting for an extended period of time (typically 90 minutes) without e-mail and chat distractions is essential for deep listening, thoughtful discussion, creative divergence and sound convergence on important issues. It also gives teams the opportunity to embrace the discomfort of the 'groan zone', the unavoidable struggle that teams go through when integrating new and different ways of thinking (Kaner, 2014).

At its heart, the team coaching session is about 'slowing down to speed up'. These sessions give teams the ability to work faster and with greater purpose once coordination and common understandings are jointly constructed. The more teams develop familiarity with collaborative problem solving and participatory decision-making techniques, the faster they produce valuable outcomes. And because time is an extremely precious resource in these settings, it is essential for coaches to introduce practices that are not only transformative but also efficiently implemented.

Transformational team KPIs

To help managers develop the perspective of a team coach, we asked them to assess the current state of their teams as indicated by the engagement survey data and by reflecting upon recent performance. Managers selected 1–2 'high impact' engagement dimensions that, if improved, would lead to significant performance improvements on the team.

From these insights, we facilitated a half-day session for the leader and team to co-create a Team Impact Plan. In these sessions, the teams developed a shared purpose, common goals, and norms and commitments. To craft the norms and commitments, teams discussed how to improve the engagement dimensions and selected behaviours to start, stop or continue in the months ahead.

We called these behaviours 'team growth edges'. In Hawkins parlance, these would be considered 'transformational team KPIs'.

Transformational team KPIs are:

- collectively created, owned, and committed to by the entire teams;
- not achieved by the current way its members currently operate; and
- require the team to change its behaviours, processes, ways of thinking and relating (Hawkins, 2017a: 351).

Over the course of five months, the teams experimented with different ways to improve their scores along these dimensions. Each team iteratively developed solutions that were tailored to their specific context and desired outcomes.

Some solutions were behavioural and others were more process- or structure-oriented. Examples of solutions include: adopting new feedback behaviours to improve individual performance, creating and developing a customer service 'wiki' for team knowledge-share, improving the tracking and evaluating of goal progress, creating protocols for cross-functional projects, clarifying roles and delegation processes, and reducing admin time for sales functions.

The power of collaborative leadership

In January 2018, Lever ran the engagement survey a second time to assess progress and uncover areas of opportunities for the subsequent team action learning cycles in the year ahead.

In terms of results, Lever increased its overall engagement score to 76 per cent (4 points above comparable tech companies). For the team transformational KPIs, teams improved their engagement scores by 20 per cent (on average) during this time period. We present the team-by-team results in the table below.

Table 12.1

Team	Transformational KPI	June 2017	January 2018	Delta
Engineering	We are encouraged to be innovative even though some of our initiatives may not succeed	54	48	−6
People	When it is clear that someone is not delivering in their role, we do something about it	22	33	11
People	Generally, the right people are rewarded and recognized at Lever	44	67	23
Product	I know what I need to do to be successful in my role	67	63	−4
Product	Most of the systems and processes here support us getting our work done effectively	50	88	38
Marketing	I know what I need to do to be successful in my role	50	100	50
Marketing	At Lever there is open and honest two-way communication	40	38	−2
CS – Corp/ SMB IS	When it is clear that someone is not delivering in their role, we do something about it	33	83	50
CS – Corp/ SMB IS	The information I need to do my job effectively is readily available	67	67	0
Customer Support	When it is clear that someone is not delivering in their role, we do something about it	33	50	17

(Continued)

Table 12.1 (Continued)

Team	Transformational KPI	June 2017	January 2018	Delta
Customer Support	The information I need to do my job effectively is readily available	67	50	−17
Sales – Corp/ SMB	I have access to the learning and development I need to do my job well	33	80	47
Sales – Corp/ SMB	I'm appropriately involved in decisions that affect my work	37	40	3
Sales – SDR	I have access to the learning and development I need to do my job well	33	100	67
Sales – SDR	When it is clear that someone is not delivering in their role, we do something about it	33	75	42
Average		44	65	21

As evident in the engagement data, some teams improved their scores considerably, while some progressed minimally or reversed slightly. To understand this variance, it is important to keep in mind that each engagement dimension is an outcome of interacting behaviours, processes and structures within each team. Some behaviours, processes and structures are easier to implement (and generate faster outcomes) than others. In addition, some managers were more skilled in implementing and integrating insights from the team coaching sessions (particularly the mid-level managers that were in the Leadership Accelerator), than others, for these managers had a deeper familiarity with the tools and techniques and more deftly put them to use with their teams. Lastly, it must also be remembered that this is the first time that the company had run an engagement survey cycle – and it was also the first time for managers and teams to collectively take ownership of that data and implement solutions to make progress.

As a result of this work, each of the eight teams is now led by a skilled manager-coach and has a set of collaborative leadership practices to draw from to raise issues quickly and solve problems collectively. Beyond these immediate results, there is a broader recognition within the organization that managers and teams have developed something with far greater implications – *the ability to lead collaboratively*. Lever's managers and teams have created the foundation for a dynamic and responsive organizational environment.

Bailen explains:

It's been really cool to see managers and teams diagnose areas of opportunity and then take action to drive up engagement together. Some went from 50 per cent to 100 per cent, which is just ridiculous over the course of 5 months. What has made this more powerful is that managers and teams worked together to make this happen – instead of the managers taking up the burden of having to come up with all the solutions, especially when they don't have all the answers or the full context to do so. As a manager myself who went through the programme, I would say the biggest change has been the ability to elevate the team's thinking so that team members say, 'I am here to not only contribute to my own growth and development and success, but for the team's growth and success'. It's been really transformative because we actually produce better outcomes as a team as a result.

The shift in mindset and behaviours from heroic to collaborative leadership, where team members take responsibility for their role and function, as well as for team and organizational goals, is ultimately what we're aiming for in this work (Hawkins, 2017b: 18). As a result of equipping managers with one-to-one and team coaching skills concurrently, and giving managers the opportunity to practise and apply those skills within the context of the real work of their teams, the organization is seeing benefits that go beyond the immediate goals set for the programme.

Below are a few reflections from managers about the experience:

'I feel empowered to give my direct reports more timely, actionable feedback because of our time in LAP and the GROW coaching model. In addition, feeling empowered to make changes in my team and our processes has helped us achieve a higher percentage of our goals, which has in turn made me feel more effective as a leader.'

'I always preached professional development, but it's hard to know what feels impactful and how to build on that continuously in a way that benefits each rep in an equal way. With the Individual Impact Plans, I have a clear structure and a framework for having conversations with my team that they've been craving.'

'I'm proud that I've set my team up for success with challenging but achievable goals that impact the business. They feel more connected to our team and the company because of the work we've been doing together.'

'The biggest change has been my ability to hold people accountable, while being direct and understanding (without being a pleaser or a pushover). I think I've done a better job being what the team needs and expects, and so I've been able to deliver better.'

'I am digging deeper into the drivers of our business and asking my team to dive deeper and be more thoughtful about their work in this way. By diving deeper, we've been able to uncover important insights that are helping shape our strategy and execution both in the short and long term.'

'I am more willing and committed to take those small steps toward achievement or goals instead of getting caught up in the details and failing to execute.'

'I am more prepared to manage my team, which allowed people to ramp more quickly and make a more immediate impact on our goals and thus our company.'

Recognizing that development is a journey, Lever plans to support its leaders and teams in flexing their newly created distributed leadership muscles in the near future and beyond

Conclusion

In returning to the questions posed at the beginning of the chapter, I'd like to draw out a few relevant insights for furthering the systemic team coaching craft in startup environments.

What does systemic team coaching look like in a fast-moving startup environment?

To do this work well in a startup, team coaches need to think like organizational development practitioners. Because most startups have yet to implement robust performance development systems and because most startup managers are relatively new to people development, there are rich opportunities to consider how to build a performance culture that is rooted in collaborative leadership principles from the ground up.

Startups are interested in cultivating their own unique approach to culture, while also hungry to learn what works well in similar contexts. To meet this need, it is helpful to offer approachable and customizable team coaching tools based on sound research. Startups are also very interested in building internal team coaching capacities. The conventional team coaching approach, which relies exclusively on an external provider, is not very compelling. Rather, startups are hungry to internally develop managers with these skills so that they can increase their value for the organization and save resources over the long term.

Also worth noting is the added value for startups when all teams engage in this work simultaneously. When conceived and implemented as a company-wide initiative, startups benefit from 1) shared learning and accountability amongst managers and within teams and 2) improved cross-functional capabilities.

Bailen remarks:

> In most organizations, you have some teams that are strong performers and really advanced in their development and other teams that are weak performers and are more junior in terms of experience. When they try to work with one another, they have totally different playing fields. The frameworks we now have create a system that optimizes cross-functional outcomes. Teams can deploy these frameworks as they are entering into team-based work or as they are interfacing with other parts of the business and it is not foreign to anybody.

One additional thing to consider when doing this work in a startup is that it is not necessary to start with the executive team. While it's essential to have executive sponsorship of the work, it's not a prerequisite for executives to have the experience of team coaching prior to successfully implementing these tools and frameworks with the rest of the organization.

In the case of Lever, we initially contracted to engage in executive team coaching when we started the mid-level management training. However, due to a series of events, the executive team was not able to meet for four of six planned sessions. Despite this turn, Lever successfully rolled out its team performance toolkit. Even though executives have yet to use these tools with each other, they have been using them with their functional teams.

Towards the end of 2017, the executive team expressed desire to pick up the team development work in the year ahead. Lever will also be running another Leadership Accelerator for its recently hired mid-level managers in early 2018 so that this knowledge is shared by subsequent waves of leaders.

How is team coaching approached by a new generation of leaders committed to purposeful work and personal growth? What are the critical few behaviours that startup leaders need to enable their teams to operate at peak performance?

Because of the generational affinity of today's young leaders to practices that foster greater collective purpose and harness 'the wisdom of the crowd', we have found that managers and team members alike are excited to learn these techniques and use them in their daily work. The power of setting and making progress on 'transformational team KPIs' has also had a marked impact on engagement levels within Lever and this influence will likely increase in the years ahead as teams develop greater familiarity and finesse with their applications.

In terms of the critical few behaviours, we have found that the skill sets described herein for owning one's growth, developing people, and empowering teams are essential for today's new managers. We have since developed a new module for leading the business that entails skills related to visioning, strategic planning and self-forming teams. Each of these skills build a leader's capacity to tap the collective intelligence of his/her team in order to further business objectives.

It's also worthwhile to consider inclusive behaviours as they relate to team performance. As mentioned, Lever has made significant inroads to ensure that its workforce is representative of diverse backgrounds. How does building a high performing, collaborative team culture further this mission? Google's Project Aristotle research (2012; see Rozovsky, 2015) identified two critical inclusive behaviours for team performance: distributed airtime and empathy. Amy Edmondson (1999) uncovered a third factor – psychological safety. This notion refers to a team environment where people feel safe to take risks. These three factors – distributed airtime, empathy, and psychological safety – are all foundational to the team performance approach we espouse within our work.

How can systemic team coaching enable startups to leap ahead of their competition and embrace agility in the face of an uncertain future?

We now turn to the final question posed at the beginning of this chapter. We surmise that a systemic team coaching approach that is complemented by a robust people analytics platform could be truly game-changing for organizations. The more reliable data an organization has about its internal dynamics, the better able it is to respond to its external environment.

Mike Bailen elaborates:

Many organizations go from point a to point b in a straight line. In contrast, we've set up a system where we can sense things along that path and move dynamically when we encounter different roadblocks, challenges or variables. We have to consistently look for ways to collect data points from all different angles along the way so that when we enter into structured conversations as a team, we can surface tension, take action quickly, and optimize success for the long run. Ultimately, we want to get the best inputs into our system so we can get the best outputs for our stakeholders – customers, investors and employees.

As a next step in developing its responsive organizational system, Lever will be implementing the goal tracking software solution, 15Five, to surface performance data at the individual, team and organizational levels. This data, especially when corroborated with engagement data, could be quite illuminating for leaders and teams in thinking strategically about how to focus development efforts.

Simply having access to this data is not a competitive edge. Most organizations are awash in data. What gives companies like Lever an edge is that they now have the frameworks and tools to deftly use that data to identify and shift behaviours as needed – whether that is to increase performance, improve an engagement dimension or decrease turnover. These are the kinds of things that most startups simply don't know how to target and improve in any significant or predictable way.

This is the real utility of systemic team coaching – it is the ability to perceive cause and effect relationships and successfully intervene in ways that continuously improve a team's capacity for results. Companies that do this well, when aided by reliable and signal-worthy data, will leapfrog ahead of their competition.

It is truly an exciting time to do this work. I am proud to be a part of its evolution, alongside a whole new generation of my peers who are called to lift the team coaching torch in the decades ahead.

Evaluation and assessment of teams and team coaching

13

PETER HAWKINS

Coming together is a beginning. Keeping together is progress. Working together is success.

(ATTRIBUTED TO HENRY FORD)

Introduction

In training and supervising team coaches for many years, I have become very aware of the challenges for team coaches in assessing the teams they are asked to work with, in both deciding whether to work with them and what approach would be most beneficial. In the early years of my own practice as a team coach, I would carry out the traditional approach of talking to each team member and asking them what they wanted from the team coaching. Too often, team members would answer by telling me what was wrong with their team leader, or their colleagues, and would be unsure what the purpose of the team was. More than one team member said: 'If we knew what development we needed, we would not need to employ you as team coach!'

I now realize the foolishness of my early approach, as (a) it is seeing the team members as the clients rather than the team as a whole, (b) it is based on the assumption that the team members know the development the team needs, and (c) it fails to start from the needs of the wider context that the team is there to serve. I started to ask more questions that were an open inquiry that started 'outside-in' and 'future-back':

- Who does your team serve? And who are your team's critical stakeholders?

- What do they value about your team and what do they need your team to do differently?

- What are the biggest challenges your team is likely to face over the next couple of years and how does your team need to change to face these challenges?

- In two years' time, what will your team regret not having dealt with today, or be pleased it did address in this team coaching?

The other big development in my craft was developing illuminative evaluation (Parlett and Dearden, 1977) tools that allowed the voice of the collective team to emerge. These included a Descriptor Analysis (Hawkins, 2017: 305–07), a High Performing Team Questionnaire (Hawkins, 2017: 301–05) and embodied and creative methods for the team dynamic to display itself (see Chapter 15). All these approaches were a means of enabling the team to listen to what the collective team was saying, not the team leader, team members or team coach, about their collective strengths and weaknesses, areas of development and the journey they needed to go on.

Increasingly I began to bring in the voices of the team's key stakeholders: their commissioners, investors, regulators, customers, partners, suppliers, employees, communities in which they operated and the 'more than human world' that provided the resources and the wider eco-system that sustained them. This I did by building wider 360° feedback elements into the diagnostics, having team members go and interview different stakeholder representatives and then, at a team session, step into the shoes of different stakeholders and speak from their perspective. Sometimes I would arrange for stakeholders to engage in person with the team coaching events.

The initial contract for the team coaching may just be with the team leader or the gatekeeper, such as the HR director. The fuller contract needs to be with the whole team and all its members, and the focus of the work needs to be larger still, based on the whole organizational, business, socio-economic and ecological systems in which the team operates and fulfils its purpose.

It is important that the team coach, be they the team leader, an internal team coach or an external team coach, starts their engagement with an inquiry that spans at least three levels of nested systems (see Chapter 16). These are:

- the ecological, business and socio-economic niche in which the team receives its commission, fulfils its purpose and operates;

- the team as a living system, with its own dynamics, interdependencies, life cycles etc;
- the team members, with their own histories, profiles, motivations and values.

This phase of inquiry can produce such rich and multi-layered seams and streams of data that it can become overwhelming, and to make sense of its richness without being overwhelmed, the team coach and team leader need strong assessment frameworks to shape the data.

Team Connect 360

Since the first edition of this book, I have worked with John Leary Joyce and the Academy of Executive Coaching, to create an online team 360° feedback instrument called 'Team Connect 360' (http://www.aoec.com/training/team-coach-training/team-connect-360/).

This is a powerful 360° diagnostic tool, which will provide the team (and the team coach) with valuable data and insights into the strengths and development areas of the team as a whole. It generates team feedback from both team members and a range of stakeholder groups, chosen in discussion with the team.

The tool is designed specifically around the Five Disciplines model so the questions cover:

- stakeholder expectations (Commissioning) – what the team is required to deliver by its stakeholders;
- team tasks (Clarifying) – what the team does to meet those expectations;
- team relationships (Co-Creating) – the interpersonal and leadership dynamics;
- stakeholder relationships (Connecting) – how the team connects with those it serves;
- team learning (Core Learning) – how the team grows and develops to meet future challenges.

There is an additional question set that covers:

- overall productivity – a summary of the team's record on their capacity to deliver. This gives a clear picture of how well the team is connected within its organizational system and what it can do to be more effective.

This is a great instrument to use in the Inquiry stage of team coaching, to generate data about the team instead of, or alongside, one-to-one interviews. It gathers data in a straightforward and user-friendly way for presentation to the team leader and team members, enabling conversation into key areas of focus for development. It is also an excellent measure of success by repeating the questionnaire at the end of the Systemic Team Coaching process.

What are the benefits?

- The requirement to seek stakeholder involvement sets the tone and approach for the systemic nature of the team coaching.
- Data is offered in a concise, tangible format, which is user-friendly and could be read and understood with minimal guidance from the coach. Once they read and explore the report, the team are able to quickly identify where team coaching can most add value.
- It is direct data so removes challenge of coach bias from interviews.
- The team coach or team members can still interview specific respondents for more clarity on their comments and additional feedback.
- It resolves issues of geography and time difference as data is collected online.
- Consistency – data is presented in a consistent format that is easy to understand by team members

How is the data gathered?

- Up to 50 respondents can be invited to complete a short online questionnaire that addresses the six areas for highly effective teams.
- For stakeholders there are just 3 questions in each of the 6 areas – simply requiring a numeric score between 1–5 plus an invitation to include written commentary in each discipline.
- For team members there are a further 2 questions in each area specifically addressing what is happening inside the teams that only they will know about.

Other useful assessment approaches

Zaccaro *et al* (2001), Hackman (1987), Salas *et al* (1992) and Gladstein (1984) all provide insight into how a team can be studied from many different perspectives and they outline four distinct perspectives:

- team cognitive processes;
- team motivational process;
- team affective processes;
- team coordination processes.

Most work on high-performing teams focuses on team coordination processes – how the team and the team leader organize the work of the team: their team purpose and objectives, how the team meets, its communication and so on (Kaztenbach and Smith, 1993; Wageman *et al*, 2008). Much less has been written about the collective cognitive, affective and motivational processes of the team and how these can be developed, whether by the team leader, the team coach or the team itself.

In this chapter I provide five such frameworks:

1 how to assess whether the team is a real team or just a reporting or work group or pseudo team;
2 the functional organization of the team and how it deploys its time and resources to carry out these functions;
3 the team energy and motivation;
4 the team in relationship to its commissioners, purpose, each other as fellow team members, its stakeholders and its own development;
5 the team maturity in both its cognitive and affective development.

Is this a team?

As mentioned above, there has been much more research and academic studies on teams and team performance than there has been on team coaching. What constitutes and defines a team is still a contested area and this has affected both clarity and consistency in the literature and the research.

Schippers *et al* (2014) refer to definitions of Tannenbaum *et al* (2012), Cohen and Bailey (1997), Devine *et al* (1999), Hackman (2002), Salas *et al* (2007) and West (2012) and point out how they include subtle yet theoretically meaningful differences. They then argue that:

> The problem of unclear or contested definitions raises crucial questions: What
> characteristics distinguish an authentic or real organizational team from
> a loose group of individuals perhaps co-acting in close physical or virtual
> proximity? Which individuals constitute team members and which individuals

are simply other organizational members who interact more or less closely with the team? How can we ensure that there is conceptual precision when accumulating and synthesizing research findings across studies on teams in organizations? Without greater precision about what characterizes a team, we cannot identify the types of collectives that warrant inclusion in our studies.

Following a comprehensive content analysis of existing definitions of teams, and a careful assessment of relevant theory, Richardson (2010: 86) defined a real team as:

> A group of people working together in an organization who are recognized as a team; who are committed to achieving team-level objectives upon which they agree; who have to work closely and interdependently in order to achieve those objectives; whose members are clear about their specified roles within the team and have the necessary autonomy to decide how to carry out team tasks; and who communicate regularly as a team in order to regulate team processes.

She went on to identify six criteria for assessing real teams:

1 Interdependence – the team has collective tasks that require them to work together.
2 Shared objectives – they have agreed collective objectives.
3 Autonomy – the team have defined areas where they can collectively decide.
4 Reflexivity – the team meets to reflect on how it is performing against its objectives and how it can learn and improve.
5 Boundedness – the team has clarity about its boundaries.
6 Specified roles – the team members perform different roles contributing to the collective performance.

Schippers *et al* (2014) contrasted real teams with what they termed pseudo teams, which they defined as:

> A group of people working in an organization who call themselves or are called by others a team; who have differing accounts of team objectives; whose typical tasks require team members to work alone or in separate dyads towards disparate goals; whose team boundaries are highly permeable with individuals being uncertain over who is a team member, and who is not; and/or who, when they meet, may exchange information but without consequent shared efforts towards innovation.

In Hawkins (2017: 32–34) I presented a useful tool for deciding whether the team was a real team or a work group. I have further developed this as I believe it is important to distinguish between:

- a reporting team where team members report into the team leader on their area of responsibility;
- an advisory team where team members also make suggestions to the team leader on areas where the team leader will then decide;
- a decision-making team where the team have some areas where they will make collective decisions, but the implementation will be done by individuals;
- a performance team where the team will also generate new thinking together and implement some of the decisions together;
- a leadership team where team members will represent the whole team in their engagement with a range of stakeholders.

In Chapter 8 Jarrett describes a team that started being a 'hub and spoke team' and gradually became an integrated leadership team.

The questionnaire in Table 13.1 can be completed by the team members, the team leader or the team coach and can give an indication of where the team is on the above continuum. The team leader or team members can also be asked where the team needs to be to meet the requirements of its commissioners and stakeholders as well as its own aspirations.

Table 13.1

Work group	Strongly agree	Agree	Neutral	Agree	Strongly agree	Real team
The team members have individual tasks which they report back on.						The team has collective tasks that require them to work together.
Strong clearly focused leadership.						Shared leadership roles.
They all have separate individual objectives.						They have agreed collective objectives.
Individual accountability.						Individual and mutual accountability.

(continued)

Table 13.1   (*Continued*)

Work group	Strongly agree	Agree	Neutral	Agree	Strongly agree	Real team
The team members make suggestions and the team leader decides.						The team have defined areas where they can collectively decide.
The group's purpose is the same as the broader organizational mission.						Team purposes are different from both the organizational mission and the sum of individual team member's objectives.
The team leader tells the individuals how they are performing.						The team meets to reflect on how it is performing against its objectives and how it can learn and improve.
Individual work products.						Collective work products.
The team performance is just the sum of the individual performances.						The team members perform different roles contributing to the collective performance.
Runs efficient agenda-based meetings.						Creates generative dialogue, with open discussion and active problem solving.

(*continued*)

Table 13.1   (*Continued*)

Work group	Strongly agree	Agree	Neutral	Agree	Strongly agree	Real team
Measures its effectiveness indirectly by its influence on others (eg financial performance of the business).						Measures performance directly by assessing collective work products.
Discusses, decides and delegates.						Discusses, decides and does real work together.
Members are only part of the group when they are together.						Members still act as part of the team when they are not together.
The group is task focused.						The team is task, process and learning focused.

Assessing the functions of the team

One relatively simple way to look at team functioning is to look at how it allocates its time, both in meetings and also in its functioning outside of meetings. I have developed a simple framework for exploring the functional tasks of teams, which can be used to carry out an analysis of where the team focuses its activity and time (Table 13.2). Renewal Associates has another version for board functions as well as one that looks at the use of time between meetings.

The model divides team functions into eight categories:

Coordinating: organizing how the team will operate; deciding who will do what; allocating time, people, roles, resources etc; agreeing priorities.

Briefing: communicating to the team updates on important news from other parts of the organization or the stakeholder context.

Table 13.2   Team function analysis

Team function	Percentage time spent on this function in our meetings	Percentage time we need to spend on this function in our meetings
Coordinating		
Briefing		
Informing		
Decision making		
Planning		
Generative thinking		
Nurturing and bonding		
Reflecting and learning		

Informing: team members feed back on their activities, progress and outcomes.

Decision making: making proposals, debating them, deciding.

Planning: planning how decisions will be communicated, implemented, monitored and evaluated.

Generative thinking: jointly creating new thinking and approaches that are more than the sum of individual team members' previous thinking.

Nurturing and bonding: any activities that help develop the commitment, loyalty, morale and relating within the team.

Reflecting and learning: reflecting on the team's actions, performance and behaviours and how these could be developed; feedback to team members or the whole team; team development.

Having filled in the Questionnaire, the individuals complete the following sentences:

1 We need to decrease our time on....

2 We could do this by....

3 We need to increase the time we spend on....

4 We could do this by...

The data is then collated, presented back to the team and explored.

This instrument helps the team to review, reflect and consciously shift the focus of their collective team time and efforts. Coyne and Nicol in Chapter 7 show how the team recognized that they needed to spend time on their reflection and learning and in Chapter 5 Carr's team were aware of how they needed more time devoted to generative thinking and less to briefing and informing.

Assessing team motivation and affective levels

Bruch and Vogel (2011) have developed an innovative approach to looking at organizational energy, which they define as:

> the force which an organization uses to purposefully put things in motion. Organizational energy is the extent to which a company, department, team has collectively mobilized its emotional, cognitive, and behavioural potentials in pursuit of its goals.

This can be applied to looking at the energy of the team. This combines looking at the motivational and affective elements of the team. Their model is based on a two by two matrix which distinguishes between the level of the intensity of the energy and the quality of the energy in producing positive or negative outcomes (see Figure 13.1).

Figure 13.1 What is the state of energy in your business, unit or team?

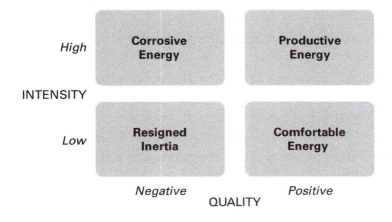

Figure 13.2   OEQ (Organizational Energy Questionnaire)

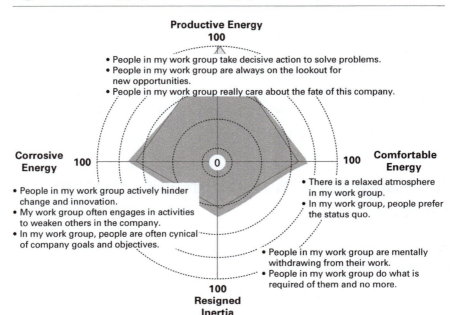

They have developed a questionnaire that is filled in by all team members and the collective scores can then be plotted on the team energy grid (Figure 13.2).

This helps plot where the team is on the matrix. Bruch and Vogel then provide a number of strategies for looking at how teams can move their energy to greater intensity and positiveness. These include:

1 Slaying the dragon (Bruch and Vogel, 2011: 62–85) – identifying and tackling the collective challenge that the team must address;

2 Winning the princess (pp: 85–101) – identifying the collective prize the team can achieve together, which mobilizes greater commitment and energy;

3 Detox your business (pp: 105–37) – identifying the processes and behaviours that creating corrosive energy and collectively deciding how to address them;

4 Sustaining the energy (pp: 173–233) – once the team has productive energy, the teams needs to create strategies for sustaining and building on this positive and productive climate.

If we look back at the case studies in this book, we can see how the different teams adopted different approaches based on the current context within which they were operating. Finnair, in Chapter 8, were focused on 'slaying the dragon' of the economic and business threats to their business, and Bruntwood in Chapter 7 utilized the economic recession to mobilize team energy. The Australian pharmaceutical company in Chapter 9 was focused on 'winning the princess' of greater innovation and in Chapter 4 the 'princess' was 'becoming a consultancy business with a strong identity and performance'. Both Jarrett (Chapter 8) and Peters (in Chapter 5) describe ways they surfaced the mistrust and toxic processes in their teams and developed processes for 'detoxing' the team's processes and behaviours. O'Sullivan and Field in Chapter 9 show how team coaching can help to 'sustain the energy' when there is a change in leader.

Team relationship to Hawkins' five disciplines of teams

In Chapter 2 I outlined useful evaluation questions for each of the five disciplines. I have since turned these questions, which you can use to evaluate either case studies or your own work with teams you lead or coach, into a questionnaire with a Likert-rating scale (see Likert, 1932). This can be used by team coaches or team leaders to assess the quality of the team's relationship with each of the five disciplines.

I invite you to fill in the questionnaire (Table 13.3), based on one of the earlier case studies, and/or on the team you lead and/or coach.

Scoring

Each item is scored (as shown in Table 13.4).

Calculating

The collective team score for each question is then calculated by adding the scores and dividing the total by the number of people in the team. For example, a team of seven people score +8 on a discipline, which when divided by 7 gives a score of 1.1429, which can be rounded up to a number with no more than two decimal places, which in this case is 1.15.

Table 13.3

	Strongly Disagree	Disagree	Neutral	Agree	Strongly Agree
1.1 The team has created an agreed-upon and inclusive list of all their commissioners (all those who have a right to require something from the team).					
1.2 This list includes the past and future commissioners – such as founders, future customers, possible potential buyers of the company.					
1.3 The team has a clear sense of what each commissioner needs from them to succeed and how they could inadvertently fail this commissioner.					
2.1 The team has co-created a mission, including purpose, strategy, core values and vision, that is better than the team leader or any team member could have created by themselves.					
2.2 The team has envisioned possible future emerging challenges.					
2.3 The team has stepped into the shoes and experience of each of their key stakeholders and clarified what their stakeholders need from them.					
2.4 The team has clarified their own aspirations.					
2.5 The team has field tested their emerging clarity through dialogue back with their commissioners, with their stakeholders and with those they lead.					

(continued)

Table 13.3 *(continued)*

	Strongly Disagree	Disagree	Neutral	Agree	Strongly Agree
2.6 The team has tried to live their aspirations and behaviours in their own meetings and in their engagements with staff and stakeholders and have refined them in the light of these trials.					
2.7 The team has at least 2 to 3 Team Key performance Indicators that they are collectively accountable for.					
3.1 There is shared ownership and leadership of the collective endeavour, team objectives and goals.					
3.2 The team members hold each other mutually accountable for individual and team agreements.					
3.3 The team generates new thinking together that is better than the individual thinking brought into the meetings.					
3.4 Team members intervene in a way that enables improvements in the process and functioning of the team, by for example: interrupting old stuck patterns; raising awareness of what is happening live in the room; reframing problems or challenges; mediating conflict; enabling new connections; and so on.					
4.1 The team has a clear, shared and inclusive list of all their key stakeholders.					

(continued)

Table 13.3 *(continued)*

	Strongly Disagree	Disagree	Neutral	Agree	Strongly Agree
4.2 The team has clarified who will take the lead responsibility for each stakeholder connection on behalf of the team.					
4.3 The stakeholders feel well informed, communicated with and engaged by the team.					
4.4 The stakeholders feel able to influence what the team does and how it engages.					
5.1 Team members can say what they have learnt and/or the capabilities and capacities they have developed in the past year that they would not have learnt or developed without their involvement with the team.					
5.2 The team can identify what they have learnt together and the collective capacities they have developed in the past year.					
5.3 The team has a plan for how they will enable the learning and development of each team member going forward.					
5.4 The team has a plan for how they will enable the learning and development of the team as a whole going forward.					

Table 13.4

Question	Strongly disagree −2	Disagree −1	Neutral 0	Agree +1	Strongly agree +2
1 Questions 1.1–1.3 can be added up and divided by 3 to give an average score for the Commissioning discipline.					
2 Questions 2.1–2.7 can be added up and divided by 7 to give an average score for the Clarifying discipline.					
3 Questions 3.1–3.4 can be added up and divided by 4 to give an average score for the Co-creating discipline.					
4 Questions 4.1–4.4 can be added up and divided by 4 to give an average score for the Connecting discipline.					
5 Questions 5.1–5.4 can be added up and divided by 4 to give an average score for the Core Learning discipline.					

Analysing

If the score is:

Between +1.5 and +2: the team has a strong hold on this discipline.

Between +1 and +1.5: the team functions well with this discipline – but not strongly established.

Between 0 and +1: this discipline is engaged with by the team but not yet established.

Between −1 and 0: this discipline is beginning to be perceived by the team, but not yet developed.

Between −2 and −1: this discipline is not yet perceived by the team.

Team maturity

The past 50 years have seen a great deal of study and publication about levels of adult development, with the recognition that we can continue to develop way beyond growing up, right until we die. This has often built on foundational work by psychologists Loevinger and Blasi (1976) and Kohlberg (1981), who all studied the capacity of adults to engage with moral and ethical complexity. In the past 20 years there has been a good deal of research and publication on how stages of adult development apply to levels of leadership maturity. My colleagues and I have worked a great deal with the model of leadership maturity developed by Bill Torbert (2004) and have written about this in Hawkins and Smith (2013: 62–70). His model can be viewed as being paralleled by other writers on leadership maturity levels, who describe, in ways that are simultaneously similar and different, the same maturational journey (Joiner, 2006; Collins, 2001; Jaworski, 2012; Laske, 2010; and Barrett 2010). My own model of Team Leader Maturity (Hawkins 2017 Chapter 12) can also be put alongside these models, as it shows how team leaders move from Team Manager, to Team Leader, to Team Orchestrator, to Team Coach.

I have created a table (Table 13.5) which shows these models alongside each other – each describing with slightly different language the journey from being merely self-serving, to being a contributor who is outer-directed, to someone who contributes some craft expertise, to a goal-focused manager or leader, and then moving into higher levels of leadership with more awareness of connecting task and process, being able to create transformation of thinking, and being able to innovate and creatively relate, live in the moment. Finally, several of the writers point to the highest stage of maturity being one that is of humility and service to a greater cause (Torbert, Collins, Jaworski and Barrett).

Levels of team maturity and development

Above we have mentioned six writers on leadership maturity, but the only one who has specifically applied his model to look at the collective maturity stages of a team is Richard Barrett (2010: 248–59), although a number of the other writers do refer to team development (Collins and Laske). Barrett suggests there are seven levels of team maturity, all of which build on each other:

Level 1: Survival Consciousness. Here the team is focused on its own survival; the need to have a mandate to operate; to have adequate resources, including: funding or income; people; technology; and the health and safety and well-being of employees.

Level 2: Relationship Consciousness. The team focuses on harmonious relationships between team members.

Level 3: Self-esteem Consciousness. This involves the team focusing on its performance and building collective pride in both its ways of operating and its outcomes.

Table 13.5 Leadership maturity models

Bill Torbert (2004)	Bill Joiner (2006)	Jim Collins (2001)	Jo Jarworski (2012)	Richard Barrett (2010)	Otto Laske (2010)	Hawkins (2014/2017)
Alchemist	Synergist	Level 5 Executive	Renewing Leaders	Service		Team Coach
Strategist	Co-creator	Level 4 Executive Leaders	Servant Leaders	Making a difference	Level 5 Leader	Team Coach/ Orchestrator
Individualist	Catalyst	Levels 3–4	Servant Leaders	Internal cohesion	Levels 4–5	Team Orchestrator
Achiever	Achiever	Level 3 Competent Manager	Achieving Leaders	Transformation	Level 4 Manager	Leader
Expert/ Technician	Expert	Level 2 Contributing Team Member	Achieving Leaders	Self-esteem	Levels 3–4	Team Manager
Diplomat	Conformist	Level 1 Capable Individual		Relationship	Level 3 Group communicator	
Opportunist			Self-centric Leaders	Survival	Level 2 Individualist	

Level 4: Transformation Consciousness. At this stage the team is more able to reflect on its own collective processes and engage in being a learning team. Team members start to take more responsibility, not just for their own area but also for the collective performance of the team.

Level 5: Internal Cohesion Consciousness. 'The focus is on developing a shared sense of team mission and a shared set of team values that align the overall vision and values of the organization and unleash the commitment and enthusiasm of team members.' All team members have a clear sense of how their work contributes to the team's success.

Level 6: Making a Difference Consciousness. Here the team is focused on building collaborative partnerships with all its key stakeholders. These include:

- other teams in the organizations, whether they be more senior, or junior in the hierarchy, or peer teams they need to work well with;
- customers and suppliers;
- investors and regulators.

The team is focused on delivering excellent product and service to these stakeholders and having a good reputation in their eyes. At this stage the team becomes more interested in a team 360° feedback from all its stakeholders and in inter-team coaching.

Level 7: Service Consciousness. Here the team is focused on being a collective force for good, creating sustainable value for all its stakeholders, not only those listed in level 6, but also the local communities in which the team operates and the 'more than human world' of the wider natural ecology.

Barrett goes on to describe what he calls a 'full spectrum team', which is a team that can deal maturely with all seven levels of team consciousness. These are teams that can hold all seven foci and therefore have:

1 a clear mandate, financial stability and funding as well as concern for the health and well-being of the employees;

2 harmonious relationships and good communication;

3 results, quality, systems and excellence that engender team pride;

4 joint responsibility and shared leadership within the team and the team engages in joint reflection, learning and development;

5 clarification of the team's collective endeavour and team charter, including its vision, values and behaviours;

6 regular, effective connection and collaboration with teams up, down and across the organization and also with their key stakeholders;

7 a focus on how they can make a sustainable difference in the world and leave a lasting legacy.

The ability of a team to move through these developmental stages and achieve full-spectrum maturity will depend on a number of factors, including:

- Its stage of historical development – is it just forming, a relatively new endeavour or a team that has been together for some time?
- Its organizational context – does it have a clear mandate from the wider organization, with the necessary funding, resourcing of people and technology?
- Its business context – for example, is it fighting to survive in a declining competitive market or well placed in a growing market?
- The maturity of the team leader – where is the team leader functioning as seen through the lens of the Hawkins team leader maturity model (see Hawkins, 2017) with its four stages of (a) a team manager, (b) team leader, (c) team orchestrator, (d) team coach? In this model a team manager will mainly focus on levels 1 and 2; a team leader on levels 1–3; a team orchestrator on levels 1–6; and a team coach on levels 1–7.
- The time and attention given to the team's coaching and development.

If we look back at the case studies, it is possible to chart the maturation of a number of the teams that are presented. For example, in Chapter 10 on the hospital leadership team, the team started off at level 1, focusing on how they survived and reached their externally set targets, and then built internal cohesion among the team members and with the three new team members, who were clinical directors (level 2). Together they built a sense of their objectives for developing the hospital's strategy, culture and leadership (levels 3, 4, 5) and then worked collaboratively with other parts of their system (board, governors, directorate leadership teams, local hospital partners, local community-based health practitioners and so on) to build collaborative partnerships and focus on how they could transform the wider health system (level 6) and leave a lasting legacy (level 7).

I invite you to use the model for one of the other case studies and then try applying it to the team you lead and/or coach.

Aligning team coaching approaches to levels of team consciousness

I am often asked 'How do you know if a team is ready for team coaching?' by coaches who have had as part of their coach training the concept of 'coaching readiness'. I now reply that there is a better question: 'What type of team coaching do they need considering their level of development?'

This question necessitates that we have a good assessment framework for ascertaining the level of development of the team (as above). Then as team coaches we need to have a framework for applying different team coaching designs to the differing needs and development levels of the team.

So if we look at the seven levels of team consciousness outlined above, we can look at how this can connect to the Hawkins five discipline model of both teams (Hawkins, 2017: 45–60) and team coaching (Hawkins, 2017: 100–122) and how the discipline focus will change at different developmental stages (Table 13.6).

We can then look at what team coaching processes and methods would be most useful to help the team develop within the level of consciousness for that particular stage (Table 13.7).

It is also useful to look at the team coaching interventions that help a team shift their consciousness from one level to the next. These need to

Table 13.6   Linking levels of team conscious to the five team disciplines

Level of team consciousness: Barrett (2010)	Team coaching discipline: Hawkins (2011, 2014, 2017)
Level 1: Survival Consciousness	Discipline 1: Commission
Level 2: Relationship Consciousness	Discipline 3: Co-creating
Level 3. Self-esteem Consciousness	Discipline 2: Clarifying
Level 4: Transformation Consciousness	Discipline 5: Core learning
Level 5: Internal Cohesion Consciousness	Disciplines 2 and 3: Clarifying and Co-creating
Level 6: Making a Difference Consciousness	Discipline 4: Connecting and Collaborating
Level 7: Service Consciousness	Disciplines 1–5: Iterative and Integrated

Table 13.7 Possible coaching methods for the various levels

Level of team consciousness: Barrett (2010)	Team coaching discipline: Hawkins (2011, 2017)	Examples of team coaching methods
Level 1: Survival Consciousness	Discipline 1: Commission	Coaching the team leader and organizational sponsors on achieving a clear commission and appropriate people and resources for the team.
Level 2: Relationship Consciousness	Discipline 3: Co-creating	Shared psychometrics and 360s; clarifying team roles; interpersonal feedback; Cape Cod approach/process consultancy
Level 3. Self-esteem Consciousness	Discipline 2: Clarifying	Coaching the team to clarify their collective endeavour, agree their strategic focus; set team and individual goals and key performance indicators
Level 4: Transformation Consciousness	Discipline 5: Co-learning	Use of team assessments – High Performing Team Questionnaire, Descriptor Analysis. Reflecting on the team's past, current and future – timeline mapping; team culture; three-way sort
Level 5: Internal Cohesion Consciousness	Disciplines 2 and 3: Clarifying and Co-creating	Clarifying the fuller aspects of the team charter, including values, behaviours, commitments
Level 6: Making a difference Consciousness	Discipline 4: Connecting and Collaborating	Stakeholder mapping; obtaining stakeholder feedback, agreeing lead and development for each key stakeholder relationship
Level 7: Service Consciousness	Disciplines 1–5: iterative and integrated	Addressing: Who does the team serve? What can it uniquely do that the world of tomorrow needs? What is the legacy it is committed to creating?

speak to the level the team are currently focused upon as well as engaging them with the next level of maturity:

Level 1 transforming to level 2: Once you have the necessary mandate and resources, how will you need to connect together to fulfil the mandate?

Level 2 transforming to level 3: Now you are connecting and forming as a team, what do you want to collectively achieve together?

Level 3 transforming to level 4: Having clarified your purpose and collective endeavour, how does this require you to function differently as a team?

Level 4 transforming to level 5: How does the team become more than the sum of its parts to deliver the transformation that is needed?

Level 5 transforming to level 6: How do your stakeholders need you to step up to the next level of value creation?

Level 6 transforming to level 7: What is the legacy this team could create in the world? What and whom can the team uniquely serve?

Assessing team maturity

I have developed and tested a method of assessing the maturity level of a team:

a simple Likert (1932) rating-scale test against the seven key statements listed. This is filled in individually by each team member. From these individual scores a team profile is produced.

Table 13.8 The Brief Team Maturity Questionnaire

		Strongly disagree	Disagree	Neutral	Agree	Strongly agree
1	The team has a clear mandate, financial stability and funding as well as focusing on the health and well-being of the employees.					
2	The team has harmonious relationships and good communication.					

(continued)

Table 13.8   (*continued*)

	Strongly disagree	Disagree	Neutral	Agree	Strongly agree
3 The team focuses on its collective results, quality outputs, and systems and this engenders team pride.					
4 The team takes joint responsibility and shared leadership within the team and the team engages in joint reflection, learning and development.					
5 The team clarifies the team's collective endeavour and team charter, including its vision, values and behaviours.					
6 The team regularly connects and collaborates effectively with teams up, down and across the organization and also with their key stakeholders.					
7 The team has a strong focus on how they can make a sustainable difference in the world and leave a lasting legacy.					

Scoring

Each item is scored:

Table 13.9

	Strongly disagree	Disagree	Neutral	Agree	Strongly agree
Question	−2	−1	0	+1	+2

Figure 13.3   A team graph of maturational levels

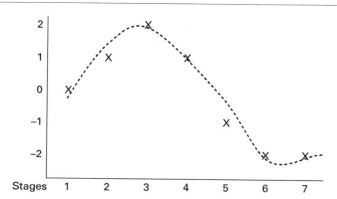

Calculating

The collective team score for each question is then calculated, by adding the scores and dividing this by the number of people in the team. For example, a team of seven people scores +8 on a question, which when divided by 7 gives a score of 1.1428, which can be rounded up to a number with no more than two decimal places, which in this case is 1.14.

Analysing

The various scores for each of the seven questions, each linked to one of the seven stages, can be placed on a grid as in Figure 13.3. From this the sense of the dominant level of team maturity is assessed. The example shows a team who are very strongly in the stage of 'self-esteem' moving into the transformation stage.

Conclusion

In this chapter I have explored a number of ways of assessing and evaluating teams, including:

1   how to assess where the team is on the continuum between a work group, reporting team, decision-making team and performance team;

2   the functional organization of the team and how it deploys its time and resources to carry out these functions;

3   the team energy and motivation;

4 the team in relationship with its commissioners, purpose, each other as fellow team members, its stakeholders and its own development;

5 the team maturity in both its cognitive and affective development.

Each of these provides signposts and guidance for what team coaching process might be most helpful, both to match the current state of the team and also to help the team focus on the transition to their next stage of development.

In using any of these methods it is important to remember:

- They are just perspectives and never tell the full story.
- The team is much richer and more complex than can be captured by any instrument.
- The development of a team is never a linear journey.
- Team development is not always progressive and teams sometimes go backwards before making new progress.
- Many windows on a team is much more illuminating than a single approach.

My hope is that this chapter will add to your current perspectives and produce more light.

Coaching the board

14

How coaching boards is different from coaching executive teams, with case examples from the private, public and voluntary sectors

PETER HAWKINS AND ALISON HOGAN

The contribution of the board to the continued future of the organization is principally dependent on the behaviour, experience and skills of its members.

(KAKABADSE, KNYGHT AND KAKABADSE, 2013: 360)

The difficult task is to respectfully change corporate board's mind-sets in the currently competitive geo-political environment in which humanity may face risk.

(WORLD ECONOMIC FORUM, 2012)

Introduction

We invite you to go on to the world wide web, choose a range of well-known or local companies from different sectors and look for the section of their website on the board of the company. Notice what they say and what they feature. We randomly chose 10 companies in different sectors and with different country headquarters. Every one featured photos of individual board members – mostly men in dark suits – with short biographies listing their achievements. None of them started by looking at why the board existed, whom it served, nor what it was collectively there to achieve. None showed the board as a team together.

When commenting on this to several boards with whom we have worked, many responded by mentioning, somewhat defensively, that they talked elsewhere about the organization's vision, values, and commitment to customers, employees, the environment and so on. We then asked them how this was echoed in presentations made by their board. Interestingly, one board then acknowledged that this pattern was echoed in how they did their AGM – a series of individual talking heads speaking down at the investors from the stage, with no visibility of customers, sustainability nor employee focus in the room, except in words.

The global context in which boards operate

Never have boards been more powerful, more challenged or more in the public gaze. The Swiss Federal Institute has suggested that international corporations control 40 per cent of global wealth (Vitali *et al*, 2011). Kakabadse and Kakabadse (2008) argue that we are seeing unprecedented weakened government control against increasingly dominant corporations. Many sectors have seen enormous consolidation. Just one example would be the UK food industry, where 70 per cent of market share is with just five companies whose boards are in the hands of no more than 140 people (Welch, 2012). Many international companies have much greater GDP than many countries, and more global influence and control.

Boards carry accountability for organizations that are ever more complex, with greater diversity of stakeholders, global interdependency, in a more volatile and unpredictable world. Boards have great responsibility but very limited control.

This growth in power, combined with much-publicized corporate scandals such as Enron, Lehman Brothers, British Petroleum, Royal Bank of Scotland, The Co-operative Group in the UK and many others, has led to demands for greater transparency, accountability and governance. Business leaders have a very low level of trust from the general public; far lower than those in the traditional professions of medicine, law and accountancy and only just ahead of politicians and journalists.

Public trust in large companies and their boards fell even lower following the economic crisis of 2008–9 and, although in some countries it has recovered a little, in Western Europe and North America, less than half of respondents trust business leaders to tell the truth (eg UK 42 per cent and United States 38 per cent (Edelman, 2012). Between 2016 and 2017 The Edelman Trust Barometer reported that trust in the credibility of boards had fallen from 45 per cent to 35 per cent (Edelman 2017), even slightly lower than CEOs! It also showed a growing support globally for governments to bring in more controls on business.

In response to the outcry from investors, lobby groups, campaigners and others, there has been a proliferation of corporate governance codes from governments, professions and regulatory bodies (including the Sarbanes–Oxley Act 2002; UK Codes of Corporate Governance 1992–2018; Financial Regulatory Commission 2012; Vienot Reports 1995–99, 2000; Organisation for Economic Co-operation and Development 1999, 2004).

Much of the response to the boardroom crisis has been to focus on the form of the board rather than the substance of how it works: to focus on the inputs to the board rather than the performance that creates the positive outcomes. Corporate codes and legislation have demanded changes in board membership, training, reporting, evaluation and so forth, but for some organizations this has been met with a conformance response, ticking the necessary boxes.

Never have boards been so in need of help and support in developing their collective capacity to rise to the growing challenge and expectations. Leadership and Systemic team coaching is still in its infancy (Hawkins, 2011, 2014, 2017). Board coaching is even further behind. Very few boards have ventured beyond carrying out a board evaluation exercise every two or three years to receive ongoing help in how they can systematically develop their collective effectiveness over time. In this chapter, we will explore the growing sophistication of the board evaluation process and how this can lead to development plans supported by ongoing board coaching. But first we must be clear about the role and purpose of boards and how we understand board effectiveness.

The role of the board and board effectiveness

To coach the board of a listed or unlisted company, a partnership, or a governmental or not-for-profit organization requires first that the coach can help the board to be clear about its purpose and its unique role in the organization and the wider system of which it is a part. Also, if the board coach is to help the board become more effective, the coach needs to understand the nature of board effectiveness.

Bob Tricker, back in 1984, provided a very simple definition of the board's role when he said that if management is about running the business, governance is about seeing that the business is run properly.

Chait, Ryan and Taylor (2005) take the concept of governance further in reframing the work of non-profit boards. They propose that governance is seen as leadership. While leadership has become a dynamic, multidimensional concept, 'the tendency with governance has been to clarify and codify conventional practice. The conversation centres more around lists of "dos and don'ts" than around compelling or competing concepts of governance.' They suggest that leadership and governance are more closely related, and the more clearly this linkage is seen, the brighter the prospects will be for better governance (Chait *et al*, 2005).

While the focus of their work is on not-for-profit boards, their insights are equally relevant to corporate boards. Likewise, much of the corporate governance guidance for limited companies is equally relevant for public sector and not-for-profit boards and as far as the work of the board coach goes in helping boards to become more effective and high performing, there is much in common.

The range of stakeholders may vary but what they share is the responsibility to know who those stakeholders are and to know that their organization is 'run properly in the service of whom and what'.

Van den Berghe and Levrau (2013: 156, 179) consider 'a board to be effective if it facilitates the creation of value added for the company, its management, its shareholders and all its relevant stakeholders'.

This fits with the stewardship theories of boards and the approaches advocated by the 'Tomorrows Company' organization since its inception by the Royal Society of Arts Manufacture and Commerce in the UK in the 1990s. They argue that a board should be able to account for the value an organization has received from each of its key stakeholder groups and the added value it has returned to each group. At a minimum, these stakeholder groupings include investors, customers, regulators, suppliers, business partners, employees, communities within which the organizations operate, and the natural environment or 'more than human world' which provides the wider eco-system and most of the primary resources for the organization.

Van den Berghe and Levrau (2013: 163–64) posit four key roles for the board:

- making sure the organization has the right leadership;
- deciding on the strategic direction of the company and how this is realized;
- monitoring execution and results (including the governance scan and board evaluation);
- advisory/support function.

This academic perspective echoes the view of Niall Fitzgerald, who, soon after moving from the position of CEO and Chairman of Unilever to become Chairman of Reuters, defined the role of the board as follows:

1 Decide which skills are needed on the board.

2 Agree the strategy and keep it under review.

3 Focus on profitable growth with acceptable risk.

4 Safeguard the brand and corporate reputation.

5 Give directors access to detailed information.

6 Expose the board to younger talent in the company.

7 Discussion should be open, candid and trusting. (Boardroom Agenda, Niall Fitzgerald, *Financial Times*, 27 September 2005)

From board evaluation to board coaching

There has been an increasing call for all boards to have regular board evaluation, but for many boards this has been a somewhat cursory scan of their governance and a tick-box exercise to check that the important regulatory processes were in place. Carter and Lorsch (2004) advocate the importance of evaluations going beyond reporting on governance processes: 'Fancy statements about the company's corporate governance practices may look good in the annual report and make some shareholders feel good, but they don't in and of themselves make boards more effective.'

Increasingly, boards are introducing more thorough evaluation processes, using a board evaluation questionnaire and/or interviews with each of the individual board members. The themes and issues are then fed back to a board meeting agenda on board performance and process. Some boards carry out this process internally, led by the chairman or the senior independent director. Other boards commission an external board evaluator to carry out the process. This has the advantage of bringing in someone who is independent of the internal politics, culture and collective ways of thinking of the board, as well as having evaluated other boards and so be able to draw out similarities and contrasts.

The Walker report (2009: 4.39) into board governance emphasized both the independence and the capability of the board evaluator to create a robust and effective evaluation process. This has become easier to assess as the wider adoption of evaluation has resulted in there being more evaluators with greater experience. Indeed, some boards select a different evaluator every few years to ensure that the consultant has not become too close to the organization.

Further rigour and sophistication can be added to this evaluation through 360° feedback on the collective board. This can be collected from a variety of sources, including the executive teams that report to the board, key investor or membership groups who elect the board and a review of analysts' and press commentary on the company and its governance. We have developed a simple 360° questionnaire that can compare data from the board members with external perspectives and can be filled in online.

Kakabadse and Kakabadse (2008) recommend complementing this process further with the use of assessment and profiling tools for individual directors. While this may not be necessary annually, it provides: an overview for the chairman of the range of skills, experience and participation of individual board members; some evidence from which to offer feedback on their performance; and also as an input into succession planning. Many companies will include a process for appraising the chairman, which will typically be conducted by the vice chairman or senior independent director.

Board evaluation, although a great improvement on governance scans, provides only the foundation for board development. Van den Berghe and Levrau (2013: 145) argue that follow-up appraisals, on the items that are selected for improvement, are essential. A quality board evaluation, whether done internally or externally, should lead to a board development plan with specific commitments to change processes, actions and behaviours. It should also include how the board will take forward its own development, based on what has emerged in the evaluation.

The quality of improvement in board effectiveness will depend on the commitment and openness of the board to take on board the feedback and address the developmental issues that are raised. The role of a skilled board coach can be pivotal in this developmental process.

Thus, evaluation is the first phase of a board coaching process and covers the CID phase of the team coaching process model (Hawkins, 2017). This includes (C) initial Contracting, (I) Inquiry and investigation (the evaluation process) and (D) the Diagnosis, discovery and design phase in which the board co-create and commit to the development plan.

The subsequent coaching process will vary depending, in part, on the openness of the chairman and board to committing to their own development and to accommodating the presence of an external coach. The focus may be on coaching the chairman on how they lead the board; working jointly with the chairman and CEO on their relationship; attending some board meetings and providing live process consultancy and feedback;

facilitating board development workshops; facilitating inter-board workshops where two boards need to work together on a joint venture, merger or other collaboration; or coaching board members before and after important presentations to stakeholders.

The board as a leadership team

The board of an organization is a very special form of leadership team. It consists of a number of directors who are accountable, in law, for the good governance of the organization. While the precise role and composition of a board will vary, there are some underlying principles that are common to all, including their purpose, which, as outlined in the UK Corporate Governance Code, is to facilitate effective, entrepreneurial and prudent management that can deliver the long-term success of the company (Financial Reporting Council, 2011: 1).

This is a particular challenge for any board, as its members do not have day-to-day responsibility for the operational management of the company. The scale of this challenge has become all the greater in recent years as the level of scrutiny of boards has increased against a backdrop of an uncertain global environment, economic turmoil and a series of corporate crises. Stakeholders have become more vocal and active in their concerns – as shareholders, customers, employees and citizens. The concept of stewardship, by the board on behalf of its stakeholders, has emerged as a much clearer and defined responsibility for companies, from global enterprises to family-owned businesses.

The growth, in many countries, of governance codes and increased regulation and scrutiny has sought to establish higher standards of board practice and effectiveness. However, as corporate crises and organizational failures continue, it is clear that improved structures and processes are insufficient on their own. Equally important is the human dynamics within the board: that members understand and embrace the spirit as well as the letter of their governance code.

Against this backdrop of change and uncertainty, boards are increasingly seeking external help to improve their own performance in four key areas:

1 To build a board that consists of the best individuals available who have a complementary mix of skills and experience and to reinvigorate the board continuously by managing recruitment and retirement procedures.

2 To create a climate of openness, challenge and productive dialogue encouraging the right group dynamics.

3 To facilitate a regular board review of structures and processes to ensure that the board can demonstrate its adherence to standards of good governance and is continually improving levels of performance and effectiveness.

4 To draw on the combined experience of all members, bringing the outside in and future back, to offer insights and guidance on strategy and risk and to engage with the wider organization and its stakeholders through periods of significant change.

Chait *et al* (2005), in proposing governance as leadership, describe three modes of governance – fiduciary, strategic and generative – that together enable board effectiveness:

- *Type I, Fiduciary*: includes the stewardship of tangible assets, technical oversight to ensure accountability based on performance metrics of facts, figures, finances and reports.

- *Type II, Strategic*: includes analysis, the shaping of strategy, the review of performance and management plans, the ability to envision and shape institutional direction.

- *Type III, Generative*: includes generative thinking, reflection, sense-making, framing questions.

They suggest that the most effective boards will have the ability to work effectively and move appropriately across all three modes. The benefits of the Fiduciary and Strategic modes are widely recognized. The payoffs from the Generative mode are not as broadly appreciated, because fewer boards regularly practise Type III governance.

Chait *et al* also offer a useful lens through which to appraise the value a board brings, conceptualizing it as a source of capital, beyond money. The four forms of capital are Intellectual, Reputational, Political and Social. The value realized rests on how well their potential as a resource is optimized. The forms apply equally to corporate and not-for-profit boards and whether board members are trustees, directors or governors. (See Table 14.1.)

Such a lens, when introduced in the process of board coaching, can help boards to consider whether they are, indeed, realizing their full potential as a resource to the organization.

Table 14.1   The four forms of board capital

Form of capital	Resource optimized	Traditional use	Enhanced value
Intellectual	Organizational learning	Individual board members do technical work	Board as a whole does generative work
Reputational	Organization legitimacy	Organization trades on board members' status	Board shapes organizational status
Political	Organizational power	External heavyweight: board members exercise power on the outside	Internal fulcrum: board balances power on the inside
Social	Efficacy of the board	Board members strengthen relationships to gain personal advantage	Trustees strengthen relationships to bolster board's diligence

The five disciplines of a highly-effective board

Boards may draw on external expertise in recruitment, board evaluation and strategy. However, to address all these areas of performance in an integrated way that also addresses behaviours requires systemic team coaching skills tailored to the unique characteristics of a board. To demonstrate this, we draw on the five disciplines of a high-performing team, which, with some refining, are as applicable to a board as they are to any other kind of team. They also demonstrate some of the shared characteristics and endeavour of all boards, be they listed companies, start-ups, charities or others in the not-for-profit sector.

In this chapter, we will describe each of the disciplines as they apply to a board, drawing on real examples. While acknowledging that a board is not a team in the more widely accepted definition of a team (see Chapter 1), the evidence shows that an effective board shares many of the characteristics of a team. Like teams, they flourish when there are high levels of openness, transparency and collaboration, and some chairmen are quite explicit in encouraging a team spirit. According to one FTSE 100 chairman, 'They're not teams in the same sense of an executive team but they need to be really constructively working together.' Another suggests that 'it is a bit like being a conductor in an orchestra' (Hogan, 2012: 8).

We have intentionally chosen to give examples from different countries, many of which have different governance codes and board structures; from different sectors; and from different sizes and types of organization. In *Leadership Team Coaching* (Hawkins, 2017), the companion to this book, detailed descriptions of the various board structures that different countries and sectors use are provided.

In spite of differences in structure, all boards share in common a commitment to good governance. A succession of corporate crises and failures in corporate governance has resulted in a body of guidance that is the culmination of extensive consultation and review. In those boards who aspire to excellence, they acknowledge the need to fulfil the spirit as well as the letter of codes of best practice. This overarching commitment to good governance can be mapped to the five disciplines of Commissioning, Clarifying, Co-creating, Connecting and Core Learning. This includes the underlying principles of corporate governance reviews and codes of conduct. Thus, statements from the proposed revisions to the UK Corporate Governance Code, Financial Reporting Council, 2018, can be matched to the five disciplines:

Commissioning 'A successful company is led by an effective and entrepreneurial board, whose function is to promote the long-term sustainable success of the company, generate value for shareholders and contribute to wider society. The board should establish the company's purpose, strategy and values, and satisfy itself that these and its culture are aligned.'

Clarifying 'The board should ensure that the necessary resources are in place for the company to meet its objectives and measure performance against them. The board should also establish a framework of prudent and effective controls, which enable risk to be assessed and managed.'

Co-Creating 'The board sets the framework within which a healthy corporate culture can develop, that underpins the way in which the company operates. It then satisfies itself that the culture throughout the organization is consistent with that framework, leading by example and taking action where it spots misalignment.'

Connecting 'Companies need to respect a wide range of stakeholder interests and take account of the impact of their decisions on them. To do this, directors must develop and maintain an understanding of the interests of these stakeholders.'

Core Learning 'It is vital that non-executive directors make sufficient time available to discharge their responsibilities effectively. They should devote time to developing and refreshing their knowledge and skills, including those of communication, to ensure that they continue to make a positive contribution to the board.'

Developing a highly-effective board

In looking at the development of a high-performing board, we draw upon examples from a wide range of boards we and our colleagues have coached in various sectors and parts of the world, in particular an international company board headquartered in Europe, the board of one of the UK's largest housing associations and the governing body of a school, the Supervisory Board of one of the big four professional services firms, and the Board of the largest fruit companies in South Africa.

In each of the examples, a board evaluation was undertaken at the outset based on the Five Disciplines Questionnaire. The questionnaires were supplemented with individual interviews of board members. This process of inquiry was helpful in highlighting the areas that were working well and where there was room for improvement. It also provided a benchmark against which to measure the board's development over time, individually and collectively.

Commissioning

Coaching a board on the discipline of its commission is essential at the establishment of an organization and its board and is an area that must be revisited at every board evaluation.

Some questions that are helpful in this area include:

a Who appoints the board? (Shareholders, partners, members depending on the nature of the board). What are they looking for the board to achieve?

b Who else does the board serve? (Employees, customers, suppliers/partners, regulators, local communities and environment). What do they need the board to achieve?

c Does it have enough clarity in its mandate? Is it clear what it must deliver, to whom it is accountable?

d What are the core functions of the board? Is there clarity of expectation in how these should be prioritized and carried out?

e Does it have the requisite diversity and capabilities? How are members selected, appointed and inducted?

In all examples, the coaches supported the boards in developing or revisiting their purpose, values, vision and strategy for the organization. For example, the housing association recognized that, with significant changes in its sector, they needed to look to the future and agree who they were here to serve today and tomorrow, and how to ensure that the customer voice would be heard. The international company recognized that the changing focus of the business required a change in its ownership structure and governance.

The discipline of Commissioning ensures that the board has clarity in its mandate and boundaries and the necessary resources to fulfil the mandate.

Clarifying

Once clear on its Commission, the board is better placed to clarify its collective endeavour and shared accountability: its roles and responsibilities to achieve good governance on behalf of the organization and all its stakeholders.

It can be helpful to start by facilitating the board to complete some key questions or statements. This can be done in open debate or through a collective build. The collective build is a dialogical process that encourages individuals to first write down their own completion of proposed beginning sentences by themselves, in between 3–5 bullet points. When they have done this the coach asks one member to share their top point and then others add to it so that a collective response is built, generatively. Once a response has been fully developed, someone offers a new idea and the process is repeated.

A collective build has the advantage of ensuring that the board taps into the diversity of individual independent thinking. Many boards and much board literature talk about the importance of independent thinking by directors and board dialogue, but few institute processes that enable this.

Statements for clarifying could include:

a This board creates value for the rest of the organization and its stakeholders by....

b To achieve our purpose this board needs to focus on....

c The objectives by which we will measure our achievement are....

d By when and by whom....

In the case of the school governing body, the board considered their individual and collective roles, the unique contribution that they could make and how best this would be achieved. Similarly, the housing association board considered how they could best contribute, individually and collectively, so that they could be better leveraged as a resource.

There are a number of tools and frameworks that board coaches can draw on to encourage boards to understand and clarify their functions, roles and responsibilities. For example, a simple functional analysis questionnaire provides a list of key board functions and asks each board member to list the percentage of time the board is currently spending across the functions and the percentage of time they think they should be spending. This exercise has enabled a number of boards to radically reconstruct their meeting agendas.

The final area of board Clarifying is about roles and structures. This includes what should be dealt with by standing or ad hoc board committees and what should come to the full board; the roles and expectations of individual directors, including chairman, senior independent director, subcommittee chairs, non-executives and executive directors.

The board coach to the school governing body facilitated a process whereby the board discussed the unique contribution that they could make and how this was best achieved. In one example, a governor with significant financial experience was not a member of the finance committee because at the time of his appointment, there was not a vacancy. This was rectified.

The board coach can play a very important role in facilitating the feedback to individuals by other board members and also the two-way inter-group feedback between executives and non-executives. Thus, in the case of the international company, the chairman and managing director were coached on how to take forward the development of the board, the executive team and the relationship between the two.

Another critical area for clarification is for the board to understand how it represents different stakeholder perspectives and brings them 'live' into board meetings. The international company board undertook the following exercise. They were divided into four teams each representing one of their key stakeholder groups. Each group spent some time preparing questions and challenges for the board from their stakeholder perspective. In turn, they presented back in role to the others who acted as the board. Each group highlighted two to three critical issues for the board to address.

The impact of the exercise was dramatic. It enabled board members to stand in the shoes of competitive groups and clearly identified a critical stakeholder contention and the importance of finding a solution to enable the business to move forward.

Co-creating

One of the most challenging areas of board development is in addressing interpersonal and team dynamics. The chairman should take the lead in encouraging a climate of openness and transparency but the support of the board coach can be pivotal in encouraging the board to co-create a culture of collaboration and shared accountability. Board reviews consistently show that group dynamics are the hardest element of board effectiveness to address. However, the clearer the board is about its purpose, collective endeavour and its roles and responsibilities, the easier it becomes to address any behavioural issues.

A constant challenge for a unitary board is how to create an environment in which non-executive directors have sufficient knowledge to be able to provide constructive challenge and fresh perspectives to the board and the executive members have sufficient grasp of operational and financial detail to represent the wider organization and the particular issues that are being brought to the board for consideration and/or decisions.

In exploring how they work together, the housing association board expressed some of these common dilemmas. They had trust and respect for each other but wondered if they could sometimes be less consensual and more challenging. They were cautious and risk averse, which had served them well, and also wondered if they could be more creative and innovative, spending more time on the future and 'blue sky' thinking.

The board had traditionally been very large, and regularly included all members of the executive team. They decided to transition to a smaller board with only the CEO and finance director as full members. The board coaches were able to support the smaller unitary board in acknowledging their concerns about being equipped to take important decisions without having all executive members present at their meetings. Large boards tend towards a process of rubber stamping rather than generative dialogue. To shift to a different level of discussion and debate requires the agenda to be revisited so that the focus is on the most important issues that require the collective input of all the board and cannot be dealt with outside of the board meeting. For executive directors it means being more open to genuine challenge and alternative propositions. For non-executive directors, it is no longer sufficient to base their input on a reading of the board pack. They are expected to stay abreast of key developments in the organization, through regular briefings and face-to-face contact with executives beyond the board.

Van den Berghe and Levrau (2013: 162) emphasize the importance of focusing on how the board fulfil one of their core functions, that of making decisions. They offer a simple typology of board decision-making roles (see Table 14.2).

Table 14.2   Board decision-making roles

Type of board	Decision-making role
Ceremonial board	No formal decision-making role
Rubber-stamping board	Only role is agreement with finalized decisions
Statutory board	Discussions limited to formalistic role of the board (with limited role in the strategy process)
Proactive board	Much more active involvement of directors in strategy and decision making, with board committees, independent directors and so on
Participative board	With open debate culture, striving to reach consensus between management and the board, and harmony and complementarity between board and management

This a useful continuum to help boards be more choice-full about their decision-making role vis-à-vis other parts of the organizational system, particularly executives and investors.

The coach has an important role in helping the board step back from a process in which they have become immersed and to notice the cultural patterns of the boardroom. This is very hard to do as an insider without skilled help. One of our favourite definitions of team or organizational culture is: 'what you stop noticing when you have worked somewhere for three months' (Hawkins and Smith, 2013: 110).

A way of surfacing these cultural patterns is to use a Descriptor Analysis (Hawkins, 2017: 305–307), where board members are independently asked to describe the collective board in three adjectives or phrases as it is today and how they think it needs to be in two years' time. This technique has worked with many different forms of board and highlights the perceived need for a change in culture. It is also used as a 360° feedback process with key stakeholders who interact with the board and who are asked to complete a word search. This provides an illuminating contrast between internal and external perspectives. On some unitary boards, the analysis has shown the collective response of the executive directors in contrast to the non-executives.

An additional benefit of using any evaluative instrument such as Descriptor Analysis is that, by repeating it every year or two, it offers a mechanism to evaluate development against the plans for improvement the board has agreed on.

The role of the board in strategy is both contentious and complex. Some argue that the board should leave strategizing to the executive and keep to an approving, monitoring and scrutiny role (Thomsen, 2008; Acharya, 2008). Others argue that this is an abrogation of one of their core functions, which is to focus on the long-term stewardship of the business and value creation for all stakeholders (Van den Berghe and Levrau, 2013; Kakabadse and Kakabadse, 2008; Carter and Lorsch, 2004).

Clarifying their role in the strategy creation, implementation and monitoring process is an important board process. We would argue that the board is responsible for:

1 clarifying the various stakeholder groups for whom the organization must create added value;

2 ascertaining the needs and aspirations and feedback from these various groups;

3 being clear about the core long-term mission of the organization (its purpose, core values, distinctive identity, vision and so on), which guides and frames the strategy debate and creation;

4 setting the strategic challenges that must be addressed by the executives;

5 hearing back from the executives their proposals to meets these challenges, challenging and debating the proposals with them and deciding in which strategies to invest in;

6 setting up monitoring and evaluation processes that will provide clear and quick feedback and learning on whether the strategies are working and how they need to be adapted and evolved;

7 supporting management, as needed, in the implementation of the strategies and regularly reviewing them.

How this cycle works out in practice will vary due to the nature of the organization, the challenges it is facing and the type of board governance it has chosen. For example, there is clear evidence (Acharya, 2008) that large publicly listed organizations operate very differently in strategic decision making than private equity-backed companies, the latter playing a much more active strategy role.

As board coaches, we have facilitated the strategizing processes between boards and the organization's executives and other key players, being clear that the role of the coach is to enable the richness of the dialogue and the most effective process and not to have views on the strategy content.

Connecting

Coaching the discipline of Connecting with stakeholders and the wider environment is rare in the fledging work of board coaching. However, there is a growing need for this form of help as boards recognize the need to engage key stakeholder groups in radically new ways if they are to be effective in helping their organizations transform themselves to meet the ever-changing challenges of their environment. Here are some illustrations of how this has emerged from a board coaching process.

The boards of Outspan and Cape fruit (Unifruca) in South Africa, through their merger process, realized that the majority of the shareholders, who were fruit farmers mostly supplying the business, were deeply suspicious of the other company and perceived loss of control. For the merger to happen there had to be a major transformation in the hearts and minds of these shareholders. The boards were insightful enough to recognize that just telling the shareholders why merger was good for the company and for the shareholders was not going to work. So the two boards requested that the board coaches partner them in designing and facilitating large events (100 shareholders at a time), which would actively engage the shareholders in working through the challenges facing the company and exploring different scenarios.

In coaching the board of a mid-size technology company through a major transition from their founders, it became clear that this was causing a great deal of rumour and feelings of unsettledness among the staff. Retaining skilled employees and future leaders through periods of transition was a priority for future success. How the board engaged the staff before everything within the board was resolved was critical. Coaching the board on how they would show up and collectively create confidence in their staff was important. Just getting the agreed script right, they decided, was not going to be enough, so they asked the board coach to be present and facilitate live when it came to the question and answer process.

A FTSE 100 financial company had realized that the process it had used to appoint its previous CEO had been very costly. Although he had led a successful period in the firm's history, the process had left several internal candidates for the role semi-detached. There had been no transparent process, no clear criteria and no feedback to the failed candidates on why one of their colleagues and not them had been appointed. The chairman asked the board coach to facilitate a different process. It included sensitive discussions between the board sub-committee and internal candidates before appointments were made and direct feedback to the successful and unsuccessful candidates afterwards.

Core Learning

As explored extensively in the rest of this chapter, boards are reluctant to stop and look at themselves; and those that do, often limit their self-reflections to the easier-to-discuss structural and process issues rather than the more personal and behavioural elements of the board's functioning.

In the case of a major professional services company supervisory board, made up of elected senior partners of the firm from different countries, the board coaches were somewhat shocked to discover that there was no formal induction process or training for the newly elected board members. Most of them were senior partners with great expertise in corporate finance, law, taxation or auditing, but nearly all of them had no previous board experience. Many admitted that, in their culture of 'expertise', you did not dare own up to not knowing how to understand the financial spread sheets or complex governance issues with which they were presented. Only the board coach, talking separately to each board member, was able to surface this dynamic and encourage the board to explore how to address it.

In Chapter 7, Coyne and Nicol look at how Core Learning is nearly always the lowest-scored area for executive boards and how they helped an executive board explore their core learning. With supervisory and unitary boards, this is even more the case. It is a hard task to build continuous, reflective learning into business as usual. It requires constant practice and support and new habits and processes, such as pauses or 'time-outs' to reflect on board process in the moment and end-of-meeting structured reviews. It also requires a shift in the culture to one where direct feedback is welcomed, the ability to reflect is developed, the importance of generative dialogue is recognized and where failure is the seedbed for learning, not blame.

Conclusion

In Chapter 14, we quote Paul Hawken (2007) who stresses that business and industry are increasingly the only institutions large enough and powerful enough to address the complex economic, social and ecological challenges facing the world today. At the beginning of this chapter, we showed how boards' responsibility is growing faster than their capacity to step up to the challenge. There is a great and growing need for effective systemic board coaches and for boards to have the humility and openness to seek their help. We hope that this chapter has made a small contribution to this urgent cause.

Reflections four years on

This chapter focuses mainly on board coaching emerging out of board governance reviews. Increasingly in the past four years we have found board coaching also emerging as a necessary connected activity of working with the executive team of the organization. Rarely can an executive team become highly effective unless it is supported in developing the right relationship with its board. This has led us to engage with more systemic team coaching, not just of boards and executive teams from the same organization, but also coaching their inter-team relationship and joint working (see case example in Chapter 10).

In Chapter 16 of the first edition of this book (Hawkins, 2014b), I proposed four levels of board maturity.

1 **Boards focused on conformance,** managing risk and ensuring compliance – both externally to the legal and fiduciary requirements of the countries in which they operate, and internally in monitoring performance and adherence to agreed strategy and processes.

2 **Boards focused on managing performance** – setting targets for growth, market share, profitability, shareholder return and company value.

3 **Boards focused on managing connections and relationships** – ensuring the organization has the right internal connections to ensure effective and timely responsiveness to all stakeholders and a culture of 'can do' attitude and leadership at all levels. Externally focusing on connections with the wider eco-system: up-stream with the suppliers and down-stream with the customers, with partner organization, potential mergers and acquisition organizations.

4 **Boards focused on sensing the emerging future** through listening deeply to all parts of the organization and the wider stakeholder eco-system and orchestrating collaborative inquiries across the internal and external systems about what 'the organization can uniquely do, to contribute with others to what the world of tomorrow needs.'

Increasingly the global situation requires boards to develop quicker to high levels of functioning and to sustain their functioning at this level. This is where board coaching can make a valuable contribution.

Embodied approaches to team coaching

15

PETER HAWKINS AND DAVID PRESSWELL

Introduction

Have you ever had the experience of being at a team meeting where everyone has agreed to a decision and an action, and you have then come back a month later and it has not happened? In talks throughout the world, when I (Peter) have asked this question, nearly everyone present has had this experience.

I then invite those at the talk, and you can do this now for yourself, to close their eyes and picture the meeting room where this last happened. Who was present? How were people sitting? What was the body language? What eye contact and connection was there round the room? What was the quality and energy of the voices that were speaking – the emotional rhythm of their voices – the quality of the listening and engagement? What was the energy at the point of decision?

Then I ask:

If you had attended to the non-verbal communication at the time, would you have known that the action was not going to happen?

If the answer is yes, how come everyone pretended it was going to be done?

What could you have done as a team member to address the gap between what was being said and what was being enacted, to avoid the month's delay and the recriminations and disappointment when you next met?

Agreements are cognitive and cerebral, but commitment is always embodied. Most teams fail to recognize the difference between these two very different processes and spend all their time in the cerebral domain of talking about what needs to be done, and then when the team fails to create the desired change at the next meeting, they all blame each other for the action not having happened.

When teaching team coaching one of us (Peter) will often ask how many of those present have taken part in 'offsites' with their team. Most hands will go up. He will then ask how many of the actions agreed at the away day actually got translated into action afterwards. The results are depressingly low and typically between 0 and 30 per cent. This matches a pattern that we have repeatedly found in individual coaching, where the biggest frustration of coaches when they come to supervision is how often their clients have had a new insight in the coaching and planned how they will handle their challenges differently, only to come back a month later having not followed through with their agreed actions (Hawkins and Smith, 2013). In transformational coaching we have adopted two important adages:

> If the change does not start in the coaching session it is unlikely to happen afterwards.

> Insight and good intention are not sufficient to produce change, which always involves the body and the emotions.

Hamill (2013) shows how the natural learning process moves from cognitive to embodied knowledge and applies this to leadership. One way or another, it is the job of the external facilitator to bring fresh perspectives and opportunities into the room, so as to help create a more energized and productive collaboration that moves away from cerebral speculation to a tangible shift in behaviour. Effectively nothing changes in a team unless behaviour changes, and an embodied approach to learning significantly improves the chances of gaining and sustaining the commitment necessary to achieve that.

One particularly elegant methodology is the creation of a collectively held, living map. It uses the people in the room as representatives of entities (groups, principles, goals, and so on) within a system and places them in space according to what 'feels true'. In effect, just two factors are in play: each representative's distance from other representatives, and the direction in which they face – whether towards the same point, towards each other or away. Each representative is then asked to report on the thoughts and sensations they experience when taking their place in the map, while the facilitator might comment on the representation of the system as a whole.

At the most basic level, getting team members up out of their seats and looking at a problem from (literally) different angles can be energizing and refreshingly new. But there is additional value that comes from teasing a problem apart into its constituent parts and then looking at these in a systemic context. New perspectives are adopted and the relationships between entities (rather than simply the entities themselves) become evident. As a whole system is represented in the room, it becomes immediately apparent how adjusting any one part affects others and, with this, previously unseen implications and possibilities reveal themselves. Meanwhile, the role of the consultant is no longer to advise, but to support a team to articulate its own understanding of an issue, collectively – a process likely to yield far more sustainable results.

In this chapter we will share a range of methods we have used, with a wide variety of teams, to move from talking about change to enabling change to happen in an embodied and emotionally engaged way, live in the room. We will also share how we have used a range of embodied approaches in supervising team coaching, on the basis that, for supervision to be helpful, change in the coach or coaches is a prerequisite to adding value to their work with a team.

The history and focus of three approaches

Psychodrama, sociodrama and systemic constellation all use a similar range of embodied action techniques, facilitated by a trained practitioner, to enable breakthroughs in addressing human challenges. Each has different historical roots and applies itself to a different focus.

Psychodrama

Psychodrama is an action method, most known for being used as a psychotherapy, in which clients use spontaneous dramatization, role playing and dramatic self-presentation to investigate and gain insight into their lives. Psychodrama was developed by Jacob Moreno, MD (1889–1974), a contemporary of Freud, who many now see as one of the founding fathers of humanistic psychology and the greatest developer of embodied action techniques, not only in the field of psychotherapy and group therapy but in education, all forms of development and social and community relations.

In 1912, Moreno attended one of Freud's lectures. In his autobiography, he recalled the experience:

> As the students filed out, he singled me out from the crowd and asked me what I was doing. I responded, 'Well, Dr Freud, I start where you leave off. You meet people in the artificial setting of your office. I meet them on the street and in

their homes, in their natural surroundings. You analyse their dreams. I give them the courage to dream again. You analyse and tear them apart. I let them act out their conflicting roles and help them to put the parts back together again.' (Moreno, 1985)

Focus: here the focus is on the protagonist, the individual who with the help of the psychodramatist and other group members is dramatically exploring an aspect of their current, past or future life. The psychodrama is in service of their individual development or therapy, although most psychodramatists would argue that 'when practised in a group setting' the whole group benefits from each individual's psychodrama.

Sociodrama

Moreno termed his application of embodied action techniques to groups, teams, organizations and whole communities 'sociodrama':

> Sociodrama has been defined as a deep action method dealing with intergroup relations and collective ideologies. The true subject of a sociodrama is the group. The concept underlying this approach is the recognition that man is a role player, that every individual is characterized by a certain range of roles which dominate his behaviour and that every culture is characterized by a certain set of roles which it imposes with a varying degree of success upon its members. (Moreno, 1959)

The British Psychodrama Association defines sociodrama as:

> A group interaction process used to assist all types of populations in meeting specific group goals. The method draws upon a person's ability to learn with their whole body and mind. It is a kinaesthetic, emotional and cognitive educational methodology.

Sociodrama is part of the wider field of study that Moreno termed 'sociometry', which is 'the study of social relations between individuals – interpersonal relationships' (Borgatta, 2007).

Sociodramatic and action method techniques are actively used in a broad range of educational, health and business environments throughout the world.

Focus: here the focus is on what needs to be explored, resolved, developed or healed within the group, team, organization or wider community. The protagonist is normally a particular collective group, which is facilitated by a sociodramatist to explore, and work through, a particular challenge.

Systemic constellations

Systemic constellations were developed by Bert Hellinger in the 1970s out of his work with the German perpetrators and victims of the Second World War and their decedents. Hellinger was a priest, missionary and psychotherapist who was planning his retirement when the psychiatrist, Gunthard Weber, persuaded him to publish something on his innovative therapeutic approach. He has since written or co-written over 30 books on the subject.

Hellinger's work (1998, 1999) draws off many theoretical sources in addition to Moreno's work, including Janov's primal therapy, neuro-linguistic programming (NLP) and Virginia Satir's family reconstruction, while his integration of dead ancestors into family constellations draws upon his experiences as a missionary among the Zulu of South Africa. Above all, he takes a phenomenological approach: eschewing theory in favour of observing and acknowledging what is experienced in the moment.

Hellinger is severely critical of the 'therapeutic relationship', seeing it as too often serving the therapist rather than the client. He has in turn been the subject of much controversy in the psychological community, largely in response to the briefness of his interventions (rarely more than an hour), his emphasis on recognizing the perpetrator in all of us, and what is perceived to be a dogmatic interpersonal style. He remains as contentious as he is influential.

Focus: here the focus is again on the individual, but exploring their issues in the context of a wider system and through the 'felt sense' of independent and often uninformed representatives. Constellations may stretch over time, and may also include wider stakeholders and abstract elements such as team purpose, values, revenue, performance and so forth. They have been developed to supervise team coaching and also adapted to help teams explore their own dynamics and collective patterns.

Key concepts

The three approaches mentioned above share a range of key concepts, although they may use different terms for them. We have drawn on all three traditions as well as transformational coaching and the latest neuropsychology to develop some of the following key concepts for embodied transformational team coaching.

Tele: 'Tele is contact at a distance enabling an exchange of emotional messages.... unity of action, time and space that is applied both in theatre and in psychodrama' (Djuric, 2006).

Limbic resonance: This is the capacity for sharing deep emotional states arising from the limbic system of the brain. These states include the dopamine circuit promoted feelings of empathic harmony, and the norepinephrine circuit originated emotional states of fear, anxiety and anger. The concept was first advanced in the book *A General Theory of Love* (Lewis *et al*, 2000). It refers to the capacity for empathy and non-verbal connection that is present in animals, and that forms the basis of our social connections as well as the foundation for various modes of therapy and healing. According to the authors, professors of psychiatry at the University of California, our nervous systems are not self-contained but rather demonstrably attuned to those around us with whom we share a close connection. 'Within the effulgence of their new brain, mammals developed a capacity we call "limbic resonance" – a symphony of mutual exchange and internal adaptation whereby two mammals become attuned to each other's inner states.'

Felt awareness: Gendlin (1982) gave the name 'felt sense' to the unclear, pre-verbal sense of 'something' – the inner knowledge or awareness that has never been consciously thought or verbalized – as that 'something' is experienced in the body. It is not the same as an emotion. This bodily felt 'something' may be an awareness of a situation or an old hurt, or of something that is 'coming' – perhaps an idea or insight. Crucial to the concept, as defined by Gendlin, is that it is unclear and vague, and it is always more than any attempt to express it verbally. Gendlin (1979) also described it as 'sensing an implicit complexity, a holistic sense of what one is working on'.

According to Gendlin, the 'Focusing' process makes a felt sense more tangible and easier to work with. To help the felt sense form and to accurately identify its meaning, the focuser tries out words that might express it. These words can be tested against the felt sense: the felt sense will not resonate with a word or phrase that does not adequately describe it.

Gendlin observed clients, writers, and people in ordinary life ('focusers') turning their attention to this not-yet-articulated knowing. As a felt sense formed, there would be long pauses together with sounds like 'uh...'. Once the person had accurately identified this felt sense in words, new words would come, and new insights into the situation. There would be a sense of felt movement – a 'felt shift' – and the person would begin to be able to move beyond the 'stuck' place, having fresh insights, and also sometimes indications of steps to take.

This 'felt sense' was further developed by Hellinger, recognizing that when representatives are placed into 3D maps, they often have access to truly remarkable levels of insight – even though they might not even know whom or what they are representing. It is the constellator's job to gather these perceptions and then, through repositioning the representatives and the use of tailored sentences, to move from accurate diagnosis of an issue – when possible – towards resolution.

Experimentation

Central to all embodied team coaching methods is the principle of 'experimentation'. Bateson (1972) posited that all learning is stochastic, that it emerges through a process of trial and error and retrial – a process of learning through embodied doing. Rather than analyse an issue and then cognitively plan how to respond, in transformational team coaching we encourage teams to try out new ways of working together and then review what worked and was helpful that they could take forward into their future ways of meeting. Otto Scharmer and Katrin Kaufer (2013) echo this sentiment when they encourage teams and organizations to 'iterate, iterate, iterate'.

Fast-forward rehearsals

This is a term coined by Hawkins and Smith (2006) and used in team coaching in Hawkins (2017) to describe the process of inviting the team not just to talk about what they will do differently, but to step into the future and enact how they will be different. Hawkins and Smith (2013) write:

> If coachees do not rehearse the way in which they want to behave differently, and do not practise it and, in the process, receive clear feedback on how they are coming over, they are less likely to do things differently outside the coaching session. So the action stage requires the relational skills of inviting the coachee to embody that change, live in the room. 'So you will confront this issue with your colleague when you meet with them next Tuesday. Show me how you will do that. Try out your first few sentences. Talk to me as if I am the colleague.' This would be followed by direct feedback from the coach and an encouragement to do a second and third rehearsal. The coach focuses on the coachee creating an authentic, embodied shift in how they relate to the other person. This will manifest in new ways of breathing, posture, eye contact, and a different energy, as well as new language and metaphor.

The same process is also true for team coaching.

The methods (each with a case example)

1 Floating team sculpt

This is an approach Peter has developed based on sociodrama for experientially exploring the underlying dynamics of teams. He has named it 'a floating team sculpt' as no one person is doing the sculpting, and the sculpt is the product of the emergent team dynamic:

> *Stage 1.* The team is asked to find objects or symbols that represent what is at the heart or core of the team. These are placed in the centre of the room.
>
> *Stage 2.* Without discussing it, the group members are asked to stand up and move around until they can find a place that symbolically represents where they are in the group, ie how far are they from the centre? Who are they close to and who are they distant from? Then they are asked to take up a statuesque pose that typifies how they are in the group. This often takes several minutes as each person's move is affected by the moves of the others.
>
> *Stage 3.* One by one, each person is invited to make a statement beginning: 'In this position in the team I feel....'
>
> *Stage 4.* All the members are given the opportunity to explore how they would like to move to a different position in the team and what such a move would entail for them and for others. For example, one person who has sculpted herself on the outside of the team might say that she would ideally like to be right in the middle of the team. Having stated this desire, she would be invited to find her own way of moving into the centre and seeing what that shift felt like for her and for the others in the middle.
>
> *Stage 5.* Team members are asked to reframe the team by being asked: If this team were a family, what sort of family would it be? Who would be in what role? Or if this team were a television programme, which programme would it be? Who would be in what role and what would be the transactions? (It is possible for the teams to try out their own frames. There are countless possibilities – meals, animals, countries, modes of transport, myths, Shakespearean plays, and so on.)
>
> *Stage 6.* The team members are given the opportunity individually to leave their position in the team sculpture and stand on a chair and view the whole matrix structure that has emerged. On this chair they are the creative coach to the team and can deliver a statement: 'If I was coach

to this team I would....' I encourage people not to think what they will say until they stand on the chair, and to notice their first 'blink' response.

Example

A global marketing team in a FTSE 50 company gathered for a one-day offsite. A year previously, a new leader had taken over in order to implement a radically different vision. As a result, the brand's internal and external reputation had been transformed and sales figures were indicating an extraordinary uplift. But it had come at significant cost. The leader had achieved this turnaround through a sometimes autocratic style, the loss of most the original team and a growing disenchantment among the new, capable recruits in the face of so many last-minute orders from the top. Something needed to be done.

As part of an embodied learning approach, I (David) suggested each member 'mapped' where they felt themselves to be within this team, taking the circle of chairs on which we sat to represent the boundaries of the team, and one particular chair to represent its 'purpose and direction'. I suggested this was done in silence and that each team member simply find a place they felt to be right in relation to that purpose and the team as a whole – not how they wanted to feel, or how they felt they should, but just what was true for them.

Despite initial protests that this could not possibly work and that more instructions were clearly needed, they did so. The leader of the team positioned himself in front of the 'purpose', while his deputy took up her place directly behind him. Around her gathered many of the new recruits, vying for her attention, while those with less defined roles or with 'dotted' reporting lines elsewhere found their places on the edge of the group. A form emerged which surprised everyone with its 'accuracy'.

This provided a great basis for discussion, in and of itself, with individuals reflecting upon the hidden dynamics the map had surfaced. Individuals noticed the appropriateness of who they were close to and where connections were missing. The deputy was particularly struck by the realization that it was impossible to fulfil her role if she continued to be drawn in so many different directions. She looked exhausted just standing there.

I asked how this team might be reconfigured into a more productive pattern. Various alternatives were explored, with representatives reporting back on whether new positions felt better, worse or no different. I then suggested that the team leader move to the back of the group so that, rather than dominating the purpose from the front, he 'led from behind' and delivered his vision through others. His deputy instinctively placed herself in front of him, and her reports found positions fanned in front of her – all facing the team purpose.

This was immediately felt to be a more empowered team in which junior members comprised a new 'frontline' with both the opportunity and responsibility for delivery – albeit with a powerful sense of support from the senior players behind them. Those with key stakeholders outside of the team took places that allowed them to connect more broadly within the organization. It was a structure that worked for the team as a whole.

So much so that a number of team members took out their phones to photograph the view from where they stood, by way of a reminder, and a discussion began about how this map might be made real in their working lives. Everyone had a place that felt appropriate and productive and, with this, the team's commitment to making these changes a reality rose.

2 Modelling the wider system

We have so far considered examples in which a group maps itself. The team can also map a far broader system, with those present representing specific entities or even principles beyond the team. In doing so, discussions of systems and stakeholders come alive, not least because the act of physically taking another's place in a system and standing in their shoes seems to give access to an uncanny degree of emotional and psychological insight. Previously Peter has referred to this method as 'enacted role sets' (see Hawkins and Shohet; and Hawkins and Smith, 2013).

The key shortcoming is that the process seems so inherently improbable that representatives might discount the sensations they feel as 'made up', or override them with more 'likely' ones. This is particularly the case in situations of long-running misunderstanding or conflict where the various parties have become comfortably attached to assumptions about their antagonists. One way to overcome this is to set up what is known as a 'blind constellation' in which the participants simply do not know the entities they are representing.

Example

It is an approach I (David) took with the four-person partner team from John Lewis: an iconic and extremely successful British retailer founded in 1929 as 'an experiment in industrial design'. Its constitution is based on the principle of co-ownership and explicitly states that the Partnership's ultimate purpose is, rather than shareholder value, the 'happiness of all its members' through the sharing of 'profit, knowledge and power'. The Partner team reports at Board level and is specifically charged with upholding these radical principles.

Needless to say, it is no easy task reconciling the empowerment of 85,000 'owners' with the need to run a retailer that has an annual turnover of almost £10 billion. It is made all the more complex by having to balance two distinct trading divisions in the form of John Lewis (department store) and Waitrose (supermarket). The Partner team faces the particular challenge of finding its best place within this system whilst remaining true to the company's founding principles.

But this was also a familiar dilemma for them and, in asking the four team members to represent the key elements of the John Lewis system, there was the risk they might 'play out' preconceived notions. So I wrote the name of four systemic elements, each on a separate piece of paper, folded them up and shuffled them so that even I did not know which was which. I then asked each to pick one piece of paper and, without opening it, to position themselves in the room according to their felt sense.

They did so, despite their understandable incredulity, and their behaviours became immediately distinct: one person started pacing around the room, looking inquisitorially at the others, another half-hid behind a curtain, another wandered aimlessly, while the last faced away from the others, busying themself with all kinds of inconsequential activity. It was an example of what almost always happens: that setting up a system in a spatial way, with an issue holder who has a genuine stake in that system, releases distinct energies that even a novice representative detects.

After a couple of minutes, I ask each team member to look at their paper to see the part of the system they represented. As a result, their actions became more confident and distinct, but remained essentially the same: the person pacing did so a little more frantically, the person behind the curtain hid all but their face.

When each announced which part of the system they represented, there was an audible expression of surprise at the 'rightness' of what was being expressed. As the facilitator, I was no longer dealing with reluctant sceptics, but with a group keen to process what they felt to be new, valid information. But there was also something that went powerfully beyond intellectual recognition of a familiar dynamic, namely an emotional connection with the experience of being part of this particular system, both one's own and others'.

Jane Burgess, Partners' Counsellor (Team Leader), John Lewis Partnership, said:

> *Having experienced the constellation methodology, I have become an advocate. Initially I was quite sceptical of the suggestion that an individual could play the part of an organization, but very quickly that act of physical movement puts your mind in a different place as it is reflective of feelings and emotions rather than words. It also enabled more constructive discussion, as when speaking it was not about your own view but the view from an organizational perspective, which did not feel personal and gave rise to better challenge and a genuine wish to understand the relationships of the varying parts. The approach also created a dynamic that made it easier to test options and 'what ifs'. If an opportunity presents itself, I would recommend exploration of the approach – it is very powerful.*

Note: it is always important to represent roles and functions within a system, rather than specific individuals, if one is to avoid being drawn into the complexities of individual psychology.

3 Constellating the values

The methodology outlined above allowed the Partner team to experiment with different configurations of the John Lewis system until they found the best position for their own team within it. Having established a configuration that worked better for all parties, they used sheets of A4 paper to capture the place and direction of each representative, thereby creating a map that could be used as the basis for further discussions.

It is standard practice for teams to use away days to discuss their 'purpose' as a team (the 'what') as well as the values by which they will work (the 'how') and to do so on a series of flipcharts (see Hawkins, 2017: chapter 6). Here we did exactly that. But what the constellation map allowed us to do was then to 'test out' these statements by means of the representatives, each in turn, stepping back into the constellation and viewing the flipcharts from the perspective of that particular stakeholder. As they did so, certain words and phrases resonated much more so than others – and they were able to share this valuable information with the rest of the team.

This was far from what can often be a somewhat dry analysis of stakeholder needs. Instead, it became an in-the-moment exploration of a system and how flow and energy might be restored. The whole process was more 'real' and emotionally engaging than anyone – including me (David) – had anticipated. Moreover, it was a collaborative process in which the team collectively mapped the problem and owned the eventual solution.

4 Clock of when people arrived

An example of bringing hidden preference to the surface is to be found in asking a team to order itself according to various aspects of time, with the person who joined the organization first sitting at '12' and so on around to the most recent joiner at '1' – who may well be the consultant themselves. As the group members take in their own and others' positions, unstated hierarchies become explicit. Typically, those who have been with an organization longest can feel a sense of burden as well as a certain authority, while the most recent can feel a sense of lightness and freedom or exclusion, alongside a desire to learn from others' experience.

But this 'order of belonging' almost invariably clashes with other hierarchies such as one's role in the team, age, level of contribution or positional status. This is particularly evident when the team leader is a relatively recent joiner. As a general rule, one learns that such tensions are rarely avoided in any organization, but that they become far more positively productive when they are respectfully acknowledged – at its simplest, with a clearly stated expression of appreciation or gratitude. It can also be extremely valuable and settling to acknowledge the contributions of previous members of the team.

5 Embodied psychometrics

An embodied approach can be used to bring psychometric results alive so that each individual sees where they fit on a particular dimension in relation to their colleagues, as well as how the team as a whole compares against the psychometric norms. An exercise that might otherwise be individual and somewhat abstract becomes both tangible and shared.

With one large team that had all received feedback on their Myers–Briggs psychological profile, I (Peter) laid out, on the floor of a large room, a framework of taped areas. On the vertical axis I put 'Thinking' in the north and 'Feeling' in the south. On the horizontal axis I put 'Sensation' in the west and 'Intuition' in the east. Each resulting quadrant was divided, with the extroverts near the centre and the introverts further out, and further divided to distinguish those who are into whether they are perception orientated from those who are more judgement orientated (Figure 15.1).

Figure 15.1 The personality Myers–Briggs floor map

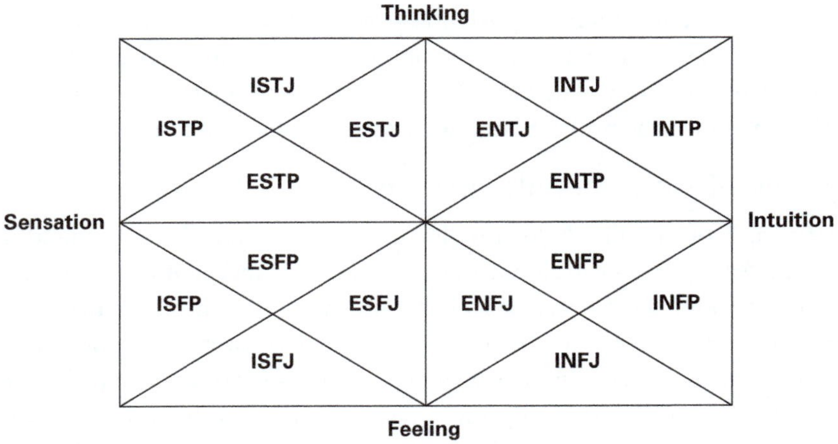

Once people have taken up their location on the map, they are invited to speak from that position, each saying: 'From this psychological perspective, this is how the team looks to me.' This helps people hear these perspectives less personally and understand how they derive from the diversity of psychological types. The team members, or the team facilitator, can then enter some of the psychological spaces that are not represented in the team and speak from that perspective. This can help the team gain fresh perspectives and also recognize areas of lack of diversity within the team and look at how they might develop themselves or recruit new members to address these.

There are many other team coaching approaches throughout this book that can be developed into an embodied and enactment method. For example, the process of working with triangulating thinking to overcome stuck 'either–or debates' (Hawkins, 2005: 29–31) can be constellated in a way that generates engagement and new perception (see also Sparrer and Von Kibed, 2001).

Methods for supervising team coaching

Embodied methods, including sculpting and constellating, can also be used in the supervision of team coaching (see Hawkins, 2017: chapter 16). Here we describe just two of the possibilities:

1 A constellation or sculpting approach can be used in one-to-one supervision to explore three key dynamics relevant to working with a team:

a The client system: what is happening within the team, or between the team and its broader organizational context?

b The client relationship: what is happening between the team coach and the client and/or their system?

c The team coach themselves: what is it within the team coach that means they are constantly drawn into the same dynamic, albeit with different teams?

The supervisor invites the team coach to set up the specific system using either furniture or floor-markers or directional objects. These can be anything from arrow Post-it notes, to Playmobil figures, to cups where the handle marks the direction of focus. Initially one might investigate what is happening at each location before then exploring where would be the most productive position for the team coach to place themselves.

2 In group supervision the team coach being supervised can be invited to use other supervision group members to represent the various team members and team stakeholders, as well as a person to represent themself as the team coach. They are invited to place each person, using their felt sense, and explore the emerging patterns and how these might be addressed. (For a full description of sculpting see Hawkins, 2017: 289–90.)

When to use embodied approaches in team coaching and when not to

We are clearly enthusiasts for an embodied approach to team coaching, but there are times when it is more or less useful or appropriate.

It is helpful when:

- a team has gone around an issue several times without making progress, possibly with too much intellectual analysis, judgements and opinions;

- to make progress an issue needs to be considered in a broader systemic context and the team needs to move from its own perspective to one that is 'outside-in' and/or 'future-back';

- the team needs help to connect with a deeper and intuitive 'knowing'.

It is unhelpful when:

- a resolution just needs rational problem solving;

- decision making and detailed action planning are what is required;

- there is no ownership of an issue or commitment to working it through;
- the team coach has not had the experience or training in using embodied approaches and/or is not feeling confident;
- either the team coach or client is not prepared to look with an open mind at a difficult situation.

For further guidance on when to use an embodied approach, see also Francis (2009).

Key attributes and capabilities for somebody using embodied methods

The role of facilitator, psychodrama or sociodrama director or constellator is deceptively difficult in that it requires an individual to support a client while keeping their system fully in mind, and to do so without judgement or commitment to a particular outcome. In doing so, the team coach needs to develop the 'beatitudes' mentioned in Chapter 16. They will also benefit from the following:

- A balance of empathy for the client with a respect for the broader system –identifying strongly with neither.
- Constantly stepping back to see the whole: the interconnectedness as well as any possible entanglements or potential resources.
- A playful detachment that is comfortable with 'not knowing'.
- Agreeing to everything even if they don't agree *with* everything, moving beyond a binary choice between right or wrong, to a concern for what the system requires.
- Not wanting to 'help' too much as this all too often incapacitates the receiver, but rather trying to be 'useful' so that the client emerges as more independently capable.
- A stillness that allows one to observe and listen intently. Trying too hard can stifle a receptive openness.

Whittington (2012) also includes a section on the key capacities of a constellator.

Conclusion

If, as we argue, agreements are cognitive and cerebral, but commitment is always embodied, then an embodied approach to learning provides a significant head-start – or perhaps, more accurately 'heart-start' – to shifting behaviour. It both stimulates and requires commitment from the outset.

But it can do more than this. The mapping process places issues in a systemic context so that we are less likely to be chasing symptoms, fixing the system in one place only to disrupt another aspect, and rather become more attuned to solutions that work for the whole. We can work collectively and we can tap into rich sources of emotional and somatic wisdom.

Once the team has co-created a map of their system that they all recognize, it is possible to experiment with changes within the map and to prototype and rehearse possible ways of developing the system. This can help uncover potential unintended consequences of changes or potential blockages to the change happening (Kegan and Lahey, 2009).

After the mapping, experimentation and prototyping, we can return to our system, seeing it and experiencing it differently; in shifting each of our individual perspectives, and the team's collective perspective, we shift the system itself.

Developing the personal core capacities for systemic team coaching

16

PETER HAWKINS

The most important task today is, perhaps to learn to think in a new way.

(GREGORY BATESON, 1972: 462)

Re-evaluation and transformation of our business paradigm is fundamental to successful evolution, not only of business, but of our species as a whole.... Transformational times call for transformational change.

(HUTCHINS, 2012:17)

Introduction

In this book I have more fully defined systemic team coaching than in my previous writings.

> Systemic team coaching is a process by which a team coach coaches a whole team over an extended period of time both when they are together and when they are apart, in order to help them improve both their collective performance and how they work together, and also how they develop their collective leadership to more effectively engage with all their key stakeholder groups to jointly transform the wider business and eco-system.
>
> The systemic team coach contracts with the whole team and its key stakeholders, then co-inquires and co-discovers how the team is currently

functioning internally and externally and how the team and its eco-system need the team to develop, then coaches the team to find these new ways of responding and engaging to create the needed difference.

The systemic team coach brings to the work a relational and systemic perspective, where they relate to the team, not as a client or subject of their coaching, but as a partner with whom they go shoulder to shoulder, leaning into the future, sensing the emerging needs in their wider eco-system and experimenting with new ways of responding.

However, just learning the theory, models and methods is not sufficient, for as Bill O'Brien, who was the modest but transformational CEO of Hanover Insurance, in the United States, said: 'The success of an intervention depends on the interior condition of the intervener' (quoted in Scharmer, 2007: 27). So at the core of becoming a systemic team coach is a maturational development that involves developing our basic assumptions, core beliefs and motivations, as well as maturing our ways of perceiving and being in the world.

This chapter also sets out the core principles of an eco-systemic leadership approach to leading team and organizations as suggested in the first chapter of this book, where leadership is focused on seeing the team or the organization in dynamic relationship with its wider eco-system:

> Just as an organism fills a niche within its ecosystem and food web, so does an organization fill a niche within its business eco-system (the stakeholder community across the social, economic and environmental landscapes within which the organization operates). (Hutchins, 2012: 53)

Simon Western (2010: 36–44) provides a great introduction to eco-leadership:

> Eco-leadership shifts the focus from individual leaders to leadership... in an attempt to harness the energy and creativity in a whole system.
>
> A key-role for eco-leaders is to be an organizational architect, taking a spatial leadership approach. ... The concept of space is essential to eco-leadership, refocusing our attention on the spaces within ourselves, our organizations, and in our social networks, where the emergent capability lies.

Systemic team coaching core capacities

Systemic team coaching cannot just be defined by its processes, intentions and activities, for at its heart is a range of beliefs and ways of being in the world, which are not generally common in our current ways of thinking and relating, but which, given the range of global challenges that face all of the human species and the organizations throughout the world, are urgently needed.

Through my work I have discovered and developed 13 systemic team coaching core capacities, because these are not just cognitive beliefs or competencies, but embodied ways of thinking and being in the world. I will explore how these manifest and show up in how the team leader or team coach engages with the team, and also how these capacities need to be developed and nurtured within the whole team. Systemic team coaching is only successful if it is happening between the times when the systemic team coach is present with the team, and also after they have finished their contracted engagement. So the systemic team coach not only needs to develop these core capacities in their own way of being, but to facilitate team members in developing them as well.

1 A relational perception

In the last chapter of *Leadership Team Coaching* (2017), I showed how Gregory Bateson (1972) wrote very clearly of the problems we have created by choosing the wrong unit of survival:

> In accordance with the general climate of thinking in mid nineteenth century England, Darwin proposed a theory of natural selection and evolution, in which the unit of survival was either the family line or species or sub-species or something of that sort. But today it is quite obvious that this is not the unit of survival in the real biological world. The unit of survival is organism plus environment. We are learning by bitter experience that the organism that destroys its environment destroys itself.

One of the first things a new team leader or new team coach needs to do is to learn to see the team as a living system, not just as a group of individuals working together. However, moving from coaching individuals to coaching the team as a system will not be enough if all we do is move our individualistic self-centred thinking from the individual to the team or tribal level and compete to be the highest-performing team on the block. As Bateson indicates, we need to recognize that the unit of survival, the unit of high performance and the unit of well-being and flourishing is the team in dynamic relationship to their environment, ecological niche, their systemic context. This is why I have throughout my writings on team coaching (Hawkins, 2011, 2012, 2014, 2017, 2018) argued for team coaching being as much if not more focused on the external relationships of the whole team as on the internal relationships between the team members; and more focused on the contribution of the team to the wider eco-system than on the team feeling good about themselves.

As a human community we have a parallel but bigger challenge. We have to move from just fighting for saving one species or another, to working with the preservation and development of living ecologies; from thinking of the environment as a thing, to seeing that it is a complex web of connections; from seeing it as 'other' to experiencing it as part of us, and ourselves as an inextricable part of the environment. This is not an easy task and will require collective effort. To constantly serve the individual and team clients as well as their organizations and wider business ecosystems is not an easy task, and to be effective all coaches constantly need to be reflecting on their work and expanding their coaching capacity. This requires the ability to stand back from the presenting issues and see the repeating patterns in the wider system. This continual need for process reflection and systemic awareness means that all coaches should undertake regular personal and professional development, including quality supervision from those who are specifically trained in supervising systemic team coaching.

Therefore, as systemic team coaches we need to focus less on the individuals or even the team and focus more on the relational spaces: between the team members; between the team and the rest of the organization; the team and its wider stakeholders; the team and its wider eco-system; and the team coaching system formed by the team and the team coach. To focus on the dance not the dancers, the drama not just the actors, and the relationships not the just the relata.

2 Being in service to the larger whole

In the final chapter of *Leadership Team Coaching* (2017) I wrote about the Parsifal trap:

> The Parsifal trap is named after the legendary Knight of the Round Table Sir Percival or Parsifal, who left home very early in his life and went on his adventures in search of the Holy Grail. His courage and innocence served him well and, while still very young, he arrived at the Grail Castle, where he saw the awesome Grail Procession, carrying the much sought after Holy Grail. He was intoxicated with excitement and with the splendour and privilege of having got there. But the next morning he awoke on a damp, cold, open field and the whole castle, procession and grail had evaporated into the mist. He had failed to

ask the question that would have allowed him to stay. Parsifal took many more years of travails and searching to find his way back to the Grail Castle but this time, with the wisdom of experience, he knew the question that must be asked: 'Whom does the Grail serve?'

Many teams fall into and stay in the Parsifal trap. They believe that getting on well together and having efficient meetings are the goal. They can fall into the trap of believing success is improving their scores on a High Performing team questionnaire. This book has set out to show that a team only has a successful and meaningful life if they are serving a need beyond themselves, and have stakeholders who require them to deliver something beyond what can be done by the team members working separately.

Team coaches too fall into the Parsifal trap of believing that team development or team coaching are an end in themself and fail to ask: 'Team coaching in service of what?' When we fail to ask this question we, like the young Parsifal, may well find ourselves waking up in a cold misty barren field, wondering why our dream has evaporated and are condemned to many more long years of searching. If as a team coach I am going to create sustainable value, I must be clear about what and who my work is in service of. As a minimum I need to ensure that my coaching is in service of the team members, the team as a whole, their organization and the wider eco-system that the organization serves. In addition I must be in service of the relationships that connect and weave between all these parties, for none of these entities can be successful by themselves and their value is intrinsically bound together. I need to be focused on the unrealized potential in all parties and the connections between them and assist in that potential being realized. However, in serving the individual team members it is important that I am not just serving their fragmented or egoistic self, but helping each person find their calling, their service, their purpose in doing what is necessary in the world. In serving the team, the team becoming high performing is not an end in itself, but merely a means to the team being better able to create 'shared value' for their stakeholders (Porter and Kramer, 2011) and improve the well being of their eco-system.

In serving the organization I need to ensure that the work with the individual or team is not an end in itself, but is enabling that individual and team to more effectively lead and manage the organization through its next phase of development, so that the organization can fulfil its potential and make a better contribution to the wider world. Only the team that is in service of their wider eco-system will continue to flourish and thereby meet their own needs and aspirations.

3 Being able to perceive multiple nested systems

It is never enough to focus on just one level of system. To understand the human individual, we need to understand the subsystems that comprise the individual; these include the vast community of non-human micro-organisms that many estimate to be greater in number than the human cells within us; the physical organs that are necessary for their physical well-being, or the many roles and sub-personalities that are integral to their way of being in the world. We also need to look at the systems the individual is part of – their family of origin, their current family, the team and organization they work within, the national, local and ethnic culture they are part of. As Wendell Berry, the great American farmer philosopher, beautifully shows, we all live within 'a system of nested systems: the individual human within the family, within the community, within agriculture, within nature' (Berry, 1983: 46).

Also:

> So long as the smaller systems are enclosed within the larger, and so long as all are connected by complex patterns of interdependency, as we know they are, then whatever affects one system will affect the others. (Berry, 1983: 46)

With a team, one needs to consider the individual members who are the subsystems of the team system, as are the various functions that comprise the work of the team. One also needs to consider the wider systems of which the team is just one part. This includes their organization and the stakeholder eco-system that they both serve and are served by. It might also include the professional culture and system they operate within.

However, in today's world, where the human species has pushed beyond the limits to growth and risks doing irreparable damage to the earth's bio-system, every leader, leadership team and organization also needs to be able to continually live and act with the awareness of how all human systems are nested within the wider ecological systems of the earth. The environment is not just something external to us as humans to be plundered as resources, managed, or even stewarded, but the system which enables, contains and shapes our very existence. We as a species are only at the very beginning of discovering how to live non-competitively and interdependently with this wider eco-system in which we all are housed:

> The definitive relationships in the universe are thus not competitive but interdependent. And from a human point of view they are analogical. We can build one system only within another. We can have agriculture only within nature, and culture only within agriculture. At certain points, these systems have to conform to one another or destroy one another. (Berry, 1997: 47)

4 'Leaning into the future'

In our research on 'Tomorrow's Leadership' (Hawkins 2017b), one CEO who was interviewed said: 'As organizations, we need to best equip ourselves to deal with today, tomorrow and the future. At present, there is too much focus on the short term, and not enough on how we transform our ways to become more able to embrace the future'. Interviewed CEO Bill Sharpe, author of *Three Horizons* (Sharpe and Williams, 2013), explores how leaders need to simultaneously hold three horizons while steering the organization. These are:

1 managing business as usual;

2 innovating continuous improvement in products, processes and engagement for tomorrow ;

3 creating the business for the future.

He advocates that we need to think in the order of 1 to 3 to 2, otherwise we are trapped in micro improvements to today's processes, products and ways of operating, rather than finding innovation that is formed by the 'future desired state'.

> It is a process of locating ourselves and our area of concern within the broader patterns of life... that helps us act more skilfully together in the present moment towards our shared future.
>
> (Sharpe and Williams, 2013)

This is parallel to my emphasis on helping leadership teams think 'future-back and outside-in', always asking: What does our stakeholder world of tomorrow need that we can uniquely provide? (Hawkins, 2017).

Our usual way of attending is to start from the present, to perceive it through our past experience and work out how to solve the presenting problems and strive to create what we or others want. Team coaching traditionally started by asking what the team leader and/or team members wanted from team coaching, or about the difficulties they were facing that they wanted to address. Systemic team coaching in contrast always starts 'future-back and outside-in' – asking what the eco-system of the team's stakeholders needs the team to learn and develop, and what new challenges the future will bring that will require a new response from the team. Starting with these questions, we can stand alongside the team in co-inquiry and co-discovery, inviting them to lean with you into the future, sensing what is emerging (Scharmer, 2013) and listening to the soft signals in the wider eco-system.

5 Listening to the field

A systemic team coach needs to listen to the field. This involves listening at multiple levels and in several different dimensions and this requires enormous training, practice and discipline.

Elsewhere I have written (Hawkins and Smith, 2006, 2013) about the four levels of listening that I originally developed 40 years ago when training psychotherapists. This was based on the experience of the listener (see Table 16.1).

More recently I have developed this model, influenced by Otto Scharmer and his Theory U (Scharmer, 2007, 2013), as he also has four levels of listening which are very parallel to my own but the wording is more focused on the discipline, consciousness and intention of the listener and provides another indication of how we can develop our listening capacity. He also indicates the team listening mode for each level as well as the awareness and attitude that each level requires (see Table 16.2).

The systemic team coach not only needs to be able to listen at depth to the team and its members but also to listen to other parts of the wider stakeholder system not in the room and listen back into the past and forward into the future; to hear what is heard and what is important, within the team's wider systemic context, but only half-heard and not yet addressed by the team.

Table 16.1 Levels of listening

Level of listening	Activity of listener	Outcome in the person being listened to
Attending	Eye contact and posture demonstrate interest in the other.	'This person wants to listen to me.'
Accurate listening	Above plus accurately paraphrasing what the other is saying.	'This person hears and understands what I am talking about.'
Empathic listening	Both the above plus matching their non-verbal cues, sensory frame and metaphors; feeling into their position.	'This person feels what it is like to be in my position, they get my reality.'
Generative listening	All the above plus using one's own intuition and felt sense to connect more fully what one has heard in how one plays it back.	'This person helps me to hear myself more fully than I can by myself.'

Table 16.2   Levels of listening: Hawkins and Scharmer

Level of listening	Hawkins model	Scharmer	Scharmer team activity	Field: structure of awareness	Scharmer attitude
1	Attending	Downloading	Downloading	Habitual awareness	
2	Accurate listening	Factual	Debate	Ego-system awareness	Open mind
3	Empathic	Empathic	Dialogue	Stakeholder awareness	Open heart
4	Generative	Presencing	Collective creativity	Eco-system awareness	Open presence

6 Presence

Scharmer and colleagues (Senge *et al*, 2005) have created a new verb, presencing, which is made up of two other words: present and sensing. The systemic team coach needs to be fully present to the team's purpose and reason for being (Discipline 1), its plans and intentions (Discipline 2), all that is within the team, its dynamics, culture and internal relationships (Discipline 3), in the relationships between the team and all the team's stakeholders (Discipline 4) and what the future is requiring from the team and how the team develops, learns and changes to be future-fit over time (Discipline 5). The systemic team coach also needs to be able to sense the relational patterns within the team, between the team and its eco-system and what the future is calling forth from the team. To have presence is to be fully present with all one's receptors open, listening and seeing and feeling with one's whole body (see resonance below and also Chapter 15).

7 Being open to emergence and non-attachment

Fritjof Capra (2003: 104) writes that: 'Throughout the living world, the creativity of life expresses itself through the process of emergence.' Emergence is the process where the parts of a system interact with each other synergistically to create a more complex or cohesive pattern. 'Emergence is how complexity and diversity are created from simplicity, and how apparently chaotic behaviour of swarms can result in self-organizing super-organisms' (Hutchins, 2012: 58). Emergence is at the heart of the evolutionary process and central to how teams become more than the sum of their parts. However, as Hutchins (2012: 59) so clearly articulates:

> Successful emergence at the organizational level requires deeply understanding what 'good' looks like, 'letting go' of predictability, and stepping out of comfort zones, being okay with ambiguity, working with dynamic tension, being flexible and patient and operating a higher level of trust and intellectual and moral maturity than is typically found in the firms of the past.

It is possible to listen at another level beyond the four mentioned in the listening capacity above. This fifth level is called pure listening (Amidon, 2012) and only comes into being when we stay presencing and open to all that is emerging in and around the team, but can at the same time stay unattached to the stories the team tell you, or your own ideas about the team and how it should change. One of the maxims I learnt in my coaching training was, 'never know better and never know first'. This requires a discipline of non-attachment to knowing and understanding and judgement, but rather being with 'what is' at many levels and waiting upon what needs to emerge. In non-attachment the team coach notices what arises in the individual team members, in the relationships, in the team dynamic, in the team's relationship to their wider system, and within themselves, but does not cling to these noticings, but waits upon the natural emergence of connecting patterns. Non-attachment creates the space for grace, which is the next capacity.

8 Creating the space for grace

Creating the space for grace was first used by Hawkins and Smith (2006) and in our second edition (2013) we describe the capacity of the coach to create spaciousness in their relationship with the individual, team or organization, which provides the space for something to emerge, not previously conceived of by any of the team members or the team coach, but emerging from their new and fresh relating. That which comes by grace is something that emerges from the larger system we are all part of, as a gift, which is not earned or strived for, but arrives like 'manna from heaven'.

9 Resonance

A key aspect of listening is to move from listening just through the ears into the neo-cortex brain, to listening with all one's senses into the totality of one's being, including one's breathing, heartbeat, body, and all aspects of the brain, the amygdala, reptilian, limbic and both sides of the neo-cortex (see Hawkins and Smith, 2014, 2018; Brown and Brown, 2012). One is attuning one's body, multiple brains and being to resonate with the reverberations of the team members, the team and the team's wider eco-system. It is allowing oneself to be an instrument on which the larger systems can play, such as the Aeolian harp which, when hung on a tree, would play in resonance to the movement of the winds. Coleridge wrote a poem about such a harp, in which he indicates how through being like the harp we can connect the one life that is within us and outside us:

O! the one Life within us and abroad,

Which meets all motion and becomes its soul,

A light in sound, a sound-like power in light.

('The Eolian Harp', Samuel Taylor Coleridge, lines 27–29)

10 *Triangulated thinking*

All creative thinking requires three aspects to be present, and yet much of our discourse and ways of thinking are framed in opposites, polarities and dualistic thinking – light and dark, day and night, good and bad, up and down, making progress and standing still. Indeed, George Kelly (1955) developed a whole psychology and psychotherapy of understanding individuals by the polarity 'constructs' they used to differentiate one person or experience from another.

It is easy for the team coach to get caught in the characteristic duality constructs of the team, such as:

'We need to be a high performing team.' (construct: high and low performing)

'We have too much conflict.' (construct: conflict versus harmony)

'We need to be more externally focused.' (construct: internal focus versus external focus)

I have written elsewhere (Hawkins, 2005) how every leadership team I have worked in or with has had at least one stuck 'either–or' debate, such as: 'should we centralize or decentralize?', 'should we focus on our investors or our customers?', 'is the problem the strategy or the culture?' Each side of the polarity will often be represented by its passionate advocate, each very attached to their own solution. I developed the three simple laws of either–or:

a If as a team you are having the same either–or debate for the third time you are asking the wrong question.

b Both opposing solutions are wrong and so moving from 'either–or' to 'both and' will just combine two wrong solutions.

c Both opposing solutions represent important needs within the system, which we have not yet found a way of connecting.

Thus a stuck either–or debate is potentially a springboard to new fresh creative thinking, if the team coach or a team member can bring triangulated thinking to bear. They do this by first facilitating the team in why each solution by itself would fail to deliver the necessary way forward. They can then ask the team what would happen if they created a compromise between these two solutions, as this is also likely to be a false solution. Then they ask each solution advocate: 'What is the need behind your solution?' Having listed the needs represented by each of the opposing solutions, the team coach can then engage the whole team in thinking how to connect these two sets of system needs in a totally new way, outside and beyond the thinking that has created the polarity and which provides a way forward that would meet all the needs. This enables us to create a new conjunction, which is a marriage of the opposites as conceived by Heraclitus, the alchemical philosophers and Carl Jung, rather than a compromise, convergence or confluence. (Figure 16.1).

Figure 16.1   Conjunction

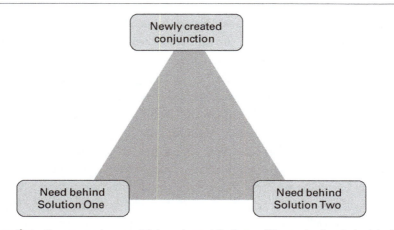

Conjunction – Here we create a new third way, beyond the frame of the previously polarized duality.

11 *Reflective practitioner*

To function systemically is to recognize that we are part of every system we perceive, Coleridge's 'one life within us and abroad', and therefore can only see the system from how it shows up from our particular perspective. This requires disciplined reflective practice, which Donald Schön first defined as 'the capacity to reflect on action so as to engage in a process of continuous learning' (Schön, 1983).

So one of the best ways of discovering the patterns and dynamics within the team is to look within oneself at how the feelings and patterns show up in parallel in oneself (for more on parallel process see Hawkins and Smith, 2013: 195–98).

Modern science has increasingly recognized that there is no such thing as pure objectivity, for the observer affects that which they are observing. This is even more true in the human sciences than it is in the material sciences, so the team coach needs to be able to reflect on themselves as part of the team or system they are attending to. However, as one spiritual teacher pointed out, the one face we cannot see is our own. Yes, we can see its reflection in a mirror, a stream or in the responses our face elicits in others, but we can never see it the way we see the faces of others. Thus we are dependent on feedback, and the team coach needs to develop the capacity to hear all feedback, undefensively and without attachment or reactivity, to hear it as one of many reflections, which inevitably will involve projection from the feedback giver, but which can help us see our part and stance within the system.

12 *A life-long learner*

I have now got to the age when people ask me when I will retire! My current answer is when I work with a team or teach a training in which I do not learn something new. I firmly believe that when we stop learning we stop being effective and work becomes stale, serving up previously cooked thoughts, rather joining the team at their learning edge where together we can create new thinking and ways of relating and being together. To stay a creative learner becomes harder the more wisdom, knowledge and experience you possess. Jesus taught that it is easier for a camel to go through the eye of a needle than a rich man to enter into the kingdom of God. It is believed by some that Jesus was referring to a gate in the walls of the city of Jerusalem, which the camel could only go through if all the baggage it was carrying was removed. The riches we have to be able to let go of are not just material riches but also the riches of knowledge, wisdom and experience, which can stop us being open to the new and previously unrecognized learning.

13 Stewardship

The ethics of stewardship entails always trying to leave behind a better state of flourishing than was there before you arrived. This can apply to the house where you live, the garden or land you inhabit, the team or organization you lead or work within, or even a space or event you temporarily occupy. In business, stewardship theory stresses collaboration to align business objectives (Sundaramurthy and Lewis, 2003), the focus on creating a sustainable business, not just short-term profit, and the focus on creating added value for all the company's stakeholders, customers, partners/suppliers, investors, employees, communities in which the organization operates and the 'more than human' natural environment. Stewardship is about leaving a legacy greater than the one you inherited in every aspect of life. As a team coach we are focused on leaving a team better resourced, capable and higher performing than when we first encountered them – to leave a team able to carry on coaching and developing themselves and a team that is co-creating increased value, with and for, all its stakeholders. As a team leader, we are focused on coaching our own team to be able to have greater shared leadership and eventually to be able to thrive without us.

These 13 capacities have become my continuous teachers. To remind myself of these capacities I made a list to pin up by my desk. I then realized that each was a blessing and could not be striven after, and that the more one consciously dwells in them the more blessings come by grace. So for each capacity I developed a beatitude, both to capture the blessing that they are and that they bring, and also because the word can be read as 'be-attitude' or an attitude of being.

Some may think that using the Christian biblical term beatitude is presumptuous, or for some offensive or sacrilegious; to any such readers I apologize in advance for any offence. The reason I have persisted is that I wanted to find a form that clearly captured the spiritual aspects of this craft.

---

1 *A relational perception.* Blessed are those who see the dance and not just the dancers, the drama and not just the actors, the relationship and not just the relata, for they shall reside in the dynamic flow of life.

2 *Being in service to the larger whole.* Blessed are they who can serve the larger system, for much will be returned unto them.

3 *Attending to at least three systems.* Blessed are those who can see the system above and the system below the one they are focusing on, for they shall reside in the stream of connection.

4 *'Leaning into the future'.* Blessed are those who can be grounded in the present but lean their attention into the future, for they shall sense what is emerging.

5 *Listening to the field.* Blessed are those who can truly listen, for they shall bring the gift of acceptance.

6 *Presence.* Blessed are those who can be fully present sensing what is in the eco-system, for they shall be in the place of power.

7 *Open to emergence and non-attachment.* Blessed are those who are non-attached to their thoughts, perceptions or attitudes, for they shall be able to pass through the eye of the needle and enter into a city of unexpected riches.

8 *Creating the space for grace.* Blessed are those who can create the space for grace, for they shall receive much blessing and be aware of the blessing they receive.

9 *Resonance.* Blessed are those who can listen with their whole being, body, mind and intuition and let themselves resonate so that the internal is attuned to the external, for they will be the musicians of life.

10 *Triangulated thinking.* Blessed are those who can constantly attend to the third implicit in every dyad, for creativity shall be theirs.

11 *Reflective practitioner.* Blessed are those who can see their own face and themselves as part of the system they are attending to, for they shall become undefensive and able to use themselves as a means of understanding the larger system.

12 *A life-long learner.* Blessed are they who continue to learn throughout their lives, for each of their days will be a new dawn.

13 *Stewardship.* Blessed are the stewards of teams and organizations, for they can rest knowing they have left a greater legacy for those who come after them.

Conclusion

To develop the 13 core capacities described in this chapter may sound like a tall mountain to climb, or a lifetime's work, and indeed that might be true. However, the good news is that they are called beatitudes because they are blessings, and as you open yourself to these ways of being, the wider system comes to meet and help you. These core capacities will also enrich every other aspect of your life and the view that will be increasingly open to you will be much deeper and broader.

In the next chapter we will further explore the journey to becoming a systemic team coach and outline training designs that can support this learning and development.

Training systemic team coaches

17

PETER HAWKINS AND JOHN LEARY-JOYCE

Introduction

We have been working together since 2009 developing one-day short courses, three-day certificate courses and 12-month practitioner diploma courses in systemic team coaching, both in the UK and internationally in over 20 countries in (**www.aoec.com; www.renewalassociates.co.uk**). In that time we have learnt a great deal from both our students and our faculty colleagues about what is helpful and what gets in the way in the complex journey of becoming a systemic team coach. Those who have been with us on the early courses have been very courageous and generous fellow pioneers, co-creating and developing the craft and the ways to learn it, and we greatly appreciate all their contributions.

This chapter is written as an imaginary letter to a prospective course participant about how he can get the best from the training and develop in the craft of systemic team coaching. It is followed by a letter to the same person four years later when he is living in a distant country and wanting to start up his own training. It integrates many of the actual conversations we have had with trainees and other international trainers and we hope that in addressing their questions we will also address some of the questions you would like to ask or at least find yourself interested in the answers.

Learning to be a systemic team coach

Dear Andrew

I am pleased to hear you are joining the diploma course in systemic team coaching and happy to respond to your request for some advice on how to get the most from the training. This has led me to reflect on the various certificate and diploma courses I have taught on systemic team coaching and review what I now believe is essential in the training to become a systemic team coach.

The most important step before you start is to develop your clear intention. Why do you want to become a systemic team coach? Brian Arthur, who was an economist at the Santa Fe Institute and before that Dean and Virginia Morrison Professor of Economics and Population Studies at Stanford University, is often quoted by Otto Scharmer and Jo Jaworski as saying: 'Intention is not a powerful force. It is the only force' (Scharmer and Kaufer, 2013: 178).

You might like to answer the following questions:

1 What are you passionate about doing and what is the difference you want to make in the world?

2 How does systemic team coaching connect to this purpose?

3 How will this training enable you to make a greater contribution?

4 What stakeholders will your team coaching serve?

5 What attributes, capacities and capabilities will each of these stakeholders need from you?

6 What would you like them to be saying in two years from now, about your work with them?

Traps

In teaching numerous trainings on systemic team coaching I (Peter) am beginning to recognize a series of traps that trainees regularly fall into. You might like to watch out for these in your colleagues on the course, but most importantly in yourself. Every time you notice a colleague in one of these traps, use it as an opportunity to explore creative projection, by asking: 'How might I also be in this state I recognize in my colleague?' The traps are probably impossible to avoid completely, and most of these I have fallen into in my own development, but the skill is to notice yourself being in them and learn the way out.

1 Attachment to your current competence

Nearly everyone who comes on to the training course will already be a successful coach, or organizational consultant, or leader, or a mixture of these. Some will be employed internally within organizations, but most will be working independently or in coaching or consulting businesses and therefore will be your competitors in the coaching/consulting marketplace. The common human thoughts and marketplace behaviours can kick in from day one: Who knows more than me? Who is more or less skilled? Whom do I need to impress as they might employ me in the future? How do I establish my standing and authority in this group?

These thoughts and behaviours become a strong barrier to 'unlearning', which is a necessary prelude to developing the capacities of a systemic team coach. It is essential to discover how to rest lightly in your past abilities and capability, without having to demonstrate them, or get others to notice, and at the same time hold these skills and beliefs loosely, without attachment, not knowing which aspects will be useful as you go forward and which you will need to unlearn and let go of.

Antidote: open mind, open heart, open will

Otto Scharmer and Katrin Kaufer (2013) have built on Otto's earlier work in developing 'Theory U' (Scharmer, 2007) by showing how to develop the necessary capacities to open oneself for the learning journey and to respond to the requirements of the emerging futures:

- Step one, they say, is to open the mind by suspending old habits of thought.
- Step two is to open the heart, to become unattached to your own feelings and perspectives and empathically step into the shoes and look through the eyes of others.
- Step three involves letting go of control and having to know what to do: 'With an open will we can let go and let the new come.'

(Scharmer and Kaufer, 2013: 22)

This is similar to what is described as 'creating the space for grace' (Hawkins and Smith, 2006, 2013) (see a description of this in Chapter 16).

2 This training will give me another product I can sell

I have frequently been asked: 'How do I sell systemic team coaching?' My answer is that I do not sell systemic team coaching, rather I talk with team leaders, senior executives and CEOs about what the world is requiring them and their team to step up to, which they are struggling to know how to do. Systemic team coaching is not and never can be a product. Nor can the systemic team coach be a supplier. Of course, many organizations may invite you to be a supplier and ask you how long team coaching will take, how much it will cost, and what are the benefits it will deliver. But as soon as we get locked into that conversation the work stops becoming systemic, which to be successful must be based on partnership and co-inquiry.

Antidote: partnership and triangulated thinking

When working with a team, it is important to start with the inquiring attitude, asking: 'What can we do together that we cannot do apart?' To remember you are not there to coach the team, but to enable team coaching to happen between you, the team leader and all the team members. Also, to ensure that systemic team coaching happens in the spaces between the team and their wider ecology (their social, political, economic and natural environment and in the relationships with all their stakeholders).

Triangulated thinking moves beyond suppliers and customers facing each other, negotiating what each can do for the other in a transactional contract, to both parties standing alongside each other, discovering their joint intention and the collective endeavour they are both in service of and what they must both do to co-create a synergistic development (see a fuller account of triangulated thinking in Chapter 16).

3 This programme is about adding to my toolkit

On some courses I have become aware of trainees measuring the value of the course on how many new tools they have added to their toolkit. Underneath this behaviour is a belief that the more tools I have the more competent I will be, and beneath that is the hope that: 'With lots of tools I will never get caught out, not knowing how to respond. I will always have something up my sleeve!' We become ruled by the archetype of team coach as magician.

If we get stuck in this trap we are in danger of losing some of the most important capacities we need to bring to the work of systemic team coaching, that is, our human vulnerability, our not knowing and our curious outsiderness.

Antidote: thinking future-back and outside-in

With the team, we start by asking them what the world of tomorrow requires them collectively to step up to. How does this require them as a team to be different? What is the work the team and the coach need to do together to enable this difference? You can practise this on the course at every module. You can internally hold the questions: 'What do future client teams and organizations need us, a community of potential systemic team coaches, to develop on this module? In the light of that, what does the learning community require to enable its development? How can I be best in service of that development right now?'

4 I need to be competent before I do it

Linked to the above can be a belief that I need to be competent before I start. Some coaching pairs contribute to the delay in getting started, as they feel they must learn enough before getting going. When encouraged to get on with the work, they can then put on a cloak of false competence in front of the client, claiming a clarity and a confidence that they don't yet own, which inevitably encourages the team members to do the same.

Antidote: practise sharing what you don't know and go for 'fast failure'

This programme is a great place to practise humility, transparency, open inquiry, and to sense what needs to emerge, learning as you go. Then to constantly experiment with the team, learning what works and what does not. Scharmer and Kaufer (2013) encourage us to 'iterate, iterate and iterate'. Great systemic team coaches get it wrong constantly, but are able to learn fast in an open and transparent way that provides learning for all parties. When you write up your case study of your team coaching, you will be assessed not just on what you got right, but more importantly, how well you learnt from what went wrong.

So what does the training consist of?

1 Developing oneself as an instrument of change

The most important instrument of change you possess as a systemic team coach is your own being. How you refine this instrument so that it can more powerfully resonate, reflect and respond is at the heart of the training. Bill O'Brien, who was the modest but transformational CEO of Hanover Insurance, said: 'The success of an intervention depends on the interior condition of the intervener' (Scharmer, 2007: 27). This is echoed by Ed Nevis at the Cape Cod Institute who wrote:

> There is a premium on digging into oneself so as to be fully in touch and as clear as possible in articulating self-awareness, but an equally important effort is required for listening to and understanding others. It is this interplay of expressed awareness among the people involved that is critical for the stimulation of energy in the group.
>
> (Nevis, 1987)

The course is first and foremost developing all the 'be-attitudes' described in Chapter 16 and the personal capacities that go along with these.

2 Shifting levels of focus

Often the first learning in team coaching is being able to see the team as a living system and not just a group of individuals who work together and have thoughts and feelings about each other. This involves being able to listen to individuals through the lens of hearing them speaking as one aspect of the collective team, rather than as expressing personal thoughts and feelings. To ask yourself: 'What are they expressing on behalf of the team and what is the particular systemic need that they represent and hold for the team?'

The next learning is to be able to see the team as one living system nested within a whole chain of systems. In Chapter 16' I (Peter) talked about the importance of always being able to see the level above and the level below the system you are focusing on. Scharmer (2013) usefully distinguishes between four levels of system: (a) *micro*, (b) *meso*, (c) *macro*, (d) *mundi*. In team coaching these can be seen as linking as follows:

micro – the individual team members and team tasks which are subsystems of the team system;

meso – the team as a living system;

macro – the organization that the team is part of;

mundi – the wider eco-system that interrelates with the team.

On the training you can practise scaling up and down these levels as they apply to the learning community you are part of, moving your focus from yourself to taking in each of the other individuals in your group (micro), to focusing on the group you are in as a living system (meso), to focusing on the system of the whole training and how the learning community task and dynamics unfold over time (macro), to focusing on the eco-system of the training (mundi), including all the necessary stakeholders (such as the client teams, the client teams' organizations and stakeholders, your sponsoring organization or own business, future clients, the team coaching profession).

You can also practise scaling up and down these levels when listening to case studies presented by your colleagues or the course faculty: the team member (micro), team as a living system (meso), the team and the team coaches (meso) plus the wider organization (macro), the team's eco-system (mundi).

We all also need to learn that interconnecting systems go well beyond these four levels. The whole cosmos is a never-ending chain of nested systems interacting with one another. Although sub-atomic physicists and astronomical scientists have both spent many years trying to discover the 'basic building block of life' (the indivisible system) and the ultimate system of the universe, which is not part of any other system, they have never been able to locate a system so small that there is no subsystem potentially within it, or a system so large that there is no system potentially beyond it. It reminds me of the story of the people who believed the world was balanced on the back of a turtle. 'What is the turtle resting on?' they were asked. 'Another turtle, who stands on another turtle' was the reply. 'What does the bottom turtle stand on?' they were then asked. They replied: 'It is turtles all the way down and all the way up.'

Bateson (1972) argues that life is 'a seamless web' of interconnected living processes; that to understand we need to apply the analytic scissors. He points out that there are more and less sensible places to apply the analytic scissors of our understanding, but that true madness is to apply the scissors, forget we have done so and believe that the cut exists in nature.

3 Learning the five disciplines

At the core of the training is the five discipline model of highly-effective teams. This framework is both a model for the different key territories of team performance as well as a map for the different areas a team coach needs to engage with a team to address. It would be helpful to start by reading about the five disciplines (there is a short summary in Chapter 2 of this book and longer descriptions in Hawkins (2017)) and then marking, on the model below, firstly the percentage of your time or attention you currently spend focusing on this aspect of the team, and secondly the percentage of time you think you should ideally spend on each of these aspects. It would be good to see how this changes over the time you are on the programme.

4 Learning the cycle of relationship between team coach and team

Another key model we use on the programme is the CIDCLEAR (Hawkins, 2017: 83–99) way of looking at the process stages of the coaching relationship. These are Contracting, Inquiry, Diagnosis/Discovery/Design, Contracting with the whole team, Listening, Exploring, Action and Review. Another version of this, the SIDER model has been developed by John Leary-Joyce and Hilary Lines (2018). SIDER stands for: Scoping, Inquiring, Discovery/Designing, Executing and Reviewing. Do not lose yourself in this map, while you are on the journey, but like all good maps, use it to discover what you might want to attend to on the next stage of the journey with the client team and also on the journey through the various stages of the training programme. Find time to explore how the journey unfolds for you and the team, how this is reflected in or aided by the CIDCLEAR model and how it goes beyond it. Often it is worth asking: 'What does this stage require? And what might the team and ourselves as coaches regret not having done at this stage, when we look back from the end of the journey?'

5 Learning to co-coach

One of the rich learning opportunities on the programme is working with a client team that is provided for you, where there is a contract that they will be open to working with you in an experimental way. Not being paid by this client gives you a lot of freedom, so make sure you make the most of that, and that the client has already contracted that they are willing to experiment alongside you.

Another rich opportunity is that you will be working with a co-coach with whom you will not have worked previously. This provides many challenges and benefits. It means that you can reflect on what is happening in the team, their context and your relationship with them from binocular rather than single-eyed vision. It also means that one of you can be working actively with the client while the other is stepping back and taking a more reflective perspective on what emergent patterns are arising and how you are both getting caught up in the system. When you systemically team coach by yourself, you have to combine both these roles and have the challenge to be both engaged and intervening as well as standing back and reflecting; focusing on the task and process; focusing at the levels of the individuals, the team, the wider context and your own responses and reactions and the dance between all of these. Quite a tall order, and easier to develop when you can play with the various positions along with a colleague.

I would really encourage you to experiment with reflective explorations between you at various ways in the work:

a Directly after you finish each meeting that you both attend: perhaps sharing what you noticed at each level; each of you in turn sharing what you appreciated about what your partner did, what you did, and the dance of your co-working; also what you sense you both could do to take your work and that of the team to the next level.

b In supervision to reflect on how the pattern of the team is being paralleled in the relationship between the two of you, and in the dance between you as a coaching team and the team being coached.

c To risk having time-out reflections between the two of you in front of the group, sharing your emerging questions and dilemmas, and modelling co-creating a way forward out of co-reflection.

6 Reading

You asked about reading and of course there is a long list of key books that the course asks you to read, but also I would encourage you to find time to read poetry (my own current favourites include Mevlana Rumi, Blake, Coleridge, Hafiz, Rilke); and also some of the great system thinkers who help take our perceiving, learning and thinking to the next level – people like Gregory Bateson (1972), David Bohm (Bohm and Nichol, 2002), Fritjof Capra (2003), Andreas Weber (2017), Malcolm Parlett (2015), Peter Reason (2017) and Giles Hutchins (2016).

For all your reading I would encourage you to read proactively and dialogically; by that I mean, rather than opening a book to passively absorb the wisdom of the author, imagine that you are going to meet them for dinner and decide before you arrive what it is you want to ask them and find out from them. Then it is advantageous to buy the book, so that you can respond when they say things you agree with, or when you disagree, or it sparks off new questions and you can write these in the margins. This way you will get far more out of each book.

Well, I hope you enjoy the programme even though I can promise it will not be a straightforward ride, but a challenging roller-coaster, with challenge, frustration, adventure, setbacks, and intellectual and personal stretch. I also hope you discover even more than you expect.

Bon voyage
Peter

Designing a systemic team coach training programme

Dear Andrew

It is now several years since you did the training and thank you for writing to us for advice on how you might run a similar training yourself in the country where you are now living and working as a systemic team coach. You ask about how the courses are structured; well, we now run two different types of course. One is a three-day certificate and one is the 12-month diploma course similar to the one you completed, so we will describe the design elements of each. From your own experience of being on the programme you will know that we strongly advocate that a systemic team coach has to develop a whole series of new competencies, but the more important learning, and indeed unlearning, involves acquiring new ways of being, perceiving, listening and sensing, new capacities and attitudes of being. These 'be attitudes' can be found in Chapter 16 of this book, but in the Appendix on page 323 we have included the competency framework that we have developed with our colleagues and course participants and which we use as a framework for assessing their work and accrediting them as systemic team coaches. So here is how we structure a basic foundation programme in systemic team coaching in a three-day programme and finally how we now structure the one-year diploma programme.

1 The three-day certificate course

This three-day programme provides participants with the basic understanding of the what and how of systemic team coaching and is useful for those starting out exploring being a team coach or those who are team leaders and want to be better at coaching their own teams.

Day One begins by seeking an understanding from you and the group members on their experience of the performance of teams and what beliefs and assumptions we bring about teams to the programme. This helps to generate a connection between participants and bring their knowledge into the room.

As with any learning context, the connecting of members at the beginning to start to build a trusting environment is crucial. So declaring relationships, expertise, background and motivation for being there is voiced and recorded. This includes ourselves as facilitators and our plan for the three days so we mirror the collective nature of our work together.

This takes us into a deeper exploration of how we will work together: how we develop our learning community and move from the customer/supplier dynamic of course participants and course providers to working in partnership. This places a big demand on you as the facilitator to be self-aware and capable of disclosing appropriately your internal world – the anxieties, fears and mistakes as well as the passions, joys and delights, thereby modelling the competencies of a team coach.

As with the CIDCLEAR model (see Hawkins, 2017: chapter 5), we need to agree our learning contract with the group – the structure of the day, time-keeping, confidentiality, the behaviours that will support learning, such as: listening, challenging, supporting, risk taking, open and trusting.

The first key positioning activity is establishing our perspective on 'What is Team Coaching and in particular Systemic Team Coaching?' – our definition, the systemic nature, position in time, as well as the role of the team coach as an enabler.

We then need to spell out the frameworks and models, tools and techniques that we can utilize, drawing on all the material you've experienced and studied on the programme yourself. This gives a structure to hold the learning experience. Finally, we come back to developing our being, our presence both as team members and as a team coach, creating self- and other awareness, as well as a sense of self as part of the system.

The difficulty of team coach practitioner training is the inability to have a live client team in the room to practise on, so we use a well-constructed team simulation of a company, 'Newcom', that has recently been acquired by ITEC, and international Technology company that is is owned by ARVO, which is listed on the New York Stock Exchange. On the one-year Diploma programme, teams of coaches have a live external client to fulfil this need.

We start with course members having the opportunity to meet the role-played key sponsors of the team coaching at Newcom, engaging in the initial *contracting* and conducting the first level of Inquiry. The exercise involves getting participants to listen to their internal response/reaction as valid data about the client. We talk about 'Standing naked in front of the data' (Hawkins and Smith, 2013; Leary-Joyce and Lines, 2017) before jumping to our pet personal or theoretical models. Questions like:

- What do you hear?
- Where are you curious?
- What distracts you?
- What connected patterns do you see?
- What do you feel?
- What is your somatic response?
- What are the assumptions you make about people in the system?

The richness then comes from exploring the wide range of perspectives shared by the participant observers and the assumptions that they carry, which can inhibit or enlighten the understanding of the client's system. Each coaching team then presents to the role-played team, how they would propose providing team coaching to address their challenges. Each team receives feedback on both their proposal and how they engaged the team and its different members.

The next layer of exploration is using the simulation to address the primary components of Hawkins' five disciplines framework.

We start with Commissioning, then Clarifying, Co-Creating, Connecting and then on the final day Core Learning.

Many attendees have reported learning a great deal from being on the receiving end of team coaching.

As each team runs their team coaching sessions, at any time the team coaches or the trainers can call time-outs, when we stop the role play and provide live supervision and feedback to the team coaches, before they go back and further engage the team.

The facilitators work with the group as a learning community using both a structured and unstructured approach, and using themselves in an intuitive as well as planned way.

On the third day we complete the model with the fifth discipline *Core Learning* both with the Newcom team and looking at what the Learning Community has learned about itself. This is charted against the contract and expectations identified at the beginning of the programme.

Finally there is the opportunity to bring the learning together in a Client Team Review session. In sub groups of three, one participant presents a live client situation and the other two act as coach/support. There is then a tightly structured exercise walking through the five disciplines and applying the work we've covered to this live client team, which brings clarity and understanding to the whole STC theory and practice.

The combination of theoretical, experiential and practitioner learning is a powerful and intense combination, and participants will come away understanding and experiencing the enormity and complexity of the task of systemic team coaching. However, you will also have provided a very sound route map for them to take forward into their team experiences.

2 The 12-month Diploma programme

The Systemic Team Coaching Diploma is designed for experienced individual coaches as well as consultants with coaching skills who are seeking to develop and expand their team coaching competence and practice while also gaining a recognized professional qualification. While the three-day certificate gives an overview of systemic team coaching, this diploma programme provides you with a deep understanding of the theory and methodology that underpins it.

To mirror the complexity of working with teams the programme learning opportunities are equally varied.

First, didactic input from the faculty stimulates discussion around the specific topics for each module. This includes multiple examples to illustrate the theory in action.

Second, being part of the large group experience challenges you to engage in the learning community and demonstrate your capability to make an impact. For many, this is a major personal experience, being part of a small dynamic, living organization. The faculty observe, facilitate and comment on the process of the community and what needs to happen for it to thrive and be effective.

Third are small practitioner groups where client case studies are discussed, theory is applied and interventions discussed. This can become an intimate, profound context in which to explore doubts and uncertainties about your capability, find ways to overcome them and discover your power and strengths. The faculty also provide supervision on client situations and insights into different interventions.

Skills practice happens in practice sessions with live 'time-outs' and feedback. Here you can safely experiment with being the team coach, but also role-play being the member of a 'client team' as well as observer of the process and provider of feedback. However, most important is the live practitioner experience between modules with an external organizational team client. Here is the opportunity to really try out those new interventions, grapple with the complexity of team functioning and get straight feedback on your style and presence. Because the client team engagement takes place over the 12 months of the programme, there is the expectation that the impact of your interventions can be measured. 'Before and after' surveys can be carried out and analysis of 'return on investment' explored.

Faculty are available as knowledge sources and examples of team coaches. One-to-one tutorials and impromptu supervision provide a great support and guidance in finding your way through the maze.

Your personal learning journey through the ups and downs of being a participant in the programme provides a rich insight into how you can develop as a team coach; a process of being in it – while going through it. Ultimately, how you 'show up' as a team coach is down to your personal 'signature presence', so the programme is designed to give you that deep personal understanding of yourself in your roles as a team member and team coach.

While you will learn prescribed models and processes, the ultimate aim is for you to create your own model of team coaching based on your background experience, academic study, learning on the programme and team coaching practice. The final module we call 'Harvesting the Learning', where you explain your team coaching model and demonstrate your learning to your peers and faculty through the case study of your client work.

The final assessment is done with a written paper on your model plus your client case study, followed by a viva with the faculty. While a demanding intellectual process, it is incredibly rich as it provides the bedrock of your team coaching work and the confidence to go forth and promote yourself as a competent and credible systemic team coach.

Conclusion

Becoming a systemic team coach is not something you can learn on a three-day or even a one-year programme, for it is a lifetime's journey. It involves acquiring new competencies, capabilities and capacities, which are diverse and varied, and integrating these into your own signature approach to being a systemic team coach, which maximizes your own unique mix of experience, skills and knowledge.

The learning journey involves constantly going around the action-learning cycle: learning new thinking; planning and practising how to use this; getting out there and coaching teams; reflecting on what has happened in a structured way, both with your colleagues and in formal team coaching supervision; and from this developing new grounded theories and methodology that support your team coaching.

Each team we coach should become our next teacher on this journey. We have often said that the day we work with a team, or indeed teach a team coaching programme and fail to learn something new, or develop a new approach or method, is the day we should retire from the field! We hope that this is still a number of years away. Meanwhile, back to new learning.

Good luck with running your programme and may you learn as much from these programmes as we continue to learn from ours. Let us know how you get on.

Peter and John

Systemic team coaching – where next?

18

PETER HAWKINS AND KRISTER LOWE

The organization of the future will be an embodiment of community, based on shared purpose calling on higher aspirations of people.

(DEE HOCK, FOUNDER OF THE VISA GROUP)

Introduction

This book has taken us on a long journey through many team lands. We have had the privilege to visit the living world of teams from Sydney, Australia, to Vancouver in Canada, and from Finnish and South African airlines to a USA technology start-up to UK hospitals. Many systemic team coaches have generously shared not only their successes but also their struggles and their learning. We hope that these travels and insights have helped all of us to learn how we might be more attuned 'teamlanders' (see Chapter 1), able to read the many layers of a team's dynamics and eco-system, and grow our own capacity to think and be in more complex systemic ways (see Chapter 16).

Whether we lead teams, are members of teams, coach a number of teams or all three, increasingly we need to be able to do so in a world that has been described as VUCA (Johansen 2007: 51–3) – that is, Volatile, Uncertain, Complex and Ambiguous and crowded – a world that is interconnected and resource constrained and facing major challenges. In my own lifetime I have lived through the world's human population trebling (from 2.4 billion to 7.6 billion) and human expectations and consumption accelerating even faster. At the same time, the Earth has seen a frightening rise in the extinction rates of species, with the majority of scientists in 1998 believing that we are currently in the early stages of a human-caused extinction (the Holocene extinction) and that up to 20 per cent of all living populations could become extinct within 30 years (by 2028). In 2012 E O Wilson went further and suggested that if current rates of human destruction of the biosphere continue, half of all plant and animal species of life on Earth will be extinct in 100 years. The current rate of species extinctions is estimated at 100 to 1,000 times the average extinction rates on Earth, although this is disputed by some as a very imprecise science (Lawton and May, 2010).

Within this macro global context of disruption, the nature of work and the workplace itself is witnessing the beginnings of a dramatic transformation. While there are 3 billion people in the global workforce, worker productivity is flat and employee engagement is declining. The old models of organization that got us here are insufficient to help us adapt effectively in the 21st century (Laloux, 2014). The Organization of the Future was reported in Deloitte's 2017 Human Capital Trends research on 7,000 companies in 130 countries as the #1 human capital issue. Ninety-two per cent of companies in their study reported that they were not organized correctly to succeed in the digital era and only 14 per cent reported having clarity on what the organization of the future would look like. As they noted 'the world is moving from a top-down hierarchical model to one of a "network of teams" in which people are iterating and solving problems in a dynamic, agile way'. As human work transforms to one that is increasingly team-centric and hybridized with technology (eg artificial intelligence, virtual reality, cognitive bots, etc), there is an explosion of demand for team-centric tools and approaches (eg Microsoft Teams, Facebook Workplace, Slack, Trello, pulse surveys, agile work methods, coaching, team of teams networks, monitoring, analytics, assessment tools and more). This changing workplace as of necessity demands not only new approaches to teams and team coaching, as have been illustrated in this book, but also new forms of individual and collective leadership that can support this transformation.

In my (Peter) first book on leadership team coaching (Hawkins, 2011, 2014, 2017), I argued that the complexity, speed and scale of leadership challenges were such that we had passed the time when the place of integration was the individual heroic CEO leader, and that we needed to move to collective leadership teams, with the CEO as orchestrator and coach of the collective capacity of the team to create integrated transformation in their organization and wider community. We can no longer afford to have teams that are not functioning at more than the sum of their parts, or spending too much time focusing on their internal politics and relationships rather than creating sustainable value for the world around them.

In this chapter we will bring to the book to a conclusion, first exploring the growing demand and professionalization of team coaching, then exploring some of the challenges the field will need to face in the future. Finally, we will argue that team coaching cannot be a field focused on its own isolated development, but must see itself as a small but significant part in transforming leadership development in service of the wider challenge of evolving human consciousness.

The continuing growth of the demand for team coaching

It is clear that there is a growing interest in, and development of, coaching in organizations in many parts of the world. The 2013 Ridler Report on coaching (with responses from 145 organizations) found only 5 per cent of organizations had no plans to introduce team coaching in the next three years. In the report they quote Lynne Chambers, the then Global Head of Executive Development for Rolls-Royce:

> I think the whole area of team-based coaching is going to grow significantly in our organization and coaches need to be agile at dealing with the shift from individual to group work, including all the boundary sensitivities and interpersonal issues that this shift may bring. (Coaching at Work, 2013: 7)

The 2016 Ridler Report, based on responses from 105 large and mostly international organizations, found that coaching as a whole represented 12.5 per cent of all learning and development spend. Although team coaching only represented 9 per cent of all coaching activity, 76 per cent of respondents expected an increase in team coaching in the next three years, the largest growth of any form of coaching.

Fifty-eight per cent of respondents currently used Team Coaching, 11 per cent were planning to deliver it within the next year and 17 per cent thought they would introduce it within 2–3 years, with only 15 per cent suggesting they were not going to use team coaching.

The main situations giving rise to team coaching included 'Teams needing to deal with organizational change' (37%) and 'teams needing to align to business strategy' (25%), suggesting that much of the team coaching has a strong systemic element.

The Sherpa Report, which is the largest and most global (over 1,000 responses, most of which were from coaches, only 10 per cent from HR professionals and only 8 per cent business executives), only started looking at team coaching in 2012 and in 2013. It said:

Team coaching is a newer concept. Large firms have not yet taken the lead in the design and development of team coaching.

Executive coaches, both internal and external, are presented with a rather large opportunity. Are they really taking advantage of it?

- 37 per cent of coaches offer established team coaching programme.
- Just 24 per cent of HR and training professionals do. (Sherpa Coaching, 2013: 9)

Henley's 2013 corporate survey of 359 senior executives from 38 countries found that 55 per cent had plans for using team coaching as a part of their learning and development plans in 2014 (second in popularity after individual coaching). See Figure 18.1.

Figure 18.1 2013 Research by Henley Business School. Based on responses from 359 executives from 38 countries; respondents were made up of a 60/40 split between HR and non-HR roles

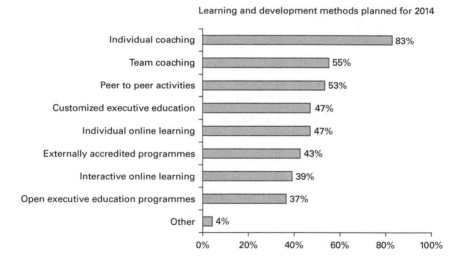

Learning and development methods planned for 2014

Method	Percentage
Individual coaching	83%
Team coaching	55%
Peer to peer activities	53%
Customized executive education	47%
Individual online learning	47%
Externally accredited programmes	43%
Interactive online learning	39%
Open executive education programmes	37%
Other	4%

In a much smaller, targeted survey I (Peter) carried out in 2014 of internal heads of leadership and development in large organizations, 82 per cent saw their efforts in team coaching growing over the next three years, 18 per cent thought they would stay the same and no one thought they would diminish.

Both the Ridler reports and my own recent smaller survey showed a wide variation in where organizations were focusing their team coaching efforts. The responses fell into three distinct clusters:

a those focusing on the board and the senior executive teams;

b those focusing on significant account teams or key project teams;

c those focusing on lower-level management teams.

Why is there a recent and continuing growth in team coaching?

From studying recent coaching surveys, research on team coaching and the recent literature on the subject, there is general agreement that team coaching is growing fast and will continue to do so. In explaining why this is the case, most studies suggest that there are three main drivers of this growth:

1 The growing need for more collective, shared and collaborative leadership in a more complex, globalized and interconnected world.

2 Nearly all companies are facing the 'unholy trinity' (Hawkins, 2012 in Hawkins and Shohet, 2012) of having to do more, at higher quality with fewer resources. This necessitates organizations having teams that are high performing and research shows that most teams perform at less than the sum of their parts. Thus some writers (Lencioni, 2002, 2006) have pointed to effective teamworking as a major competitive advantage for organizations.

3 The need for global companies to have account teams that can work in an integrated way across sectors, cultures and countries in a way that can provide added value to the customer company, beyond the products and services provided, through business foresight and/or customer/company insight (Hawkins, 2017: chapter 7).

4 Increasingly the challenges for organizations do not lie in the people, or in the individual teams or functions. As one CEO said to me (Peter): 'I have lots of coaches who coach my people, and consultants who consult to parts of my organization, but all my challenges lie in the connections' (Hawkins 2017b). Other CEOs commented on how in the next five years they would be employing fewer people, but the number and complexity of the stakeholders they will have to partner with in order to be successful will exponentially increase. This will continue to drive the need for more 'team of team coaching' (see Chapters 11 and 12) and 'Eco-systemic Team Coaching' (Hawkins, 2017 chapters 9 and 10).

These four main drivers of growth are putting pressures on organizations to adjust their designs and shift their structures to ones that are increasingly team-centric. In Deloitte's industry report on human capital management trends – HR Technology Disruptions for 2018: Productivity, Design and Intelligence Reign – they provide one notable example of how companies are grappling with this shift:

> As companies replace hierarchical management with a networked team structure, we are going to be using new tools purpose-built for teams. For example, Cisco System's team enablement leader found that while the company has 20,000 teams actively working on projects, none of their work or team-related data is in the HR systems of record – so the company has implemented a brand-new team-based management system to manage goals, performance, coaching, and more.

As this example illustrates, moving from a hierarchical structure to a team-centric structure is creating a need for an integrated and holistic approach to teams that includes organizational design, HR technology, performance management, team coaching and more. Team coaches would do well to see themselves as one important player in a larger team contributing to this sea shift in organizations. Consequently, this shift is creating a ripeness for team coaching that has been up until recently a harder sell to organizational decision makers and gatekeepers.

In sum, the time for team coaching to be taken seriously by organizations is no longer in some distant future. Its time has come and is here now. Are we as an industry and profession ready to respond? How do we need to keep developing to be fit for purpose ourselves? What disruptions do we need to proactively inject into our thinking, being and acting as team coaches to stay relevant?

Professionalization of team coaching

Team coaching is currently at the same stage that individual coaching was about 30 years ago (Sherman and Freas, 2004) – with no clarity of quality standards, little research or even accepted clear definition of terms, or established professional accreditation. However, in the same way we have seen coaching rapidly professionalize, I would predict we will see the same happen in the field of team coaching. As always, there is a strong debate for and against professionalization, and we need to be aware of the negative side effects that can come with professionalizing, such as over-standardization, increasing barriers to entry, reduction in fringe innovation and so forth. However, with the growing need from organizations to access skilled, ethically sensitive and well-trained team coaches and to have clarity about what they are purchasing and what they can expect, the drive for professionalization is inevitable.

The usual core features of a profession, according to Professor David Lane (2010) and Spence (2007), are:

- formal academic qualifications;
- adherence to an enforceable code of ethics;
- practice licensed only to qualified members;
- compliance with applicable state-sanctioned regulations;
- common body of knowledge and skills.

Bennett (2006) used these criteria to review the literature and argued that coaching had a long way to go, and yet Stephen Palmer (2008) argued that individual coaching in the UK was already a profession, rather than an 'industry', as there were:

- nationally and internationally established bodies;
- professional qualifications;
- *university or exam board accredited and professional body recognized courses*;
- national registers of coaches and accredited coaches;
- *supervision of coaches and attendance at CPD events being required*;
- codes of practice and ethics adhered to by members of professional bodies;
- national occupational standards;
- *competencies*;
- *growing research and publication of research*;
- *books and evidence-based journals*.

I have highlighted in italics the items that are already beginning to happen in the field of team coaching. In the UK, the Association of Professional Executive Coaching and Supervision (APECS; **www.apecs.org**) was the first professional body to go live with accrediting team coaches (see below). The diploma and certificate courses run by the Academy of Executive Coaching and Renewal Associates are recognized as master's-level courses and accredited by the ICF. The courses by Peter Bluckert and David Clutterbuck, just starting to run, are run in conjunction with University of Leeds Metropolitan. Over the last few years we have witnessed a dramatic increase in the number of team coaching certification programme that are being offered by team coaching consultancies and institutes (eg CRR Global, Team Coaching International, Peter Bluckert and Leeds Metropolitan, Pyramid Resource Group, Correntus, Agile Coaching Institute, Executive Coach Studio, and more…) that qualify for ICF continuing coach education units (CCEUs). Increasingly, team coaches are having specific supervision for their team coaching, and models of team coaching supervision are being developed (see Hawkins, 2017: chapter 15). The universities of Middlesex, Reading (Henley Business School) and Oxford Brookes have a number of people doing research on team coaching and indeed two of the contributors to this book completed their doctorates in team coaching through Middlesex University.

The professionalization and training of team coaches will also require the certifying organizations as well as the team coaches themselves to increasingly situate their development within the rapidly changing trends in organizations. Are we training team coaches that can work systemically, in an increasingly agile and digital work environment, at scale in a 'team of teams' approach, and in closer partnership with organizational leaders, HR, customers and other important stakeholders? These are important questions for those seeking to professionalize the team coaching industry and will separate the mediocre and good programs from the great in the years to come.

Accreditation of team coaches

As mentioned above, APECS is the first organization to have a formal process for accrediting professional executive team coaches. As with their approach to executive coaches, they expect team coaches to be able to demonstrate knowledge, competence and capability in all three legs of the coaching stool (see Hawkins, 2012: 51):

- business and organizational understanding;
- psychological training and understanding;
- training in coaching and team coaching knowledge, skills and practice.

This needs to be linked to receiving regular supervision, clear understanding of ethics in the field of team coaching and an ability to describe and demonstrate one's own signature approach to team coaching.

Development of research on, and case studies of, team coaching

There continues to be a good deal of research on team effectiveness. Google launched their Project Aristotle to study the most important ingredients of successful teams in their organization. These, in order, were:

1 Psychological safety: Can we take risks on this team without feeling insecure or embarrassed?

2 Dependability: Can we count on each other to do high quality work on time?

3 Structure and clarity: Are goals, roles, and execution plans on our team clear?

4 Meaning of work: Are we working on something that is personally important for each of us?

5 Impact of work: Do we fundamentally believe that the work we're doing matters?

(Rozovsky 2015).

Bersin (2016), in the Global Deloitte survey, found that: 'leadership now becomes a "team sport", where leaders must inspire and align the team, but also be good at connecting teams together and sharing information.'

There has been research on medical teaming (Gawande, 2011), health care (West and Markiewicz, 2016) and scientific research teams (Cooke and Hilton, 2015) as well as leadership teams (Aldag and Kuzuhara, 2015; Karlgarde and Malone, 2015; Wageman, Hackman, Nunes and Burruss, 2008).

However, as mentioned in Chapter 3, there has been a dearth of detailed case studies of team coaching in practice and this book has doubled the number readily available, as well as providing tools and guidance on how to maximize the learning from case studies. But we are still on the nursery slopes and much more needs to be done. Our hope is that this book will inspire many others to develop case studies of their work with teams and make them available, and give them some guidance and frameworks that will help them develop excellent and useful studies. A very useful new resource that is shortly to be published is *The Practitioner's Handbook of Team Coaching*, edited by David Clutterbuck, Krister Lowe, Sandra Hayes, Doug Mackie, Judith Gannon and Ioanna Lordanou, which has a range of case studies from many parts of the world.

From editing this book I (Peter) have learnt a great deal about what makes for a valuable case study and offer the following principles that I have gleaned. The case study is best when:

1 It shares multiple perspectives on the work. Many of the case studies here have been written by the team leader and the external team coach.

2 The study shows the challenges that the team were faced with and how these were addressed.

3 There are data not just on the team but on their wider organizational and stakeholder systems and attention is paid to the interaction between these levels.

4 There is evidence of how the team coaching impacted not only on the team members' relationships, the team processes and meetings, but also on the team performance and the impact on the performance of the wider organization.

5 The team leaders and/or coaches describe the models, tools and interventions they used, what worked and what did not work.

6 The team leaders and team coaches reflect on their own role, joint working and learning, and share what they would do differently next time.

7 The case study completes the action learning cycle (Kolb, 1984) and goes from theory, to planning, to action, to reflection and to new development of the starting theory.

Digitalization and team coaching

The next few years will see a dramatic development in the digitalization of many professional and support services. The legal, medical, accountancy, education and many other professions will be greatly transformed. Already there are computers that can diagnose more accurately than 80 per cent of general practitioner doctors. Coaching will not be exempt. Already we have the development of computer software that have the best coaching questions from across the world, that can read client moods and adjust their 'empathic responses and tone' accordingly, and can link clients with an enormous network of resources and contacts.

Systemic team coaching will also need to incorporate digital innovation, both because the need for systemic team coaching is already outstripping the number of trained practitioners, but also to increase effectiveness and efficiency and reduce cost. Also there is an enormous growth in virtual teams that need their team coaching to be virtual.

Already many team coaches are leveraging collaboration platforms and technologies such as Trello, Slack, Microsoft Teams, Facebook Workplace, Zoom, Skype, WebEx, Adobe Connect, and countless others as part of their regular engagements with teams. As virtual and augmented reality technologies become mainstream in the next few years, the digital landscape is going to open up exciting new tools and opportunities for teams and their coaches.

I (Peter) am working with one exciting tech start-up (www.Saberr.com) that has spent several years researching the best of team coaching and how to make it digitally available. They have looked at the enormous amount of data from dating agencies on successful and unsuccessful matches, and applied this to predict success of team relationships. They have also looked at how teams can be coached digitally by: team members filling in simple questionnaires, engaging with chat boxes, creating a collective profile of the team's strengths and challenges, providing exercises, videos, resources for each of the development challenges, providing a team room for the planned actions, and regular nudges and reminders on follow-ups.

The smart aspect of what they are developing is that it will not replace systemic team coaches, but enable them to better support and sustain their work by such features as: collecting all the thinking on a team workshop online and turning it into followed-through action; supporting the continuation of the action between team coach engagements; evaluating progress and highlighting concerns. It will also enable systemic team coaches to increase their impact, by working directly with the senior teams and providing parallel e-enabled support mechanisms for teams throughout the same organization, supporting team alignment and inter-team learning.

Systemic team coaches need to be learning from and working with digitalization. Many of our clients are needing help in developing their digital strategy and managing the culture change this requires. We need to role model that we are doing digital enablement in our own industry.

How are we in the team coaching profession disrupting ourselves now to integrate emerging technologies into our approaches? For too many of us the answer is probably 'not much'. One fact is clear: work is becoming increasingly hybridized with tighter integrations between technology and people. Team coaching has served an important role as a new disruptive social technology that promises to help with the shift from individual-centric to team-centric approaches to work and organizations. Yet if we are not proactive, the digitization of the economy may indeed quickly turn the tables and disrupt us in the coming years. What we are sure of is that team coaching five years from now will likely look and feel very different than it does today. Do we as an emerging profession have what it takes to take our team coaching game to the next level in the digital era? Accelerating our learning and culture of experimentation as team coaches in the coming years will differentiate the winners and the losers. How are you planning to stay relevant?

Team development, organizational transformation and human evolution

This book has set out the core principles of an eco-leadership approach to leading teams and organizations, as suggested in the first chapter of this book, where leadership is focused on seeing the team or the organization in dynamic relationship with its wider eco-system:

> Just as an organism fills a niche within its eco-system and food web, so does an organization fill a niche within its business eco-system (the stakeholder community across the social, economic and environmental landscapes within which the organization operates). (Hutchins, 2012: 53)

The team is both transformed by, and transforming of, its wider organization and stakeholder eco-system and only creates value through these wider engagements. I have throughout the book emphasized that every team needs to focus at a minimum on a stakeholder set that includes:

- investors, funders, commissioners;
- regulators;
- customers (and in many cases customers' customers);
- suppliers and partner organizations;
- employees (and contractors);
- communities in which the company operates;
- the natural, 'more than human' environment.

Elsewhere I have talked about the dangers of the stakeholder that is not noticed or attended to, and like the 13th fairy in the Grimms' fairy story of Sleeping Beauty, when not invited to the party, becomes the bad fairy that will later cause major problems for the organization.

A good example of this is the oil giant BP. It failed to notice, before it was too late, that fishermen off the east coast of the United States were an important stakeholder in its drilling in the Gulf of Mexico and that this stakeholder had a massive influence on US voters, customers and politicians, which eventually led to massive expenditure by BP in compensation and legal costs.

I have consistently argued that all leadership team coaching needs to be systemic team coaching, working with the team not just on its internal relating, but on its engagements with its wider organization and eco-system. This means that we need to move beyond talking about a high-performing team based solely on the team's attributes, processes and behaviours. Yes, it is important to attend to and provide coaching for these, but only as a means to an end. In Chapter 13, I suggest that:

> A team's performance can best be understood through its ongoing ability
> to facilitate the creation of added value for the organization it is part of,
> the organization's investors, the team's internal and external customers and
> suppliers, its team members, the communities the team operates within and the
> more than human world in which we reside.

This is echoed in the Chapter 14 on boards where we quote Van den Berghe and Levrau (2013: 156, 179) on what makes an effective board: 'a board is effective if it facilitates the creation of value added for the company, its management, its shareholders and all its relevant stakeholders'.

Many businesses are beginning to recognize that only by creating 'shared value' (Porter and Kramer, 2011) for all their stakeholders will they flourish and grow. The entrepreneur and leader of the large number of Virgin companies, Richard Branson (2011: 331), wrote:

> Those in businesses that do well by doing good are the ones that will thrive in
> the coming decades. Those that continue with 'business as usual', focused solely
> on profit maximization, will not be around for long (and don't deserve to be).

Tata, an even larger global conglomerate business, based in India, has creating value for all its stakeholders at the heart of its mission and values: 'Our purpose in the Tata Group is to improve the quality of life of the community we serve' (Doongaji, 2010):

> We must continue to be responsible, sensitive to the countries, communities and
> environments in which we work, always ensuring that what comes from the
> people goes back to the people many times over. (**www.tata.com**)

Dee Hock, the founder of the VISA financial services group, wrote: 'The organization of the future will be an embodiment of community, based on shared purpose calling on higher aspirations of people.'

Leadership and systemic team coaching must be part of a much wider movement to understand how we create organizations and organizational leadership fit for the future and able to create a sustainable world that is fit for life. We need to continue researching how teams can be more effective and creating and leading transformation in their wider system of influence, which enables these organizations to become more values driven, resilient, adaptive and innovative, in ways that create added value for the eco-systems they are both sustained by and sustain. (Hutchins (2012), Porrit (2007), Hawken *et al* (1999) and Porter and Kramer (2011) all give much greater detail on the business of the future.)

Systemic team coaching also needs to learn from and contribute to the growing field of new approaches to new paradigms of leadership. Much has been written about new models of leadership. What is still lacking is an integrated approach to leadership that brings together:

- strategic leadership (Hamel and Prahalad, 1994; Keller and Price, 2011);
- global leadership (Black *et al*, 2014);
- visionary, resonant and engaging leadership (McKee et al, 2008);
- values-based leadership (Barrett, 2010);
- authentic leadership (George, 2003; George and Sims, 2007; Boston, 2014);
- embodied leadership (Hamill, 2013);
- adaptive leadership (Heifetz, 1997; Heifetz *et al*, 2009; Obolensky, 2010);
- relational leadership (Lines and Scholes-Rhodes, 2013; Kellerman, 2008; Hersted and Gergen, 2013);
- sustainability and eco-system leadership (Redekop, 2010; Western, 2010, 2013; Senge, 2010; Avery and Bergsteiner, 2011);
- collective leadership (Hawkins, 2011, 2013);
- collaborative leadership (Hackman, 2011; Archer and Cameron, 2013).

There is also a much written about why leadership development is no longer fit for purpose (Kellerman, 2012; Hawkins 2017). However, there is a lack of an integrated approach that brings together all the necessary ingredients. The research I led for Henley Business School between 2015–2017 (Hawkins 2017), looked for best practice in developing 21st century collective leadership, as opposed to 20th century leaders. We found a range of 'Green Shoots – seven places where the future leadership development is already sprouting'. These included:

Challenge based leadership development – where team coaches work with diverse teams from across the business on breakthrough projects.

Deep immersion development – where a team of leaders is given a project in a very different culture and setting to do in partnership with the local people.

Team coaching a shadow leadership team of millennial young staff from across the business in parallel with coaching the senior leadership team, and then coaching the generative dialogue between the two teams.

Leaders providing team coaching and consultancy to each other's teams and businesses.

Systemic team coaching – Bridging the gap between leader development and organizational development. Developing team leadership in Deloitte UK

One of the important contributions that systemic team coaching can offer is to provide a form of leadership development that immediately translates into organizational change. We have been working for the last four years with Deloitte, the professional services firm in the UK, training their Senior Partners to develop from 'team managers and team leader' to being 'team coaches of their own team' (Hawkins, 2017: Chapter 12).

The Leading Leaders of High Performing Teams programme emerged from Deloitte's *Coaching with Impact* strategy, which identified group and team coaching as accelerators to development and organizational change.

As part of this strategy, in 2014 we were invited to train a group of internal systemic team coaches drawn from various parts of the business, and a joint inquiry began that has proved a catalyst for change. A close partnership was formed with Bath Consultancy Group (now GP Strategies) and we co-created an integrative leadership development programme with systemic team coaching at the core. The partnership modelling that has evolved in both the design and delivery of the programme actively demonstrates the qualities of teaming we are helping the leaders to develop.

Since developing this group, we have worked together with four cohorts of Senior Partners drawn from all different parts of the UK and Swiss practices. The programme starts and finishes with a team 360° questionnaire based on the five discipline model, filled in by all the team members of the team they lead, followed by a one-to-one interview with the team leader. These two steps help produce the data foundation on which the partner, with support, can build their team development and team leadership development plan.

The whole cohort then attends a two-day workshop, which covers the five disciplines of systemic team coaching from the perspective of a team leader carrying out the coaching of their own team. In each discipline they have structured exercises to apply that discipline to their own team and plan their team development. They also work in small action learning groups to support and challenge each other and learn from each other's successes and failures. They leave the workshop with specific planned actions and experiments for both their team and their own team leadership.

In their action learning cycles they are supported by one of the internal systemic team coaches. This coach helps them design and plan their changes in team meetings, roles and engagement events, and may also facilitate, with the team leader, specific team workshops or engagement with their wider partner or employee groups.

After the first action learning cycle of three months, the partners meet in their small action learning set, to review progress, co-coach around emerging challenges and learn rapidly from each other's activity. They also refresh their plan for the next cycle of action learning. This both raises the quality of their work and sustains their commitment and momentum through the process.

During this period the systemic team coaches engage in co-supervision session with the firm's team and on-to-one external supervisors. This brings an added dimension to the systemic learning for the coaches, their coachees and the organization.

After this second cycle of three months, the whole cohort comes together for the final one-day workshop. At this workshop they each present the story and timeline of their parallel journeys of their team and their own team leadership to their small group and receive help in both harvesting the learning from these two journeys and in planning how they take these development processes forward into the future. Leaders and their teams then have the opportunity to complete another team 360 and continue work with their coach for three more months to embed the learning and create sustainable change.

The whole group then explores the patterns that connect their different but parallel journeys and what that shows about the wider cultural patterns of the firm, both the positive cultural patterns that are helping the business move forward and the patterns that are holding the company back. The group then explores how they can each be active change agents not just with their own team and business unit but also with the wider firm. This has led to important new dialogues with executive teams across the firm.

Over the last four years we have partnered with Peter to design an innovative, iterative, adaptable programme that has a tangible impact to our leaders and business. For the leaders, the programme has enabled them to create capacity to focus on strategy, requiring them to trust and empower their team more, leading in a way that encourages a constructive, collective, inter-connected group ready to respond rapidly to change and challenges.

The impact of the programme keeps on giving back to the individuals, the organization and our clients in both formal and informal ways. Several have commented that because of the programme, they led a different approach with a key account generating deep insights for the client.

> *For a handful of individuals, the programme has proven to be an important launchpad for their careers and increased the level of contribution to the firm and our clients. Within months of completing the programme, I have seen leaders move from local to global roles, take on executive responsibilities and seem much more agile in their ability to adapt their leadership style and inquire collectively into the challenges of tomorrow. (Head of Coaching, Claire Davey)*

What is needed is leadership development that:

- develops collective leadership and leadership teams rather than just individual leaders;
- attends to developing the collective leadership culture not only across the organization, but all in partnerships with its wider stakeholder eco-system;
- holistically develops intellectual, emotional, social, political, ethical end ecological intelligences;
- is systemic in not only what it teaches but how it teaches;
- is focused on facing and addressing current and future challenges, connecting leadership and organizational development in a way that accelerates and deepens both;
- delivers creatively blended learning, utilizing teaching, action learning, group work, challenge and project teams, coaching, team coaching, virtual and e-learning, gaming and social media.

Leadership team coaching needs to play its part in the provision of leadership development fit for the future.

If we are leaders, systemic team coaches, executive coaches, consultants, or in the wider leadership development industry, we are an important part of necessary revolution in human consciousness, human thinking, relating and being. In Chapter 16 I quoted Giles Hutchins: 're-evaluation and transformation of our business paradigm is fundamental to successful evolution, not only of business, but of our species as a whole.... Transformational times call for transformational change' (Hutchins, 2012: 17).

For some time the 'more than human world', that is, the whole ecological system that contains and supports human life, has been sending feedback that it needs the human species to evolve to a new mode of interrelating to the rest of life with which it shares this planet. So far, the human species has been wilfully blind to the feedback and unwilling to make the changes. But while challenged by the enormity of the task, we must proceed with 'active hope' (Macy and Johnstone, 2012), always recognizing that whatever area we are specializing in, we need to focus not on its success, but on its contribution to the greater whole.

In their inspirational book *Leading into the Emerging Future*, Otto Scharmer and Karin Kaufer (2013) present a four-stage model of evolution of both human consciousness and human social organizations. One level is not necessarily better than the preceding levels and all have their place, time and function. However, Scharmer and Kaufer argue that the current world state is requiring more human beings and societies to embrace level 4.0, which is still in the early stage of emergence.

The stages of evolution of human consciousness are:

1.0   Fixed beliefs and judgements.

2.0   Scientific factual inquiry.

3.0   Collective dialogue and empathic engagement.

4.0   Collective generative dialogue – co-sensing the future needs, co-inquiring into possible responses and co-creating innovative action.

The stages in the evolution of human social organizations are:

1.0   *The state-centric model* characterized by coordination through hierarchy and control in a single-sector society.

2.0   *The free-market model* characterized by the rise of a second (private) sector and coordinated through the mechanisms of market and competition.

3.0   *The social market model* characterized by the rise of a third (NGO) sector and by negotiated coordination among organized interest groups.

4.0   *The co-creative eco-system model* characterized by the rise of a fourth sector that creates platforms and holds the space for cross-sector innovation that engages stakeholders from all sectors.

(Scharmer and Kaufer, 2013: 13–14).

These levels can be applied to thinking about the evolution of leadership teams and company boards and board functioning:

1.0   *Leadership teams and boards focused on conformance, managing risk and ensuring compliance* – both externally to the legal and fiduciary requirements of the countries in which they operate, and internally in monitoring performance and adherence to agreed strategy and processes.

2.0   *Leadership teams and boards focused on managing performance* – setting targets for growth, market share, profitability, shareholder return and company value.

3.0 *Leadership teams and boards focused on managing connections and relationships* – ensuring that the organization has the right internal connections to ensure effective and timely responsiveness to all stakeholders and a culture of 'can do' attitude and leadership at all levels. Externally, focusing on connections with the wider eco-system: upstream with the suppliers and downstream with the customers, with partner organizations, potential mergers and acquisition organizations.

4.0 *Leadership teams and boards focused on sensing the emerging future* through listening deeply to all parts of the organization and the wider stakeholder eco-system and orchestrating collaborative inquiries across the internal and external systems about what 'the organization can uniquely do, to contribute with others to what the world of tomorrow needs'.

There is much to be done and success will only emerge through new levels of collaboration: between individuals in teams; teams working collaboratively across organizations; organizations partnering more effectively across sectors and countries; not-for-profit and for-profit organizations collaborating to create shared value; and the human species learning from the more than human world how to live collaboratively with our wider eco-system.

Creating Future-fit organisations

Systemic team coaching must not become a new siloed offering. In the research I led, with global research partners, for Henley Business School between 2015–2017 on 'Tomorrow's Leadership and the Necessary Revolution in today's Leadership development' (Hawkins, 2017b), I argued that within the next five years we need to integrate the often-separate departmental functions of strategy, HR, leadership development, organizational development and coaching into one critical function, which I have called 'The future-fit function'. All of these activities including systemic team coaching have one combined purpose – to enable the organizations, and the functions, teams, relationships and individuals within them to be 'future-fit' and also the networks, partnerships and business eco-systems that the organization is within.

Thus, in this book I have specifically chosen to include two new case studies that show systemic-team coaching, integrating with leadership development, individual coaching, HR and strategy, to help their organization ride the roller-coaster of hyper-change and embrace the growing complexity of a hyper-connected world. One from a fast-growing west coast technology business (Chapter 12), and one from a well-established airline business in

South Africa (Chapter 11), that is having to transform its business.

The Tomorrow's Leadership research (Hawkins, 2017b), interviewed CEOs, HR Directors and nominated Millennial Future Leaders in over 40 companies from different sectors and countries, combined this with the data from the world's leading surveys on these three groups, over a hundred pieces of thought leadership that has been published on future leadership and the changing needs of leadership development and a number of carefully facilitated focus groups.

It showed that the seven largest challenges that organizational leaders were currently seeing were:

1 unceasing and accelerating transformation;

2 the technological and digital revolution;

3 disintermediation and 'Uber-ization';

4 the hollowing out of organizations and the growing complexity of the stakeholder world;

5 globalization;

6 climate change;

7 the need to learn and adapt faster.

It then argued that this emerging world was going to require new and different leadership capacities (not individual leader competencies, but collective leadership capacities). We began to see the shape of a number of critical tipping points, both in our assumptions about leadership (what it is, where it is located and how it operates) and in how it needs to transform to be fit for our future world.

These tipping points were:

a from 'leading my people' to 'orchestrating business ecosystems';

b from 'heroic individual leaders' to 'collective and collaborative leadership';

c leadership needing to be driven by purpose and value creation for all stakeholders;

d from serial and fragmented innovation to working simultaneously in three time frames;

e embracing multiple individual diversity and also systemic diversity;

f leader as developer;

g motivation, millennials and mobility;

h 'no place to hide' – implications of living in a transparent world;

i partnering and networking.

(Hawkins, 2017b: 17).

The report also identified 'Green Shoots' where there were examples of new leadership development approaches that were more likely to develop 21st century needed leadership, rather than 20th century leaders. These included:

- Integrating individual, team and organizational learning.
- Challenge-based leadership development – Building leadership development by getting multi-functional groups working on the future challenges of the organization, supported by systemic team coaches/trainers, who can provide 'just-in-time learning input' and maximize the learning from both the content and the group process.
- Deep immersion training – An extension of challenge-based leadership developed is development programmes that involve deep immersion in a very different culture and setting to the one you are used to.
- Systemic team coaching of intact teams and team of team coaching.
- Secondments and peer consulting – leaders going in to other areas to partner them with their transformation.
- Shadow leadership teams – where a group of young millennial future leaders, works in parallel to the leadership teams on the same agenda and then there is a facilitated dialogue that focuses each team on shifting the fixed mindsets of the other group and generating new thinking beyond both.
- Self-system awareness – developing agility, resilience, capacity and consciousness through jointly working on inner self-awareness and awareness of the wider eco-systems you are part of. This can be combined with any of the above approaches.

Systemic team coaching must not become a new silo of activity – or be seen as a golden bullet to solve complex organizational challenges. Rather it should be seen as a constantly developing new synthesis of the best of organizational development, coaching practice, and leadership development, geared to addressing the urgent need to create future-fit leadership and future-fit organizations. Organizations that can not only increase and sustain their individual success, but can constantly co-create value with and for all their stakeholders and make a positive contribution to creating the well-being world for our collective grandchildren.

Chris Fussell, who worked as aide-de-camp for General McChrystal as they developed a radical 'Team of Teams' approach in terrorist ridden, post-war Iraq, and who has gone on to apply this thinking in many commercial and public-sector organizations, ends his book (Fussell 2017: 248–9) by saying:

'Aligning teams, communicating with transparency, decentralizing decision making, these stand-alone concepts are not new. But if organizations are willing to truly embody them together, linchpinned by leaders who can assume humble, non-heroic roles and individual team members who embrace new realms of responsibility, they will set the standard for effective enterprises in the years to come.....

Those who survive this transformation into the information age wills set the standards for years to come, and those who hold tightly to the twentieth century playbook will be a footnote in history.

Conclusion

Our hope is that this book has made a small contribution to that greater cause.

APPENDIX
AOEC/Renewal Associates

AoEC/Renewal Associates

A Setting the foundation

   i   Meeting ethical guidelines and professional standards

   ii   Establishing the coaching agreement

   iii *Working ethically in an organizational context*

B Co-creating the relationship

   iv Establishing trust and intimacy with the client team

   v   Coaching presence

   vi *Managing self, individuals and team*

C Communicating effectively

   vii Active listening

   viii Powerful questioning

   ix Direct communication

D Facilitating learning and results

   x   Creating awareness

   xi Designing actions

   xii Planning and goal setting

   xiii Managing progress and accountability

Notes

Each competency listed on the following pages has a definition and related behaviours.

Essential ICF competencies: are in regular font. These are behaviours classified as those that should always be present and visible in any coaching interaction.

Discretionary advanced level competencies: are in *italics*. These are behaviours that are called for in certain coaching situations (eg in this context in team coaching) and, therefore, not always visible in any one coaching interaction.

Competencies and indicators that are especially relevant to systemic team coaching and that are over and above the competencies and indicators currently required for ICF accreditation are in **bold**.

A Setting the foundation

Meeting ethical guidelines and professional standards – Understanding of coaching ethics and standards and ability to apply them appropriately in all coaching situations:

A Understands and exhibits in own behaviours the ICF Standards of Conduct (see list).

B *Understands and follows all ICF Ethical Guidelines (see list).*

C **Is clear about the boundary of team coaching and consulting.**

Establishing the coaching agreement – Ability to understand what is required in the specific coaching interaction and to come to agreement with the prospective and new client team and sponsors about the coaching process and relationship:

A **Establishes how he/she will work to be of most value to the team.**

B *Determines whether there is an effective match between his/her coaching method and the needs of the prospective client team.*

Working ethically in an organizational context – Attending to and working with the relationship between the team and the wider context:

A **Develops contract transparently with team members, team leader and sponsor(s).**

B **Holds the wider organizational agenda as a context for the work with the client team.**

C **Draws on appropriate methods for gathering data that will help clarify the scope and progress of the coaching.**

D Helps the client team to clarify the 'collective endeavour' and outcomes they are committed to in the context of overall organizational requirements for the team.

E Manages the complexities of confidentiality within the team and between the team and its environment.

F Facilitates effective connections between the team and the wider organization.

B Co-creating the relationship

Establishing trust and intimacy with the client team – Ability to create a safe, supportive environment that produces ongoing mutual respect and trust:

A Provides ongoing support for and champions new behaviours and actions, including those involving risk taking and fear of failure.

B *Asks permission to coach client team in sensitive, new areas.*

C Helps the client team to respect and work with individual perspectives facilitating the creation of collective understanding.

Coaching presence – Ability to be fully conscious and create spontaneous relationship with the client team, employing a style that is open, flexible and confident:

A Is comfortable with 'not knowing', ie able to be open about own uncertainty without 'having to be in control'.

B Sees many ways to work with the client team, and chooses in the moment what is most effective.

C *Confidently shifts perspectives and experiments with new possibilities for own action.*

D Demonstrates confidence in working with strong emotions, and can self-manage and not be overpowered or enmeshed by client team's emotions.

E Judges when it is appropriate to intervene in the team and when it is more appropriate for the team to 'work it through' themselves.

Managing self, individuals and collective – The ability to work dynamically with both individuals and the collective, attending to the individual in the context of collective coaching goals and to manage self with awareness and integrity:

A Able to handle multiple perspectives/agendas while seeing them in the context of the collective agenda.

B Enables the client team to acknowledge and deal with changes that occur during the coaching programme (eg changes in team membership/leadership).

C Works with the team to link the various perspectives and views of team members into a collective understanding that advances their joint thinking.

D Facilitates clear, direct and honest dialogue between team members.

C Communicating effectively

Active listening – Ability to focus completely on what the client team is saying and is not saying, to understand the meaning of what is said in the context of the client team's desires, and to support client team self-expression:

A Hears the client team's concerns, goals, values and beliefs about what is and is not possible.

B Encourages, accepts, explores and reinforces the client team's expression of feelings, perceptions, concerns, beliefs, suggestions, etc.

C Integrates and builds on client team's ideas and suggestions.

D *'Bottom-lines' or understands the essence of the client team's communication and helps the client team get there rather than engaging in long descriptive stories.*

E *Allows the client team to vent or 'clear' the situation without judgement or attachment in order to move on to next steps.*

F Attends to patterns/non-verbal signals/energy flow and offers feedback that leads to learning.

Powerful questioning – Ability to ask questions that reveal the information needed for maximum benefit to the coaching relationship and the client team:

A Asks questions that reflect active listening and an understanding of the client team's perspective.

B Asks questions that evoke discovery, insight, commitment or action (eg those that challenge the client team's assumptions).

C Asks open-ended questions that create greater clarity, possibility or new learning.

D Asks questions that move the client team towards what they desire, not questions that ask for the client team to justify or look backwards.

Direct communication – Ability to communicate effectively during coaching sessions, and to use language that has the greatest positive impact on the client team:

A Is clear, articulate and direct in sharing and providing feedback.

B Able to be bold and to 'name' what is observed in the team.

C Able to retain rapport with the team while offering challenge/different perspectives.

D Can articulate the rationale behind interventions made in their practice.

E *Uses metaphor and analogy to help to illustrate a point or paint a verbal picture.*

D Facilitating learning and results

Creating awareness – Ability to integrate and accurately evaluate multiple sources of information, and to make interpretations that help the client team to gain awareness and thereby achieve agreed-upon results:

A Offers models and frameworks as part of a collaborative process with the team (as opposed to advising, leading or taking charge of the team).

B Helps client teams to see the different, interrelated factors that affect them and their behaviours (eg thoughts, emotions, body, background).

C Expresses insights to client teams in ways that are useful and meaningful for the client team.

D *Asks the client team to distinguish between trivial and significant issues, situational vs recurring behaviours, when detecting a separation between what is being stated and what is being done.*

E Uses appropriate experiments/exercises/activities to extend or deepen awareness of team effectiveness.

F Helps team members identify what they already do well collectively and what they want to change.

G Facilitates raising awareness of what is 'not being expressed' (unspoken feelings and concerns) within the team.

Designing actions – Ability to create with the client team opportunities for ongoing learning, during coaching and in work/life situations, and for taking new actions that will most effectively lead to agreed-upon coaching results:

A *Challenges client team's assumptions and perspectives to provoke new ideas and find new possibilities for action.*

B Helps the team to clarify their own objectives within the context of the wider strategic objectives.

C Invites the team to explore the wider organizational agenda ie the needs that the team exists to serve, and draw lessons for interacting with this agenda.

D Supports the team to clarify how it needs to function in order to deliver its required outcomes.

E *Advocates or brings forward points of view that are aligned with client team goals and, without attachment, engages the client team to consider them.*

F Helps the team to seek feedback on how they are seen by key stakeholders.

G Helps the team to evaluate how effectively they are engaging with their wider stakeholder system (eg upwards, downwards, sideways).

H Draws on appropriate exercises/activities to help the team see themselves from the viewpoint of their stakeholders.

I Helps the team to make decisions about what connections need to be built/strengthened.

Planning and goal setting – Ability to develop and maintain an effective coaching plan with the client team:

A Helps the team create plans/objectives that are appropriate to achievement of their desired outcome(s).

B Makes plan adjustments as warranted by the coaching process and by changes in the situation.

C *Identifies and targets early successes that are important to the client team.*

D Encourages the team to take collective responsibility for the learning and development of team members.

Managing progress and accountability – Ability to hold attention on what is important for the client team, and to leave responsibility with the client team to take action:

A Regularly invites the team to reflect on what and how they are learning.

B Helps the team decide how they will continue to support and challenge each other after the coaching programme has ended.

C Challenges the team if they are not taking collective responsibility for progress towards desired outcomes.

D *Focuses on the coaching plan but is also open to adjusting behaviours and actions based on the coaching process and shifts in direction during sessions.*

E *Is able to move back and forth between the big picture of where the client team is heading, setting a context for what is being discussed and where the client team wishes to go.*

F *Develops the client team's ability to make decisions, address key concerns, and develops himself/herself (to get feedback, to determine priorities and set the pace of learning, to reflect on and learn from experiences.*

BIOGRAPHIES OF
THE CONTRIBUTORS

Shannon Arvizu

Dr Shannon Arvizu's passion for transforming the next generation of managers into epic team leaders can be traced back to when she first gained her chops as a social scientist researching global youth movements. What she uncovered is that the next generation of leaders are motivated by a new kind of leadership, collaborative leadership, which will be the defining force of the next century. To that end, Dr. Arvizu founded Epic Teams (www.epicteams.co) to help fast-growing companies build high-performing collaborative cultures that scale and continuously improve over time.

Dr Arvizu received her PhD in Sociology from Columbia University, with an emphasis in technology and organizations. She is also certified as a positive psychology coach and teaches team leadership courses at General Assembly in San Francisco.

Gavin Boyle

Gavin Boyle joined the NHS just over 20 years ago as a general management trainee in Liverpool. This followed University and a degree in Biological Sciences, then a short period of private industry. He spent the first part of his NHS life in and around Liverpool in both primary care and organizations and hospitals, then on to Exeter and then Winchester where he was responsible for a broad range of hospital and community services. More recently he has held board level posts as Director of Operations at the Oxford Radcliffe Trust, the Queens Medical Centre in Nottingham and at Leeds Teaching Hospitals. Prior to joining Derby Teaching Hospitals in March 2016 as Chief Executive, Gavin has held the position of Chief Executive at Chesterfield Royal Hospital NHS Foundation Trust and Yeovil District NHS Foundation Trust. Gavin became Chair of East Midlands Leadership Academy in November 2013 and is Chair of the East Midlands Acute Hospitals Chief Executives forum.

Catherine Carr

Dr Catherine Carr is an innovative systemic coach who draws on positive psychology practices to inspire a bigger vision of change – personally, in teams and organizations, and in the world. She is a professional certified coach, master corporate executive coach, the Resilience @ Work lead for Canada, and registered clinical counsellor with Carr Kline & Associates, Canada.

Over her career, she has worked across business sectors with particular experience in the public sector. She has worked to inspire change as a government-wide mental health consultant and as a strategic practice lead creating an individual and team coaching programme offered to 26,000 people across government. Her ongoing work centres on creating resilient and purpose-driven leaders and teams. Her education includes a BSc in Biology and Environmental Studies, an MEd in Counselling Psychology and Leadership, a Graduate Certificate in Executive Coaching and a Professional Doctorate in Leadership Development and Executive Coaching. In 2012, Catherine won the Goulding Award given to the most outstanding professional doctorate for her work on team coaching. She is the co-author of two books on coaching: *50 Tips for Terrific Teams* and *High Performance Team Coaching*, several peer-reviewed journal articles, book chapters and magazine articles. Catherine also volunteers as an executive coach for TED Talks and Starting Bloc, organizations committed to changing the world.

Sue Coyne

Sue began her career in marketing and then spent 20 years as an owner/director of a market research agency. She led a management buy-out in 1996 and grew the business to be in the top 10 in the UK before selling it in 2002 when she exited the business. In 2003 she trained as an executive coach and added to that later by training as a systemic team coach. She brings together her business experience with the latest thinking on leadership, her advanced coaching skills and 10 years of walking alongside executives, board directors, boards and senior leadership teams to enable sustainable high performance. She published *Stop Doing Start Leading* in 2016. She adopts a holistic, systemic approach, understands the challenges faced by senior leaders and acts as a trusted adviser and sounding board. She operates her leadership development consultancy through suecoyne.com and Connectiveness Ltd.

Justin Dell

Justin Dell is the Ground Operations Manager (HOD) for Comair. He is fully accountable for the national and regional service delivery in the

Airports Airside environment and all components related to this, eg security, airside operations, and AMC, GEFB Ramp and Cargo. His primary focus is to ensure that punctuality, airside operational efficiency and aviation safety, security and quality assurance is maintained. He liaises internally with EXCO, Finance, IT HR, Operations Control and other Operational Departments regarding any matters that impact the Comair Airport Airside Operations and ensures that third party suppliers deliver and maintain standards according to SLAs in place. Building strong relationships with internal and external partners supports the effective day-to-day running of airside operations, policy compliance and amendments, budgets, customer service, safety and security and landside operations.

Carole Field

Carole Field is a partner at O'SullivanField, coaching with individuals and teams. Clients appreciate the value of her grounded presence, saying that she provokes their thinking and provides critical support as they transition and transform. She maintains special interest in coach professional development. This includes partnering with client organizations to develop the coaching capability of internal coaches and the provvision of supervision for coaches and mentors. Carole is a published author, including co-authoring *Mastering the Art of Leadership*, and contributed to *Women in New Business Leadership*.

Peter Hawkins

Dr Peter Hawkins is the international thought leader in systemic team coaching. He is the author of many books, including *Leadership Team Coaching: Developing collective transformational leadership* (third edition 2017) and *Creating a Coaching Culture* (2012). He is Professor of Leadership at Henley Business School, Emeritus Chairman of Bath Consultancy Group and Director of Renewal Associates and consults to many boards and executive teams internationally. He trains and supervises systemic team coaches from many countries through the AoEC and Renewal Associates and coach supervisors through Bath Consultancy Group.

Margaret Heffernan

Margaret Heffernan produced programmes for the BBC for 13 years and then started and ran software companies in the United States for the next 10 years. Her third book, *Willful Blindness: Why we ignore the obvious at our peril*, was a finalist for the Financial Times Best Business Book Award 2011 and her TED talks have been seen by over 7 million people. In 2015, she was awarded the Transmission Prize for *A Bigger Prize: Why Competition isn't Everything and How We Do Better*, described as 'meticulously researched... engagingly written... universally relevant and hard to fault'. Through Merryck & Co., she advises CEOs and senior executives of major global organizations and is Lead Faculty for the Forward Institute's Responsible Leadership Programme. She holds an honorary doctorate from the University of Bath and continues to write for the *Huffington Post* and the *Financial Times*.

Alison Hogan

Alison Hogan is Managing Partner at Anchor Partners, a leadership coach and consultant and Honorary Fellow of the University of Exeter Business School Exeter Centre for Leadership, specializes in organizational change, leadership development and boardroom behaviours. She has written about excellence in board leadership, co-led leadership programmes and is a graduate of courses including systemic team coaching and Gestalt international organization and systems development.

David Jarrett

David is Managing Director of Jarrett Partners Ltd. He was previously CEO of Bath Consultancy Group and a partner at KPMG as part of their Financial Services Transformation group. He is an experienced coach working with executive teams across a range of industries, including commercial businesses, professional and financial services.

He has worked with executive teams in Finland, Germany, India and China as well as the UK, with clients including a major European airline, a global minerals and metals processing leader, a global shoe manufacturer, a European postal service and logistics company, one of the Big Four professional services companies, several global financial services companies and a global telecommunications manufacturer. David has recently been exploring the impact of the digital age upon the nature of leadership and culture needed for these different business environments we are seeing.

John Leary-Joyce

John Leary-Joyce is the founder and Executive Chair of the Academy of Executive Coaching. As entrepreneurial leader, John understands the importance of teamwork and the value of team coaching. Over the past 15 years he has become widely recognized as a senior transformational coach, combining this with a 20-year career as a Gestalt group facilitator/trainer, recently authoring *Fertile Void: Gestalt coaching at work*. With substantial team building and process consulting experience, he has become a highly regarded team coach working in large organizations, especially in legal and accountancy firms. He has an MA in executive coaching, and is an accredited coach with APECS, a qualified supervisor and a frequent conference presenter. He is core faculty on the innovative Masters in Systemic Team Coaching programme, which he designed with Peter Hawkins.

Hilary Lines

Dr Hilary Lines has over 30 years' experience of working with senior leaders as an executive and team coach, as a facilitator and trusted adviser in organizational change and as an innovator in leadership development across the globe. Hilary specializes in helping senior leaders work with conflict and difference within their teams, enabling them to create new organizational cultures through working with difference in a constructive and creative way. Her 2013 book *Touchpoint Leadership* (with Jacqui Scholes-Rhodes) provides a template for leaders to build collaborative relationships and cultures that build lasting value. She is on the faculty of the Academy of Executive Coaching Diploma in Systemic Team Coaching.

Krister Lowe

Krister Lowe, MA, PhD, CPCC is an Organizational Psychologist, an Executive and Team Coach, and a Podcaster. Krister is the Host of the The Team Coaching Zone podcast – a weekly interview show that explores the art and science of team coaching – and that has a listenership in more than 125 countries around the world. Dr Lowe is a specialist in team coaching, conflict resolution and performance management and has more than fifteen years of experience consulting to diverse organizations in more than 25 countries throughout Europe, Asia, Africa, the Middle East, and the Americas. His coaching, consulting, facilitation and training interventions have reached more than 25,000 people globally. He has expertise in a number of sectors including: international organizations, professional services, financial services, information technology, foundations, pharmaceuticals and education. Krister holds both a Master of Arts Degree and a Doctor of Philosophy Degree in Social-Organizational Psychology from Columbia University.

Angela McNab

Angela McNab started her career as a speech and language therapist, progressing to general management in the UK National Health Service. She has held a variety of senior leadership roles, including Director of Public Health Delivery (Department of Health) and CEO of a national regulator. She has written a number of articles in health journals, is an executive coach and is currently CEO of Camden and Islington NHS Trust.

Tracey McCreadie

Tracey McCreadie is the Service Delivery Manager at Comair Limited. Her expertise lies in the areas of Strategic Implementation (Cabin crew and Airports), Customer Experience and Industrial Relations.

Tracey ensures within the Comair Service Delivery team that a seamless experience for Comair passengers is given from their check-in at the airport, through to boarding the aircraft, onboard services and collection of luggage at their destination. Her team comprises Airport Management, Cabin Services Management and a special service offering to high valued passengers.

Tracey is also a Director of Food Directions, a subsidiary of the Comair group, providing onboard catering to their British Airways and Kulula brands, as well as Comair's Slow Lounges in airports and city centres.

Judith Nicol

Judith Nicol started her leadership coaching practice in 2002. She has worked with many boards, CEOs, directors, talented leaders and senior leadership teams in FTSE 100, 250 and mid-cap companies as well as smaller and venture-capital-backed organizations and in the not-for-profit sector. Judith spent her early career in executive search and became a partner with Spencer Stuart, one of the leading global consultancies. She has trained in the UK and the United States and has been ICF PCC accredited since 2005. She is a qualified systemic team coach. Judith has published a paper on 'Leadership range and flexibility' with Lancaster University and in 2011 she authored the ARC Culture and Leadership Impact diagnostic tools that work with these concepts.

Padraig O'Sullivan

Padraig is Founder and Managing Partner of O'SullivanField. His reputation as a thought leader, international coach and educator has been established with over 12 years' global leadership and coaching experience. His work with executive teams guides them to high performance. At an individual level, he supports executives in transition. He is an Honorary Fellow of the Sydney Business School (UOW) where he teaches on the Masters of Business Coaching, specializing in innovation and business change, and leading teams and groups towards high performance. He is published in academic journals and is co-author of *Leadership: Helping others to succeed*. His new book, *Foreigners in Charge: Success strategies for expert leaders in Australia*, was published in 2014.

Jacqueline Peters

Dr Jacqueline Peters collaborates with senior leaders to strategically develop their individual and team leadership abilities to achieve maximum results. Drawing upon wisdom and knowledge gained over 25 years as a leadership and organizational effectiveness specialist, she focuses on action and accountability in her coaching. Jacqueline works primarily in the oil and gas, retail, financial, and telecommunication sectors. Jacqueline has completed a BSc, a diploma in career development, an MEd in adult and higher education, a professional doctorate in leadership development and executive coaching and is a professional certified coach with the International Coaching Federation. Jacqueline is an international speaker and writer on team coaching and is co-author of two books on team effectiveness: *50 Tips for Terrific Teams* and *High Performance Team Coaching*. She melds her leadership and team development expertise with her training as a couples therapist in her latest book *High Performance Relationships: The heart and science behind success at work and home*.

David Presswell

David Presswell is a partner of Aretai LLP and an executive coach. He works with senior teams and individuals in a broad range of organizations, internationally, often employing a systemic constellation approach. He was formerly Head of Global Coaching at YSC, a business psychology consultancy working with half the FTSE 100. His early career was as a TV director of factual programmes for BBC and Channel 4 in the United Kingdom, and Discovery, PBS and A&E in the United States. He read English Literature at Oxford University and studied theatre directing at The Bristol Old Vic Theatre School – from where he got much of his initial interest in an embodied approach.

Jacqui Scholes-Rhodes

Dr Jacqui Scholes-Rhodes is a freelance coach and coach supervisor, specializing in the systemic development of leaders and teams. She has held several senior leadership roles, including OD Director for a global pharmaceutical company, and in 2002 was awarded a PhD from the Centre for Action Research, University of Bath, for her work in narrative inquiry and dialogue. She has coached across private and public sectors for over 15 years, first with Korn Ferry and then with Praesta Partners, and is joint author of *Touchpoint Leadership: Creating collaborative leadership across teams and organizations*.

Danny Tuckwood

Danny is a Director and Principal Consultant with Metaco in Johannesburg, South Africa. His work with leaders and teams involves reducing complexity, achieving clarity of strategy, and enabling the collaboration and co-operation across stakeholder groups that characterizes high-performance. Originating from the UK, Danny has an extensive background in the international corporate world and has also developed a number of entrepreneurial business ventures. Danny has an MSc in Coaching and Behavioural Change from Henley Business School, is registered with the SA Board of People Practitioners as a Master HR Professional: Learning and Development, and is a qualified coach supervisor.

Erik Venter

Erik Venter is CEO of Comair. Erik joined the airline in 1996 as Financial Manager, and has held various positions within the company including Commercial Manager, Commercial Director and Financial Director. In July 2006 Erik was appointed as Joint CEO of Comair and in December 2011 he subsequently assumed the sole responsibility for the company as Chief Executive Officer. Erik has a BCom and Postgraduate Diploma in Accounting from the University of Cape Town and further completed his articles with KPMG qualifying as a Chartered Accountant (South Africa). Erik has served two terms as Chairman of the Airlines Association of South Africa from November 2013 until November 2015.

Barbara Walsh

Barbara is a director and principal partner of Metaco in Johannesburg, South Africa. Her specific interests lie in the areas of strategic planning, communication and stakeholder relationships and cultural change. She partners with senior teams and leaders for whom success depends on their ability to navigate complexity, anticipate an uncertain future, thrive through rapid change, and partner across various stakeholder groups to achieve their results. Barbara has an MSc in Coaching and Behavioural Change through Henley Business School in the UK (distinction and academic award) and several recognized practitioner coaching qualifications, including a Master Practitioner Diploma in Systemic Team Coaching. She is registered by the SA Board for People Practices as a Master HR Practitioner: Learning and Development and is a qualified coach trainer.

Geraldine Welby-Cooke

Geraldine Welby-Cooke heads up Organizational Development and Talent Management at Comair Limited, based in Johannesburg, South Africa. Her experience includes building and managing capabilities in talent management, organizational culture, performance management, change, team coaching, leadership development, and organizational design and alignment.

She is passionate about making a difference to business and individuals through identifying and leveraging people capabilities linked to business strategy. She works systemically across business to create an environment that fosters collaboration, enhances performance and enables business success.

Geraldine has a Masters Degree in Human Resource Management and is an industrial psychologist with experience in the consulting and corporate sector.

GLOSSARY

Account team: A multidisciplinary and/or a multi-regional team brought together from across a company to focus on the relationship with one key customer or client organization.

Action learning: 'Action learning couples the development of people in work organizations with action on their difficult problems... (it) makes the task the vehicle for learning and has three main components – people, who accept the responsibility for action on a particular task or issue; problems, or the tasks which are acted on; and the set of six or so colleagues who meet regularly to support and challenge each other to take action and to learn' (Pedler, 1997).

Agile Teaming: is about quickly forming (and ending) teams as needed to achieve project based commissions. They are helped by using Agile Methodology which help teams respond to unpredictability through incremental, iterative work cadences and empirical feedback.

Appreciative inquiry: 'Appreciative Inquiry seeks out the very best of "what is" to help ignite the imagination of "what might be". The aim is to generate new knowledge which expands "the realm of the possible" and helps the partners of an organization envision a collectively desired future and then to carry forth that vision in ways which successful translate intention into reality' (Cooperrider and Srivastva, 1987).

Clarifying: One of the Hawkins' five disciplines for a high-performing team which measures how the team clarifies and develops its mission, including: purpose, strategic goals and objectives, core values, protocols and ways of working, roles and expectations, compelling vision for success.

Coaching supervision: The process by which a coach, with the help of a supervisor, can attend to understanding better both the client system and themselves as part of the client–coach system, and by so doing transform their work and develop their craft (Hawkins and Smith, 2006, 2013). Supervision does this by also attending to transforming the relationship between the supervisor and coach and the relationship with the wider contexts in which the work is happening.

Co-creating: One of the Hawkins' five disciplines for a high-performing team: measures how a team is attending to the way it creatively and generatively works together. The team is noticing when it is functioning well at more than the sum of its parts and also noticing and interrupting its own negative patterns, self-limiting beliefs and assumptions.

Commissioning: One of the Hawkins' five disciplines for a high-performing team: a commission that gives the team a clear purpose and defined success criteria by which the performance of the team is assessed.

Connecting: One of the Hawkins' five disciplines for a high-performing team: measuring how the team is engaging in new ways to transform stakeholder relationships so that they drive improvement in their own and the organization's performance.

Core learning: One of the Hawkins' five disciplines for a high-performing team: measures how the team reflects on its own performance and multiple processes and consolidates its learning ready for the next cycles of engagement. This discipline is also concerned with the support and development of team member performance.

Eco-systemic team coaching: 'Sees the team as co-evolving in dynamic relationship with its ever-changing eco-system of interconnected teams, with which it co-creates shared value. Eco-systemic coaching focuses on the interplay between the team and other connected teams (inter-team coaching), its external partners (partnership coaching) and its wider stakeholder networks.'

Fast-forward rehearsals: The process of inviting the team not just to talk about what they will do differently, but to step into the future and enact how they will be different (Hawkins and Smith, 2006).

Felt awareness: The inner knowledge or awareness that has never been consciously thought or verbalized – as that 'something' is experienced in the body.

Group coaching: Coaching of individuals carried out in a group setting, utilizing the resources of the rest of the group to support the coaching.

High-performing team: A small number of people with complementary skills who are committed to a common purpose, set of performance goals, and approach for which they hold themselves mutually accountable. The common approach needs to include: ways of effectively meeting and communicating that raises morale and alignment, effectively engaging with all the team's key stakeholder groups and ways that individuals and the team can continually learn and develop.

Leadership team coaching: Team coaching for any team, not just the most senior, where the focus is on how the team gives leadership to those who report to it and also how the team influences its key stakeholder groups.

Learning team: A group of people with a common purpose who take active responsibility for developing each other, themselves, their team and the wider organization in which they operate, through both action learning and unlearning.

Limbic resonance: The capacity for sharing deep emotional states arising from the limbic system of the brain.

International team: A group of people who come from different nationalities and work interdependently towards a common goal (Canney Davison and Ward, 1999: 11).

Organizational energy: The force that an organization uses to purposefully put things in motion. Organizational energy is the extent to which a company, department or team has collectively mobilized its emotional, cognitive and behavioural potentials in pursuit of its goals.

Project team: A team brought together, often drawn from different teams, for a specific, defined and time-limited task.

Pseudo team: 'A group of people working in an organization who call themselves or are called by others a team; who have differing accounts of team objectives; whose typical tasks require team members to work alone or in separate dyads towards disparate goals; whose team boundaries are highly permeable with individuals being uncertain over who is a team member, and who is not; and/or who, when they meet, may exchange information but without consequent shared efforts towards innovation' (Schippers, West and Dawson, 2014).

Psychodrama: An action method, most known for being used as a psychotherapy, in which clients use spontaneous dramatization, role playing and dramatic self-presentation to investigate and gain insight into their lives.

Real team: 'A group of people working together in an organization who are recognized as a team; who are committed to achieving team-level objectives upon which they agree; who have to work closely and interdependently in order to achieve those objectives; whose members are clear about their specified roles within the team and have the necessary autonomy to decide how to carry out team tasks; and who communicate regularly as a team in order to regulate team processes' (Richardson, 2010: 86).

Requisite conflict: The team having no more, or no less conflict than currently exists in the system they need to respond to.

Requisite diversity: The team having a level of diversity that is equal to the diversity in the stakeholder world they need to engage with.

Systemic constellations: A way of working with issues within human systems (Hellinger, 1998, 1999).

Systemic team coaching: 'A process by which a team coach works with a whole team, both when they are together and when they are apart, in order to help them both improve their collective performance and how they work together, and also how they develop their collective leadership to more effectively engage with all their key stakeholder groups to jointly transform the wider business' (Hawkins, 2017).

Team development: Any process carried out by a team, with or without assistance from outside, to develop its capability and capacity to work well together.

Team building: Any process used to help a team in the early stages of team development.

Team facilitation: A process where a specific person (or persons) is asked to facilitate the team by managing the process for them so they are freed up to focus on the task.

Team KPIs: "Team Key Performance Indicators are measurable objectives that can only be achieved by the team members collaborating." (Hawkins 2017)

Transformational Team KPIs: are Team KPIs that; are collectively created by the team, which the whole team fully own and are committed to and to which they hold each other mutually accountable; cannot be achieved by the current way the team and it members currently operate; to be attained require the team to change its behaviours, ways of thinking and relating, its ways of partnering internally and externally, and its team processes. (Hawkins 2017)

Team of Teams: A term made popular by General McChrystal (2015) to describe how to create a network of teams that is as effective in collaboration as an effective team.

Teamlander: Someone who lives and works in a team.

Team process consultancy: A form of team facilitation where the team consultant sits alongside the team carrying out its meetings or planning sessions and provides reflection and review on 'how' the team is going about its task.

Tele: 'The contact at a distance enabling an exchange of emotional messages. ... unity of action, time and space that is applied both in theatre and in psychodrama' (Djuric, 2006).

Touchpoint: The point of difference within an organization between individuals, teams and divisions.

Touchpoint leadership: The belief that leadership does not lie in the leader or the follower, but in the relationship between them, which is formed, moulded, stretched, grown and diminished at the *touchpoint*.

Transformational leadership team coaching: 'Where any team taking leadership at whatever level, not only focuses on how they want to run their business, but also how they will transform their business' (Hawkins, 2017).

Value-creating team: A team focused on creating real sustainable value for all their stakeholders and getting regular feedback on ho well they are doing this (Hawkins 2017)

Virtual team: A virtual team, like every team, is a group of people who interact through interdependent tasks guided by a common purpose. Unlike conventional teams, a virtual team works across space, time, cultures and organizational boundaries with links strengthened by webs of communication technologies (Lipnack and Stamps, 1996).

Woodlander: Someone who lives and works in woods.

REFERENCES

Acharya, S (2008) The halcyon years, 2003–08, *The Business Standard*, New Delhi

Aldag, R J and Kuzuhara, L W (2015) *Creating High Performing Teams: Applied strategies and tools for managers and team members*, Routledge, New York

Amidon, E (2012) *The Open Path: Recognizing non-dual awareness*, Sentient Publications, Boulder, CO

Ancona, D G and Caldwell, D F (1992) Bridging the boundary: External activity and performance in organizational teams, *Administrative Science Quarterly*, 37, pp 634–65

Anderson, M, Anderson, D and Mayo, W (2008) Team coaching helps a leadership team drive cultural change at Caterpillar, *Global Business and Organizational Excellence*, 27 (4), pp 40–50

Archer, D and Cameron, A (2013) *Collaborative Leadership: Building relationships, handling conflict and sharing control*, Routledge, London

Avery, G and Bergsteiner, H (2011) *Sustainable Leadership*, 1st edn, Routledge, London

Bandler, R and Grinder, J (1975) *The Structure of Magic I: A book about language and therapy*, Science & Behavior Books, Palo Alto, CA

Barrett, R (2006) *Building a Values-Driven Organization*, Butterworth-Heinemann, Oxford

Barrett, R (2010) *The New Leadership Paradigm*, 1st edn, Lulu.com, Lexington, KY

Barrick, M, Mount, M and Judge, T (2001) The FFM personality dimensions and job performance: Meta-analysis of meta-analyses, *International Journal of Selection and Assessment*, 9, pp 9–30

Bateson, G (1972) *Steps to an Ecology of Mind*, Ballantine Books, New York

Beisser, A (1970) Paradoxical Theory of Change in *Gestalt Therapy Now*, eds J Fagen and I L Shepard, Harper Colophon, New York

Belbin, M (2004) *Management Teams: Why they succeed or fail*, Heinemann, London

Bell, S (2007) Deep-level composition variables as predictors of team performance: A meta-analysis, *Journal of Applied Psychology*, 92 (3), pp 595–615

Bennett, J L (2006) An agenda for coaching-related research: A challenge for researchers, *Coaching Psychology Journal: Practice and Research*, 58 (4), pp 240–49

Berry, J W (1997) Immigration, acculturation, and adaptation, *Applied Psychology: An International Review*, 46, pp 5–34. doi: 10.1111/j.1464-0597.1997. tb01087.x

Berry, W (1983) *Standing by Words*, North Point Press, San Francisco

Bersin, J (2016) *Predictions for 2017*. [Accessed 13 March 2017] www.bersin.com/Practice/Detail.aspx?docid=20454&mode=search&p=Talent-Management

Black, J S, Morrison, A J and Gregersen, H B (2014) *Global Explorers: The next generation of leaders*, Routledge, London

Blackman, A, Moscardo, G, and Gray, D E (2016) Challenges for the theory and practice of business coaching, *Human Resource Development Review*, **15** (4), pp 459–86. doi:10.1177/1534484316673177

Blattner, J and Bacigalupo, A (2007) Using emotional intelligence to develop executive leadership and team and organisational development, *Consulting Psychology Journal: Practice and Research*, **59** (3), pp 209–19

Bohm, D and Nichol, L (2003) *The Essential David Bohm*, 1st edn, London, Routledge

Borgatta, E F (2007) Jacob L Moreno and sociometry, *Social Psychology Quarterly*, 70 (4), pp 330–32

Boston, R (2014) *ARC: The path to authentic responsible courageous leadership*, 4th draft edn, lulu.com

Brackett, M A, Reyes, M R, Rivers, S E, Elbertson, N E and Salovey, P (2011) Classroom emotional climate, teacher affiliation, and student conduct, *Journal of Classroom Interactions*, **46**, pp 27–46

Branson, R (2011) *Screw Business as Usual*, 1st edn, Virgin, London

Britton, J. (2010) *Effective Group Coaching: Tried and tested tools and resources for optimum coaching results*, Wiley, Mississauga

Britton, J (2013) *From One to Many: Best practices for team and group coaching*, Jossey-Bass, Mississauga, Ontario

Brown, P and Brown, V (2012) *Neuropsychology for Coaches*, 1st edn, Open University Press, Maidenhead

Bruch, H and Vogel, B (2011) *Fully Charged: How great leaders boost their organization's energy and ignite high performance*, 1st edn, Boston, MA, Harvard Business Review Press

Buljac-Samardžić, M (2012) Health Teams: Analysing and improving team performance in long term care, PhD thesis, Erasmus University, Rotterdam

Cadbury Committee, The (1992) *The Financial Aspects of Corporate Governance*, Gee and Co, London

Canney Davison, S and Ward, K (1999) *Leading International Teams*, McGraw-Hill, Maidenhead

Capra, F (2003) *The Hidden Connections: A science for sustainable living*, Flamingo, London

Carr, C and Peters, J (2012) The experience and impact of team coaching: A dual case study, PhD thesis, Middlesex University, Institute for Work Based Learning

Carter, C and Lorsch, J (2004) *Back to the Drawing Board*, 1st edn, Harvard Business School Press, Boston, MA

Chait, R P, Ryan, W P and Taylor, B E (2005) *Governance as Leadership*, John Wiley & Sons, Inc, Hoboken, NJ

Chamine, S (2012) *Positive Intelligence: Why only 20% of teams and individuals achieve their true potential and how you can achieve yours*, Greenleaf Book Group Press, Austin, Texas

Clutterbuck, D (2007) *Coaching the Team at Work*, Nicholas Brealey, London

Coaching at Work (2013) Credibility voted top quality in coaches, *Coaching at Work*, **8** (4), p 7

Cohen, S G and Bailey, D E (1997) What makes teams work: Group effectiveness research from the shop floor to the executive suite, *Journal of Management*, **23**, pp 239–90

Cole, T K (n.d.) *Innovation Capital: Case study 2: Team coaching*, Retrieved from www.synovations.com/casestudies/innovationcapital.htm

Collins, J (2001) *Good to Great*, Random House, London

Cooke, N J and Hilton, M L (Eds) (2015) *Enhancing the Effectiveness of Team Science*, The National Academies Press, Washington

Cooperrider, D and Srivastva, S (1987) Appreciative inquiry in organizational life, in *Research in Organizational Change and Development*, Vol 1, ed R W Woodman and W A Passmore, JAI Press, Greenwich, CT

Covey, S R (2011) *The 3rd Alternative: Solving life's most difficult problems*, Simon & Schuster, London

Deakin, R (2007) *Wildwood: A journey through trees*, 1st edn, Hamish Hamilton, London

Devine, D J, Clayton, L D, Philips, J L, Dunford, B B and Melner, S B (1999) Teams in organizations: Prevalence, characteristics, and effectiveness, *Small Group Research*, **30**, pp 678–711

Diamandis, P H & Kotler, S (2014) *Abundance: The future is better than you think*, Free Press, New York

Djuric, Z (2006) *Psychodrama: A beginner's guide*, Jessica Kingsley, London

Doongaji, T R (2010) The legacy of Jamsetji Tata, *Business Line*, 21 September [Online] http://www.thehindubusinessline.com/todays-paper/tp-opinion/the-legacy-of-jamsetji-tata/article1004501.ece

Edelman Trust Barometer Global Survey (2012) http://www.edelman.com/trust

Edelman Trust Barometer Global Survey (2017) [online] http://www.edelman.com/trust

Edmondson, A (1999) Psychological safety and learning behavior in work teams, *Administrative Science Quarterly*, **44** (2)

Edmondson, A (2012) *Teaming*, 1st edn, Jossey-Bass, San Francisco

Edmondson, A, Bohmer, R and Pisano, G (2001) Speeding up team learning, *Harvard Business Review*, October, reprint R0109, pp 125–34

Elkington, J and Jochen Zeitz, J (2014) *The Breakthrough Challenge: 10 ways to connect today's profits with tomorrow's bottom line*, Jossey-Bass, San Francisco

Erdal, D (2011) *Beyond the Corporation: Humanity working*, Bodley Head, London

Fiaramonti, L (2017) *Wellbeing Economy: Success in a world without growth*, Pan Macmillan, Johannesburg

Financial Reporting Council (2011) Guidance on Board Effectiveness, Financial Reporting Council, London

Financial Reporting Council (September 2012) UK Corporate Governance Code, Financial Reporting Council, London

Financial Reporting Council (2012) UK Stewardship Code, Financial Reporting Council, London

Francis, T (2009) Upwardly mobile, *Coaching at Work*, June

Fredrickson, B and Losada, M (2005) Positive Affect and the Complex Dynamics of Human Flourishing, *American Psychologist*, **60** (7), pp 678–86

Fussell, C (2017) *One Mission: How leaders build a team of teams*, Macmillan, London

Gawanda, A (2010) *The Checklist Manifesto*, Profile Books, London

Geier, J (2004) Disc profiling [Online] http://www.geierlearning.com/welcome.html

Gendlin, E T (1979) Befindlichkeit: Heidegger and the philosophy of psychology, *Review of Existential Psychology & Psychiatry: Heidegger and Psychology*, **XVI** (1, 2 & 3)

Gendlin, E T (1982) *Focusing*, 2nd edn, Bantam Books, New York

George, W (2003) *Authentic Leadership: Rediscovering the secrets to creating lasting value*, Jossey-Bass, San Francisco

George, W and Sims, P (2007) *True North: Discover your authentic leadership*, Jossey-Bass, San Francisco

Gersick, C J G (1988) Time and transition in work teams: Towards a new model of group development, *Academy of Management Journal*, **31**, pp 9–41

Gilchrist, A, and Barnes, L (2013) *Systemic Team Coaching Case Study: The Living Organisation*, Retrieved from www.thelivingorganisation.co.uk/wp-content/uploads/2013/07/rocela-report.pdf

Gladstein, D L (1984) Groups in context: A model of task group effectiveness, *Administrative Science Quarterly*, **29** (4), pp 499–517

Grant, A (2012) ROI is a poor measure of coaching success: Towards a more holistic approach using a well-being and engagement framework, *Coaching: An International Journal of Theory, Research and Practice*, 5 (2), pp 1–12 [Online] http://dx.doi.org/10.1080/17521882.2012.672438 [accessed 13 May 2014]

Hackman, J R (1983) A normative model of work team effectiveness (Technical Report No. 2), Research Program on Group Effectiveness, Yale School of Organization and Management, New Haven, CT

Hackman, J R (1987) The design of work teams, in *Handbook of Organizational Behavior*, ed J Lorasch, pp 315–42, Prentice-Hall, Englewood Cliffs, NJ

Hackman, J (1990) *Groups That Work (and Those That Don't)*, 1st edn, Jossey-Bass, San Francisco

Hackman, J R (2002) *Leading Teams: Setting the scene for great performance*, Harvard Business Press, Boston, MA

Hackman, J R (2011) *Collaborative Intelligence: Using teams to solve hard problems*, Berrett-Koehler, San Francisco

Hackman, J R (2011) Six common misperceptions about teamwork, *Harvard Business Review* [Internet blog]. Available from: http://blogs.hbr.org/cs/2011/06/six_common_misperceptions_abou.html [Accessed 23 June 2011]

Hackman, J R and O'Connor, M (2005) What makes for a great analytic team? Individual vs team approaches to intelligence analysis, Intelligence Science Board, Office of the Director of Central Intelligence, Washington, DC

Hackman, J R and Wageman, R (2005) A theory of team coaching, *Academy of Management Review*, 30 (2), pp 269–87

Hamel, G and Prahalad, C (1994) *Competing for the Future*, 1st edn, Harvard Business School Press, Boston, MA

Hamill, P (2013) *Embodied Leadership: The somatic approach to developing your leadership*, Kogan Page, London

Haug, M (2011) What is the relationship between coaching interventions and team effectiveness? *International Journal of Evidence Based Coaching and Mentoring*, Special Issue No 5, pp 89–101

Hawken, P (2007) *Blessed Unrest*, Penguin, New York

Hawken, P, Lovins, A and Hunter Lovins, A (1999) *Natural Capitalism: Creating the next industrial revolution*, Little Brown, Boston, MA

Hawkins, P (2005) *Wise Fool's Guide to Leadership: Short spiritual stories for organisational and personal Transformation*, O Books, London

Hawkins, P (2010, 2018) Coaching Supervision, in *The Complete Handbook of Coaching*, ed E Cox, T Bachkirova and D Clutterbuck, Sage, London

Hawkins, P (2011, 2014, 2017) *Leadership Team Coaching: Developing collective transformational leadership*, Kogan Page, London

Hawkins, P (2011a) Systemic coaching supervision, in *Supervision in Mentoring and Coaching: Theory and practice*, ed T Bachkirova, P Jackson and D Clutterbuck, Open University Press, Maidenhead

Hawkins, P (2012) *Creating a Coaching Culture*, McGraw Hill/Open University Press, Maidenhead

Hawkins, P (ed) (2014, 2017) *Leadership Team Coaching in Practice*, Kogan Page, London

Hawkins, P (2014c) The Challenge for Coaching in the 21st Century in e-Organisations and People, **21** (4), Winter 2014, http://www.amed.org.uk/

Hawkins, P (2015) Cracking the shell: Unlearning our coaching assumptions, *Coaching at Work*, 10 (2), pp 42–6

Hawkins, P (2017b) *Tomorrow's Leadership and the Necessary Revolution in Today's Leadership Development*, Henley Business School, Henley

Hawkins, P (2017c) The necessary revolution in humanistic psychology, in *The Future of Humanistic Psychology*, eds House, R and Kalisch, D, Routledge, London

Hawkins, P and Shohet, R (1989, 2000, 2006, 2012) *Supervision in the Helping Professions*, Open University Press, Milton Keynes

Hawkins, P and Smith, N (2006, 2013) *Coaching, Mentoring and Organizational Consultancy: Supervision and development*, Open University Press/McGraw Hill, Maidenhead

Hawkins, P and Smith, N (2010, 2014, 2018) Transformational coaching, in *The Complete Handbook of Coaching*, ed E Cox, T Bachkirova and D Clutterbuck, pp 231–44, Sage, London

Hawkins, P and Wright, A (2009) Being the change you want to see: Developing the leadership culture at Ernst & Young, *Strategic HR Review*, 8 (4), pp 17–23

Hay, J (2009). *Transactional Analysis for Trainers*, 1st edn, Sherwood, Watford

Heffernan, M (2011) *Wilful Blindness: How we ignore the obvious at our peril*, Simon and Schuster, London

Heffernan, M (2013) *A Bigger Prize: Why competition isn't everything and how we do it better*, Simon & Schuster, London

Heifetz, R A and Laurie, D L (1997) The work of Leadership, *Harvard Business Review*, Jan/Feb

Heifetz, R A, Grashow, A and Linsky, M (2009) *Practice of Adaptive Leadership: Tools and tactics for changing your organization and the world: A fieldbook for practitioners*, Harvard Business Press, Boston, MA

Hellinger, B (1998) *Love's Hidden Symmetry*, Zeig, Tucker & Theisen, Phoenix, AZ

Hellinger, B (1999) *Acknowledging What Is*, Zeig, Tucker & Theisen, Phoenix, AZ

Hersey, P (1985) *The Situational Leader*, Warner Books, New York

Hersted, L and Gergen, K J (2013) *Relational Leading*, 1st edn, Taos Institute Publishing, Chagrin Falls, OH

Hogan, A (2012) Excellent board leadership, Anchor Partners, http://www.anchorpartners.co.uk/

Hutchins, G (2012) *The Nature of Business: Redesigning for resilience*, 1st edn, Green Books, Totnes, Devon

Hutchins, G (2016) *Future-Fit*, CreateSpace Independent Publishers

International Coach Federation and PricewaterhouseCoopers (2012) 2012 ICF Global Coaching Study: Executive summary. [Online] Available from: http://www.coachfederation.org/coachingstudy2012 [Accessed 27 June, 2013]

Ismail, S (2014) *Exponential Organisations: Why new organizations are ten times better, faster, and cheaper than yours (and what to do about it)*, Diversion Books, New York

Issacs, W (1999) *Dialogue and the Art of Thinking Together*, Doubleday, New York

Jaworski, J (2012) *Synchronicity: The inner path of leadership*, Berrett-Koehler, San Francisco

Joiner, B (2006) *Leadership Agility: Five levels of mastery for anticipating and initiating change*, Jossey-Bass/Wiley, San Francisco

Kakabadse, A and Kakabadse, N (2008) *Leading the Board: The six disciplines of world class chairman*, Palgrave, London

Kakabadse, A and Kakabadse, N (2009) *Global Boards: One desire, many realities*, Palgrave, London

Kakabadse, A and Van den Berghe, L (eds) (2013) *How to Make Boards Work: An international overview*, Palgrave Macmillan, Basingstoke

Kakabadse, N K, Knyght, R and Kakabadse, A (2013) High-performing chairmen: The older the better, in *How to Make Boards Work: An international overview*, ed A Kakabadse and L Van den Burghe, pp 342–59, Palgrave Macmillan, Basingstoke

Kaner, S (2014) *Facilitators Guide to Participatory Decision Making*. Jossey-Bass, San Francisco

Karlgaard, R and Malone, M S (2015) *Team Genius: The new science of high-performing teams*, HarperCollins, New York

Karpman, S (1968) Fairy tales and script drama analysis, *Transactional Analysis Bulletin*, 7 (26), pp 39–43

Katzenbach, J (2012) Look beyond the team, it is about the network, HBR Blog 10:48 am March 21, 2012, http://blogs.hbr.org/2012/03/look-beyond-the-team-its-about/ [accessed 27 June 2014]

Katzenbach, J and Smith, D (1993b, 1999) *The Wisdom of Teams: Creating the high-performance organization*, Harvard Business School Press, Boston, MA

Kegan, R and Lahey, L (2009) *Immunity to Change*, Harvard Business School Press, Boston, MA

Kegan, R and Lahey, L (2016) *An Everyone Culture: Becoming a deliberately developmental organization*, Harvard Business School, Boston

Keller, S and Price, C (2011) *Beyond Performance: How great organizations build ultimate competitive advantage*, John Wiley & Sons, Inc, Hoboken, NJ

Kellerman, B (2008) *Followership*, 1st ed, Harvard Business School Press, Boston, MA

Kellerman, B (2012) *The End of leadership*, 1st ed, Harper Business, New York

Kelly, G A (1955) *The Psychology of Personal Constructs*, Vols 1 and 2, Norton, New York

Kline, N (2015) *More time to think: The power of independent thinking*, Cassell, London

Kohlberg, L (1981) *The Philosophy of Moral Development*, 1st edn, Harper & Row, San Francisco

Kolb, D A (1984) *Experimental Learning: Experience as the source of learning and development*, Prentice Hall, Englewood Cliffs, NJ

Kozlowski, S W, Gully, S M, Salas, E and Cannon-Bowers, J A (1996) Team leadership and development: Theory, principles and guidelines for training leaders and teams, in *Advances of Interdisciplinary Studies of Work Teams*, ed M M Beyerlein, D A Johnson and S T Beyerlein, pp 253–91, JAI, Greenwich, CT

Kübler-Ross, E (1969) *On Death and Dying*, Routledge, London

Kübler-Ross, E and Kessler, D (2005) *On Grief and Grieving: Finding the meaning of grief through the five stages of loss*, 1st ed, Scribner, New York

Laloux, F (2014) *Reinventing Organizations*, Nelson Parker, Brussels

Lane, D (2010) Coaching in the UK: An introduction to some key debates, *Coaching: An International Journal of Theory, Research and Practice*, 3 (2), pp 155–66

Laske, O (2011) *Measuring Hidden Dimensions: The art and science of fully engaging adults*, IDM Press, Gloucester, MA

Lawrence, P and Whyte, A (2017) What do experienced team coaches do? Current practice in Australia and New Zealand, *International Journal of Evidence Based Coaching and Mentoring*, 15 (1), pp 94–113

Lawton, J H and May, R M (2010) *Extinction Rates*, Oxford University Press, Oxford

Leary-Joyce, J and Lines, H (2017) *Systemic Team Coaching*, Academy of Executive Coaching, London

Lencioni, P (2002) *The Five Dysfunctions of a Team: A leadership fable*, Jossey-Bass, San Francisco

Lencioni, P (2005) *Overcoming the Five Dysfunctions of a Team: A field guide*, Jossey-Bass, San Francisco

Lencioni, P (2006) *Silos, Politics and Turf Wars: A leadership fable*, Jossey-Bass, San Francisco

Lewis, Amini, F and Lannon, R (2000) *A General Theory of Love*, Random House, New York

Likert, R (1932) A technique for the measurement of attitudes, *Archives of Psychology*, 140, pp 1–55

Lines, H and Scholes-Rhodes, J (2013) *Touchpoint Leadership: Creating collaborative energy across teams and organizations*, Kogan Page, London

Lipnack, J and Stamps, J (1996) *Virtual Teams: People working across boundaries with technology*, John Wiley & Sons, Inc, Hobokem NJ

Liu, C, Lin, L, Huang, I and Lin, K (2010) Exploring the moderating effects of LMX quality and differentiation on the relationship between team coaching and team effectiveness, in ICMSE (ed), International Conference on Management Science and Engineering (17th), November 24–26, Tainan, Taiwan, pp 896–92

Loevinger, J and Blasi, A (1976) *Ego Development: Conceptions and theories*, Jossey-Bass, San Francisco

Macy, J and Johnstone, C (2012) *Active Hope*, 1st edn, New World Library, Novato, CA

McKee, A and McMillen, M (1992) Discovering social issues: Organization development in a multi-cultural community, in *Journal of Applied Behavioral Science*, 28 (3), pp 445–60

McKee, A, Boyatzis, R and Johnston, F (2008) *Becoming a Resonant Leader*, 1st edn, Harvard Business School Press, Boston, MA

McKenna, M, Shelton, D and Darling, J (2002) The impact of behavioral style assessment on organizational effectiveness: A call for action, *Leadership and Organization Development Journal*, 23 (6), pp 314–22

Meier, D (2005) *Team Coaching with the Solution Circle: A practical guide to solutions focused team development*, Solution Books, Cheltenham

Miller, S (2013) Voices from the field: Expanding coaching from leader to team and across the organization. In J. Britton, (Ed), *From One to Many: Best practices for team and group coaching*, pp 4–8, Mississauga: Wiley, Canada. Retrieved from www.from12many.com/401/login.php?redirect=/downloads.html (Use code 4411)

Moreno, J (1959) *Psychodrama*, Vol II, Beacon House, New York

Moreno, J (1985) *The Autobiography of J L Moreno, MD* (Abridged), Moreno Archives, Harvard University

Moss-Kanter, R (2011) How great companies think differently, *Harvard Business Review*, November

Mulec, K and Roth, J (2005) Action, reflection, and learning and coaching in order to enhance the performance of drug development project management teams, *R and D Management*, 35, pp 483–91

Myers, I, Briggs, M H, McCaulley, N Q and Hammer, A (1998) *MBTI Handbook: A guide to the development and use of the Myers–Briggs Type Indicator*, 3rd edn, Consulting Psychologists Press, Palo Alto, CA

Nevis, E C (1987) *Organisational Consulting: A Gestalt approach*, Gestalt Institute of Cleveland Press, Cambridge, MA

Obolensky, N (2010) *Complex Adaptive Leadership: Embracing paradox and uncertainty*, 1st edn, Gower, Farnham, Surrey

Organisation for Economic Co-operation and Development (1999, 2004) OECD Principles of Corporate Governance, OECD, Paris

Oshry, B (1995, 2007) *Seeing Systems: Unlocking the mysteries of organizational life*, Berrett-Koehler, San Francisco

Oshry, B (1999) *Leading Systems: Lessons from the power lab*, Berrett-Koehler, San Francisco

Palmer, S (2008) How you can personally contribute to the field of coaching, Paper presented at the Association for Coaching, Embracing Excellence, London

Parker, G M (1990) *Team Players and Teamwork: The new competitive business strategy*, Jossey-Bass, San Francisco

Parlett, M and Dearden, G (1977) *Introduction to Illuminative Evaluation: Studies in higher education*, Pacific Soundings Press, Sacramento, CA

Pedler, M (1997) What do we mean by action learning?, in *Action Learning in Practice*, ed M Pedler, Gower, Aldershot

Peters, J (2013) Voices from the field: Team coaching as a lever for change. In J. Britton (Ed), *From one to many: Best practices for team and group coaching*, pp 8–11, Wiley, Canada, Mississauga. Retrieved from www.from12many.com/401/login.php?redirect=/downloads.html (Use code 4411)

Peters, J and Carr, C (2013) *50 Terrific Tips for Teams: Proven strategies for building high performing teams*, InnerActive Leadership Associates Inc, Calgary, Alberta, Canada

Pittinsky, T L (2009) *Crossing the Divide: Inter-group leadership in a world of difference*, Harvard Business Books, Boston, MA

Pliopas, A, Kerr, A and Sosinski, M (2014) *Team coaching project: Hudson Institute of Coaching*. file:///C:/Users/Jacqu/Downloads/Team%20Coaching%20Project%20by%20Pliopas%20Kerr%20Sosinski%202014.pdf

Porrit, J (2007) *Capitalism as if the World Matters*, Earthscan, London.

Porter, M E and Kramer, M R (2011) Shared value: How to re-invent capitalism and unleash a wave of innovation and growth, *Harvard Business Review*, **89** (1/2), pp 62–77

Public Service Agency (2013) Voices from the field: Team coaching case study: British Columbia Public Service Agency. In J Britton (Ed), *From One to Many: Best practices for team and group coaching*, pp 11–20, Wiley, Canada, Mississauga. Retrieved from www.from12many.com/401/login.php?redirect=/downloads.html (Use code 4411)

Reason, P (2017) *In Search of Grace*, Earth Books, S.I.

Redekop, B W (2010) Introduction: Connecting leadership and sustainability, in *Leadership for Environmental Sustainability*, ed B W Redekop, Routledge, New York

Reilly, R, Lynn, G and Aronson, H (2002) The role of personality in new product development team performance, *Journal of Engineering Technology Management*, **19**, pp 39–58

Revans, R (1982) *The Origin and Growth of Action Learning*, Chartwell-Bratt, Brickley, UK

Richardson, J (2010) An investigation of the prevalence and measurement of teams in organisations: The development and validation of the real team scale, Unpublished doctoral dissertation, Aston University, Birmingham, UK

Ridler Report (2013) www.ridlerandco.com

Rozovsky, FA (2015) *Consent to Treatment*

Salas, E, Dickinson, T L, Converse, S A and Tannenbaum, S I (1992) Toward an understanding of team performance and training, in *Teams: Their training and performance*, ed R J Swezey and E Salas, pp 3–29, Ablex, Norwood, NJ

Salas, E, Stagl, K C, Burke, C S and Goodwin, G F (2007) Fostering team effectiveness in organizations: Toward an integrative theoretical framework of team performance, in *Modeling Complex Systems: Motivation, cognition and social processes: Nebraska Symposium on Motivation*, Vol 51, ed R A Dienstbier, J W Shuart, W Spaulding and J Poland, pp 185–243, University of Nebraska Press, Lincoln

Sandahl, P (2013) Voices from the field: Trends in team coaching and health care case study. In J Britton (Ed), *From One to Many: Best practices for team and group coaching*, pp 21–4, Wiley, Canada, Mississauga. Retrieved from www.from12many.com/401/login.php?redirect=/downloads.html (Use code 4411)

Scharmer, O (2007) *Theory U: Leading from the future as it emerges*, Berrett-Koehler, San Francisco

Scharmer, O with Kaufer, K (2013) *Leading From the Emerging Future: From ego-system to eco-system economies*, Berrett-Koehler, San Francisco

Schein, E H (1987) *Process Consultation Revisted: Building the helping relationship*, Prentice Hall, London

Schippers, M, West, M A and Dawson, J F (2014) Team reflexivity and innovation: The moderating role of team context, *Journal of Management* [Online] http://dx.doi.org/10.1177/0149206312441210 [Accessed 27 June 2014]

Schnell, E R and Hammer, A L (2004) *Introduction to the FIRO-B Instrument in Organizations*, CPP Inc, Mountain View, CA

Schön, D (1983) *The Reflective Practitioner*, Basic Books, New York

Schutz, W C (1973) *Elements of Encounter*, Joy Press, Big Sur, CA

Senge, P (1990) *The Fifth Discipline: The art and practice of the learning organization*, Doubleday, New York

Senge, P (2010) *The Necessary Revolution*, 1st edn, Nicholas Brealey, London

Senge, P, Jaworski, J, Scharmer, C and Flowers, B (2005) *Presence: Exploring profound change in people, organizations and society*, Doubleday, New York

Senge, P, Kleiner, A, Ross, R, Roberts, C and Smith, B (1994) *The Fifth Discipline Fieldbook: Strategies and tools for building a learning organization*, Doubleday, New York

Sharpe, K (2013) *Rebranding Rule*, Yale University Press, New Haven

Sherman, S and Freas, A (2004) The Wild West of executive coaching, *Harvard Business Review*, **82** (11), pp 82–90

Sherpa Coaching (2013) 8th Annual Executive Coaching Survey at the Summit [Online] http://www.sherpacoaching.com/pdf%20files/Survey-Executive-Coaching-2012.pdf [accessed 27 June 2014]

Silberman, M (2005) *101 Ways to Make Training Active*, John Wiley and Sons, Inc, Hoboken, NJ

Sparrer, I and Von Kibed, M V (2001) *Miracle, Solution and System: Solution-focussed systemic constellations for therapy and organisational change*, Solution Books, Cheltenham

Spence, G B (2007) Further development of evidence based coaching: Lessons from the rise and fall of the human potential movement, *Australian Psychologist*, **42** (4), pp 255–65

Sundaramurthy, C and Lewis, M (2003) Control and paradoxes of governance, *Academy of Review*, **28** (3), pp 397–415

Tannenbaum, S I, Mathieu, J E, Salas, E and Cohen, D (2012) Teams are changing: Are research and practice evolving fast enough? *Industrial and Organizational Psychology*, 5 (1), pp 2–24

The Insights Group Limited (2012) Insights Team Effectiveness [Online] http://www.insights.com/956/insights-team-effectiveness.html

Thomsen, S (2008) A minimum theory of boards, *An International Journal of Corporate Governance*, **I**, pp 73–96

Thornton, C (2010) *Group and Team Coaching*, 1st edn, Routledge, London

Torbert, B (2004) *Action Inquiry: The secret of timely and transforming leadership*, Berrett-Koehler, San Fransisco

Torbert, W R and Rooke, D (2005) 7 transformations of leadership, *Harvard Business Review*, **83** (4), pp 67–76

Trompenaars, F and Nijhoff Asser, M (2010) *Global M&A Tango: Cross-cultural dimensions of mergers and acquisitions*, McGraw-Hill, Philadelphia

Tuckman, B (1965) Developmental sequence in small groups, *Psychological Bulletin*, **63** (6), pp 384–99

Van den Berghe, L and Levrau, A (2013) Promoting effective board decision-making, the essence of good governance, in *How to Make Boards Work: An international overview*, ed A Kakabadse and L Van den Burghe, pp 211–67, Palgrave Macmillan, Basingstoke

Vienot, Reports (1995–99) Corporate Governance Codes and Principles, European Corporate Governance Institute, Paris

Vienot, Reports (2000) Corporate Governance Codes and Principles, European Corporate Governance Institute, Paris

Vitali, S, Glattfelder, J B and Battiston, S (2011) The network of global corporate control, *PLoS ONE*, **6** (10), p e25995, doi:10.1371/journal.pone.0025995

Wageman, R (2001) How leaders foster self-managing team effectiveness, *Organization Science*, **12** (5), pp 559–77

Wageman, R, Fisher, C and Hackman, J R (2009) Leading teams when the timing is right: finding the best moments to act, *Organizational Dynamics*, **38** (3), pp 192–203

Wageman, R and Hackman, R (2009) What makes teams of leaders leadable? In *Advancing Leadership*, ed N Nohria and R Khurana, Harvard Business School Press, Boston, MA

Wageman, R, Hackman, J R and Lehman, E (2005) Team Diagnostic Survey: Development of an Instrument, *Journal of Applied Behavioral Science*, **41** (4), pp 373–98

Wageman, R, Nunes, D A, Burruss, J A and Hackman, J R (2008) *Senior Leadership Teams*, Harvard Business School Press, Boston, MA

Walker, D (2009) A review of corporate governance in UK banks and other financial industry entities, The Walker Review Secretariat, London

Ward, G (2008) Towards executive change: A psychodynamic group coaching model for short executive programs, *International Journal of Evidence Based Coaching and Mentoring*, **6** (1), pp 67–78

Weinberg, R and McDermott, M (2002) A comparative analysis of sport and business organizations: Factors perceived critical for organizational success, *Journal of Applied Sports Psychology*, **14**, pp 282–98

Welch, D (2012) Ethical buyers guide to supermarkets, Ethical Consumer Report [Online] http://www.ethicalconsumer.org/buyersguides/food/supermarkets.aspx

West, M A (1996) *Effective Teamwork*, Excel, New Delhi

West, M A (2012) *Effective Teamwork: Practical lessons from Organizational Research*, 3rd edn, Wiley Blackwell, Oxford

West, MA and Markiewicz, L (2016) Effective team working in health care in E Ferlie, K Montgomery and AR Pedersen (eds) *The Oxford Handbook of Healthcare Management*, Oxford University Press

Western, S (2010) Eco-leadership: Towards the development of a new paradigm, in *Leadership for Environmental Sustainability*, ed B W Redekop, Routledge, New York

Western, S (2013) *Leadership: A critical text*, 2nd edn, Sage, London

White, A (2008) From comfort zone to performance management, White & MacLean, La Houlette 3, B-1470 Baisy-Thy, Belgium

Whittington, J (2012) *Systemic Coaching and Constellations*, Kogan Page, London

Williams, R L (2010) Leadership and the dynamics of collaboration, in *Leadership for Environmental Sustainability*, ed B W Redekop, Routledge, New York

Wilson, E O (30 April, 2012) E.O.Wilson wants to know why you're not protesting in the streets, Interview with Lisa Hymas, Grist [online] http://grist.org/article/e-o-wilson-wants-to-know-why-youre-not-protesting-in-the-streets/ [accessed 27 June 2014]

Woodhead, V (2011) How does coaching help to support team working? A case study in the NHS, *International Journal of Evidence Based Coaching and Mentoring*, Special Issue No 5, pp 102–19

Zaccaro, S J, Rittman, A L and Marks, M A (2001) Team leadership, *The Leadership Quarterly*, **12**, pp 451–83

Zinker, J (1977) *Creative Process in Gestalt Therapy*, 1st edn, Brunner/Mazel, New York

Zinker, J (1980) The developmental process of a Gestalt therapy group, in *Beyond the Hot Seat: Gestalt approaches to group*, ed B Feder and R Ronall, pp 55–77, Brunner-Mazel, New York

INDEX